MARKS THE SPOT

ON LOCATION WITH THE X-FILES

ON LOCATION WITH THE X-FILES

Louisa Gradnitzer & Todd Pittson

ARSENAL PULP PRESS

VANCOUVER

ARSENAL PULP PRESS
103-1014 Homer Street
Vancouver, BC
Canada V6B 2W9
www.arsenalpulp.com

 The publisher gratefully acknowledges the support of the
Canada Council for the Arts and the B.C. Arts Council for
its publishing program.

Canadä The publisher gratefully acknowledges the support of the
Government of Canada through the Book Publishing Industry
Development Program for its publishing activities.

Book design by Lisa Eng-Lodge
Printed and bound in Canada

CANADIAN CATALOGUING IN PUBLICATION DATA:
Gradnitzer, Louisa.
X marks the spot

ISBN 1-55152-066-4

1. X-files (Television program). I. Pittson, Todd. II. Title.
PN1992.77.X34G72 1999   791.45'72   C99-910359-8

C O N T E N T S

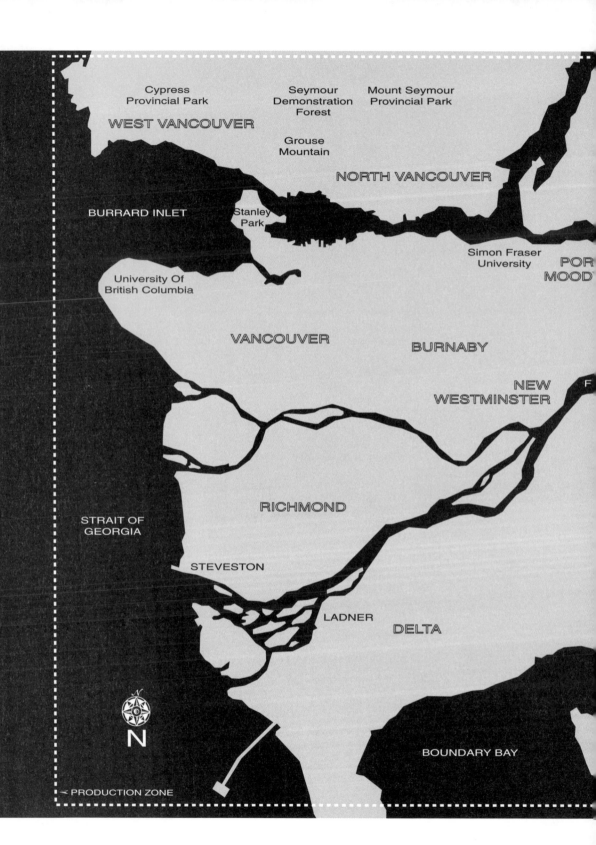

Cypress
Provincial Park

Seymour
Demonstration
Forest

Mount Seymour
Provincial Park

WEST VANCOUVER

Grouse
Mountain

NORTH VANCOUVER

BURRARD INLET

Stanley
Park

Simon Fraser
University

POR
MOOD

University Of
British Columbia

VANCOUVER

BURNABY

NEW
WESTMINSTER

F

STRAIT OF
GEORGIA

RICHMOND

STEVESTON

LADNER

DELTA

N

BOUNDARY BAY

PRODUCTION ZONE

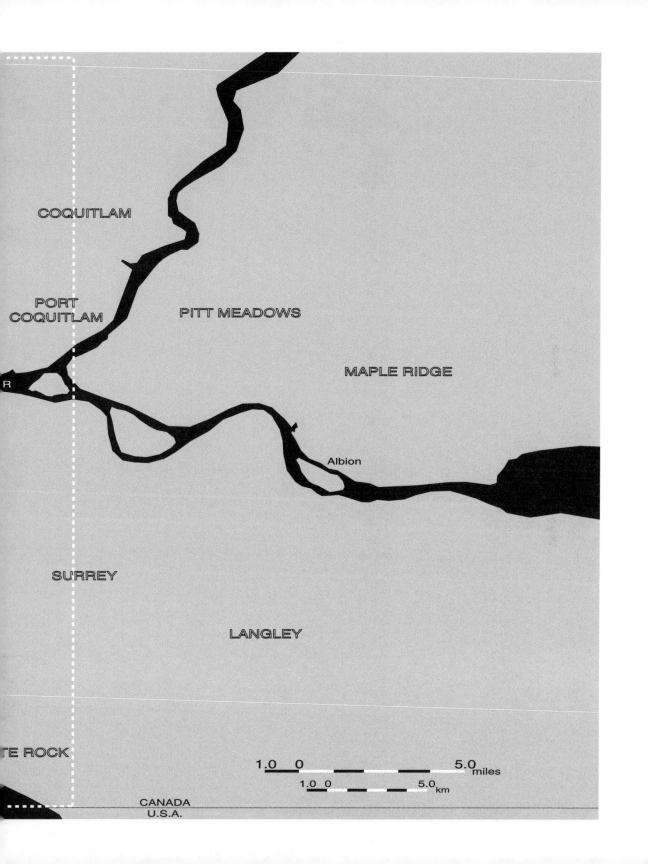

COQUITLAM

PORT
COQUITLAM

PITT MEADOWS

MAPLE RIDGE

R

Albion

SURREY

LANGLEY

TE ROCK

1.0 0   5.0 miles

1.0 0   5.0 km

CANADA
U.S.A.

ACKNOWLEDGEMENTS

Todd
To Sally for her love and patience, to my mother
for her nurturing, and to Francesca for the wonder
which is new life.

Louisa
For Mom, Dad, Kate, and Callan.

We extend special thanks to Rob Murdoch, Alan Bartolic,
Rick Fearon, Ainslie S. Wiggs, Dave Caughlan,
Michael Bobroff, Robyn Gelka, and Woody Morrison
for their years of long-term commitment
to the locations department.

Thanks to Chris Carter for providing us with the
wave of the decade and the ride of a lifetime, and
to the crew and cast members with whom
we shared five years of our lives.

Thanks to the following for allowing us
to use their photographs:
Amir Barsoum, Alan Bartolic, Michael Bobroff,
Tom Braidwood, Robyn Gelka, Frank Haddad,
Greg Loewen, Vivien Nishi, Patrick Stark

FOREWORD: THE X-PERIENCE

On a warm spring night ten thousand fans sit motionless, watching the final moments of the game. As the boy leans forward over the chessboard, a gunshot rips through the silence and his opponent is thrown back, the impact of the bullet smashing him full in the chest. Pandemonium. In a blind panic, the screaming crowd is up out of their seats and stampeding for the door. And then, above the roar, a bellowing voice yells: "Cut!"

The cameras stopped rolling and the crowd froze. Everyone calmly and quietly returned to their seats to await further instructions. I stood in the centre of Vancouver's General Motors Place, lowering the microphone to my side. Surveying the crowd as they settled back in, I was awed by the scale of the scene *The X-Files* crew was attempting to shoot. I was equally amazed at how attentive and responsive this huge audience was.

As one of the two first assistant directors on the show, it was my responsibility to maintain order and push the production forward. It required careful planning and the complete co-operation of everyone – crowd and crew alike. Really, only myself and the director were fully aware of the complex amount of work to be accomplished in the few short hours we had available. The crew and the crowd had to trust us to guide them through the confusion.

The scene at GM Place was an enormous undertaking for everyone. I remember at the time shaking my head in disbelief at the incredible challenge. But then, that was and is *The X-Files*.

It began as a dark atmospheric TV series rooted in cautionary paranoia. For those of us who started with the show in 1993 it was just another job, another notch on our resumés. But five years later we would look back and realize how this passionate and unique experience had not only changed the look of television but had changed our lives as well. Over those five years the demands of the show grew exponentially, as did our satisfaction in taking on the challenge – and winning – on a week-to-week basis.

The production of *The X-Files* became all-consuming. Twelve- to sixteen-hour days, five days a week, for ten months at a time. The crew became a surrogate family. The bottom line was rooted in loyalty and friendship and the mutual bond was working towards making the best show possible.

Aside from my production role on the show, I have also had the good fortune of acting in the series. Through a twist of fate during the first season I was asked to play the character of "Frohike," one of the triad called "The Lone Gunmen." That first brief scene I participated in started me on a journey to destinations never imagined. The continuing adventure has taken me to Los Angeles, Chicago, Milwaukee, and New York, just to name a few places. I've been to conventions, appeared on trading cards and t-shirts, and even performed in a rock video. Who would have ever thought?

And who would have ever thought that *The X-Files* would grow into the incredible success that it has? For those of us involved, the show was a unique experience. For five seasons, as an assistant director and an actor, I had the pleasure of working – on and off the set – with multi-talented producers, a myriad of wonderful actors, and an incredible crew; hundreds of gifted and dedicated people who, at the end of five years, could proudly claim a share in the success of the series.

In an odd way, the evening at GM Place was a culmination of all that was *The X-Files;* a chess game, like the game we played every week with every story and every shot. And an audience who waited patiently (and anxiously) for the outcome. That night at GM Place was much more than another day of shooting – it was an event. As I stood centre-stage, I realized that the audience – so alert and synergetic – were there not just to be part of the episode, but also to say, *thank you* to the show and all that it contributed to Vancouver.

It's curious what fragmented moments stand out in your memory. Several months later I was sitting outside Los Angeles International Airport waiting for my luggage to arrive when a young woman approached me. She looked at me for a few moments before asking, *You were at GM Place, weren't you?* I nodded. She smiled and continued, *That was your night, wasn't it?* And it struck me at that moment that she was absolutely right, but more right than she could know. Because really, she was speaking for the entire cast and crew, and for Vancouver. What she was really saying was, *That was your show, wasn't it?*

And for five years that's exactly what it was.

– Tom Braidwood
Vancouver
May 1999

AUTHORS' NOTE

The locations described in *X Marks the Spot* do not represent a comprehensive list of every location used by *The X-Files* during its five-year sojourn in Vancouver, Canada. That is not the intention of this book. The locations represented were chosen for their visual significance, their importance to the show, and their importance to us.

Some locations no longer exist. Others have been transformed beyond recognition. Sites such as Woodlands and Riverview Hospitals have played host to more sets than can reasonably be counted. Still others are not listed out of respect for the owners' right to privacy.

Similarly, views expressed herein are in no way representative of official Fox policy. They are, rather, opinions based on our varied and colorful experiences as location managers on *The X-Files* during its Vancouver run. All factual errors are ours and ours alone.

And while every attempt has been made to maintain accuracy of fact – including detail checks with former crew members and technicians – no two individuals, when asked, recounted a story in exactly the same way. This we must attribute to the vagaries of memory. Still, you can be assured that these stories are true.

We can only hope that this book will stimulate fond memories for those associated with *The X-Files* during its Canadian run, while providing others with a rare window into the making of television history from the unique perspective of the location manager.

What Chris Carter wanted, he generally got. And so it should have been, considering the time and energy he put into *his* show. That aside, a sense of loyalty developed seldom equaled in this business. And that was true for all departments. We, as crew members, were more than willing to run that extra mile, even if it meant (as it often did) more headaches and an expanded workload. The results almost always translated to the screen as unique and unusual locations, elaborate sets, very creepy visual effects and technically challenging props. In short, very big television.

It is important to explain and differentiate the use of the term "mythology" within the context of *X Marks the Spot*. For our purposes, several references are made to crew mythology, which we define as the body of fact and fiction which evolved over the course of the series into something greater than the sum total of its parts. Call it fable. Call it legend. It constitutes those behind-the-scenes elements of physical production wherein our anecdotes and stories reside. Shared experience.

In one of the numerous interviews given by series creator Chris Carter, he carefully differentiates the two basic types of shows embodied in *The X-Files*. The first is the stand-alone – or genre – show, typified by the "horror" episode. The other is the "mythology" show. These are the episodes which examine – on a continuing arc – subject matter related to covert government conspiracy and cover-up or an alien presence among us.

It is crucial not to confuse the context of storytelling within which Chris' definition of "mythology" appears with the production context from which our use of this word derives.

Visual Alchemy

Sometime in the last half-century a myth was born: the camera never lies. After all, this instrument has emerged as perhaps the most faithful documentarist of the 20th century, recording images and events just as they are revealed to the human eye. The perfect Kodak Moment, complete in every detail.

But wait a minute. There's a digital printer at my local drugstore which reproduces photographs from prints. Details can be enhanced, flaws erased. Elements of an image can be isolated and enlarged, or simply eliminated altogether. The very essence of the photographed image — that held sacred for so long — can be manipulated for under ten bucks each, with the resulting print arguably of "better" quality than the original.

This is, of course, only the thin edge of the wedge. The movie industry (which includes television) expends incredible amounts of time, money, and expertise in the recreation of reality. The technological innovations pioneered by digital effects companies in the last decade are truly amazing. Witness the ability to manipulate negative imagery by erasing and reinventing backgrounds, creating believable pitched battles in outer space, or recreating the last hours before the sinking of a famous ocean liner.

Such expertise suggests a problem with another myth: seeing is believing. If what we're seeing on the screen is a computer-generated, digitally-enhanced recreation, this can be, at best, a half-truth. A more apt saying for today's day and age might better read: the camera always lies.

INTRODUCTION

CREATIVE GEOGRAPHY

There's an aspect of movie-making which involves the manipulation of locales and geographies to portray or approximate the oft-distant "real thing." The back-streets of Malta playing a crowded Turkish bazaar (*Midnight Express*). The English countryside (with a few well-placed palm trees) playing the Central Highlands of Vietnam (*Full Metal Jacket*). A defunct gravel quarry in British Columbia, Canada playing the New Mexico desert (*The X-Files*). The term used to describe this conjuror's trick is *creative geography*.

An aerial stock shot can establish a setting such as New York, complete with distinct landmarks such as the Statue of Liberty and the Empire State Building. Icons, in a sense, which are recognizable around the world. But filming on the streets of New York is costly, frustrating, and time-consuming. That's what studio backlots are for. That's what *other* smaller, less chaotic cities are for.

Creative geography, and the use of composite imagery, informs our ability to visualize a burrough or neighbourhood in some city or country and accept it for what it is not. A few scenes shot on location in New York intercut with an action sequence shot on a Los Angeles street, intercut with many more scenes shot on a Universal Studios backlot, provide the overall impression of a story set in New York, even if virtually none of the production was, in fact, shot in New York.

Agent Scully walks down a quiet street and enters her Washington, D.C. apartment building. (A location in Vancouver's West End.) Inside, she fumbles with her keys, then enters her apartment. (A standing set on a soundstage several miles away in North Vancouver.) We accept the physical contiguity of these two elements – exterior and interior – because of the process of *seamless editing* as it relates to that other basic tenet of cinematic storytelling, *suspension of disbelief.* What makes the difference here is good direction, good production design, creative use of locations, and smart writing.

And while location filming has certainly helped to inform our perception of distant locales, it remains very much the preserve of large feature films and, in any event, a flawed process. When Jackie Chan waterskis barefoot across an urban waterway called False Creek in *Rumble in the Bronx*, those rugged mountains looming in the near background seem oddly out of place for New York. And so they should, since *Rumble in the Bronx* was filmed almost entirely in Vancouver, with only a small Second Unit being sent to New York to "establish" the locale, most notably the Brooklyn Bridge.

Television does not have the luxury of time or money to continent-hop in search of authentic locations, which is what makes *creative geography* so crucial to the process. Much has been said of the Lower Mainland's ability to double as transparent "Anywhere, U.S.A." In the last decade, countless television series and movies attest to this. What gives this region its greatest appeal (monetary exchange rates aside) is the wide range of geographical locales accessible within thirty minutes of the downtown core, whether it's the rainforests of Costa Rica and the Pacific Northwest, the flatlands of North Texas, or the wilds of Siberia.

And while the quality of light (or lack thereof) played a starring role on *The X-Files*, it is the Lower Mainland – and Vancouver itself – which must be credited with putting in a consistently strong performance. On a dark-hearted television series fictionally located in a different American city or state each week, this continued diversity of *location* and *look* has been one of the show's great challenges and achievements.

During its five-year run in Canada, residents, fans, and tourists alike were often surprised to learn that *The X-Files* had called Vancouver "home" ever since the filming of the *pilot* in March 1993. The show stands as a wonderful tribute to the scenic diversity of the Lower Mainland, running like a five-year advertisement for Tourism British Columbia.

Ironically, most viewers – particularly those in other countries – didn't see it that way. It was simply assumed by many that the imagery exported around the world each week was more or less true to the American-ness of its purported settings.

As location managers, this incredulity was perhaps the greatest possible compliment paid to us. If the truth is out there, then so are the locations.

Pilot: the first episode of what could be (but is not always) a new television series.

Often, Chris — while writing scripts — would personally call department heads to make inquiries about locations and sets.

Because so much of *The X-Files* was shot on location, the production company felt that two location managers were needed. Louisa and Todd location managed alternating episodes.

A location manager, as defined by the Directors Guild of Canada: ". . . searches, surveys, and secures locations for the approval of the Employer in consultation with the Director and arranges for the same. . . ." In reality, location managers do much more.

On the technical survey for the pilot episode, director Robert Mandel was eager to return to home and abandoned us in favour of an earlier flight to L.A. A survey without a director is like a ship without a captain, so we spent the rest of the afternoon devising our own shots, staging our own action, and idling away the hours.

The last technical survey: (left to right) construction coordinator Rob Maier, production designer Graeme Murray, Louisa, and first assistant director Tom Braidwood.

THE PROCESS

Each episode of *The X-Files* was typically allocated eight days for preparation (prep) and eight days of Main Unit shooting. Once a script was received in prep, a concept meeting was scheduled to discuss the overall look of the show, as well as any specific requirements. Technical surveys, during which department heads toured the locations to be used in filming, took place on Day Six of prep. On Day Seven, a production meeting was held. Day Eight was a mad scramble as everyone prepared for the first day of shooting.

CONCEPT MEETINGS

At the concept meeting, department heads assembled in the boardroom, adhering to the rigid seating order that evolved over the first two seasons. Nameplates in front of certain seats reinforced the importance of the "knights" around the rectangular table. A telephone connection to Los Angeles – to Chris if he was not in Vancouver, and other L.A.-based staff – was established and script discussions commenced. Each department head had a chance to ask questions and express ideas. There were sometimes murmurs about forthcoming rewrites by Chris and there were often concerns about a script's requirements given the time constraints of the schedule and air dates. The marching orders from L.A. were simple: try to stay on budget, but, most importantly, do not – ever – miss an airdate.

TECHNICAL SURVEYS

The location technical survey brought together all elements of preproduction in one (very often long) day of Q&A. The survey provided all departmental heads with an opportunity to visit each location (and sets, where applicable) in advance to discuss the director's requirements for that location and ensure that everyone was "on the same page" when it came to camera positions, lighting, special effects needs, special equipment requirements, actor and stunt actor action, and work truck and crew parking arrangements.

Technical surveys were the big day for the location manager. We had to be almost omnipresent in our ability to ferret out and decipher mumbled conversations twenty feet away, and provide real answers to the many questions being posed from all directions at once. Any last-minute "surprises" usually surfaced on this day.

Surveys typically departed the production office at 10 a.m. and returned when the itinerary was complete. Depending on the number of locations and the distance travelled, this sometimes meant as late as 8 p.m. The size of the survey crew varied from episode to episode, but generally numbered about twenty. The mode of transport evolved over the years, encompassing everything from airport shuttle buses (not a very comfortable way to spend eight hours of one's life) to small coaches (bad air conditioning and no washroom) to full-size passenger tour buses (the only way to go). Crew members became very territorial about seating, expecting the same seat each trip. This was only problematic when an additional crew member tagged along. Unknowingly sitting in someone else's "designated" seat forced a domino effect, skewing the entire arrangement.

The ability and the knowledge of the driver was very much a crapshoot at the hands of the charter bus company. On one occasion, a driver – barely able to navigate his bus off the North Shore Studios lot – quietly informed me that he had no practical knowledge of the Lower Mainland. He had been selected as a last-minute replacement while his usual run was between Vancouver and Calgary.

The "event" around which each technical survey revolved was lunch. More often than not, a good lunch meant a good technical survey and a bad lunch spelled disaster. For better or for worse, surveys came to be remembered more for their lunches than for the actual survey itself. In a way, they came to define crew dynamic and morale.

No one understood this better than executive producer Bob Goodwin, who was always ready with a dining suggestion should we come up short. True, his choices were usually at the *high* end of the dining spectrum, but they were always appreciated by a crew hungry for a new dining experience. As one unidentified crew member once postulated: "There has to be some correlation between good production values and good tech survey lunches."

The key to a good meal was three-fold: we had to be in and out in one hour, the service had to be efficient, and the food had to be of a quality and variety as to please the varying tastes of the crew. Restaurants offering such service almost always became "repeaters." Choosing a restaurant was based on the actual locations itinerary.

Bills for these lunches averaged six to nine hundred dollars (tip included) for twenty people. A *significantly* larger bill for a lunch at La Belle Auberge in Ladner

Wine complemented the technical survey lunch twice a season: before Christmas hiatus and at season's end. During the lunch for "Talitha Cumi" (3x24), equal bottles of red and white wine were placed on the table. However, only two people drank white wine: Tom Braidwood and Al Campbell. At our first location stop after lunch, Tom disappeared. He was eventually discovered dumpster diving in the alley behind Asian Imports, retrieving a supply of new wooden accordion fans. Back on the bus, and with a smile on his face, Tom distributed his gifts.

Months later we discovered that the fans were infested with termites, as evidenced by the expanding piles of sawdust in our offices.

Executive producer Bob Goodwin asked for a lunch at a top-notch restaurant during the survey for "Quagmire" (3x22). He planned to ask key grip Al Campbell to return for Season Four, and expected Al would more easily agree if he was distracted by a good meal. Unfortunately, Al's meal arrived after the rest of us had eaten and were ready to leave. Bob waited for another day to ask Al to stay with the show.

resulted in this fine restaurant being dropped from the repeater list. Another sneak visit to this restaurant on the tech survey for "The Post-Modern Prometheus" (5x06), directed by Chris, caused shock waves in the accountants.

> Overall, as the show got bigger, so did the lunch bills. Lunch at Nick's Spaghetti House during "Ghost in the Machine" (1x06) cost $231.12. Lunch at Il Giardino during "The Pine Bluff Variant" (5x18) was $997.74.

PRODUCTION MEETINGS

The final review of the entire script occurred during the production meeting. The first assistant director synopsized each scene, and allowed each department head their last chance to voice outstanding concerns in a group setting and to provide progress reports on prep.

> During these meetings executive producer Bob Goodwin would sketch architectural renderings of Victorian houses. An average production meeting lasted for ninety minutes. A short meeting usually had Bob rushing to finish his sketch.

The last supper. From left to right, top: Michael Bobroff, Rick Fearon, Alan Bartolic; middle: Shirley Inget, Louisa, Todd; bottom: Al Campbell, Bob Goodwin, Tom Braidwood, Chris Carter, "Bucky."

Another late night for Second Unit.

PROLOGUE (TP)

I remember well the day that the official announcement finally came that *The X-Files* would not be staying in Vancouver for Season Six. It was mid-afternoon Friday, March 27 and I was sitting at my desk. Louisa was at the 2400 Motel on Kingsway with the shooting crew, overseeing the filming of scenes for the "The Pine Bluff Variant" (5x18). Needless to say, there had been much speculation on this topic for months, most of it in the media. As Tom Crowe of the B.C. Film Commission explained: "We were getting 'x' number of calls a day from citizens wondering if the latest rumour they'd heard was true . . . I was telling them they'd got the wrong number . . . they should have been calling the local newspapers, who seemed to have a direct line to Fox network's executive offices."

My phone rang and when I picked it up, Chris was on the line. He sounded extremely disappointed as he informed me of the network's decision to move the show to Los Angeles. I recall saying something inadequate like, "That's really too bad, but thanks for taking the time to call in person," as we ended the conversation.

After five years of working closely with this gifted individual and our extended family, I was stunned by the sense of impending loss. And although I think most of us believed the writing was on the wall, it still came as a shock when the word finally came. This was evident by the range of emotions shown when Chris travelled to set later that afternoon to formally announce the decision to the shooting crew. It was certainly not the decision he had been pressing for and whether it came about as a result of an executive decision or a promise made to an actor mattered little. It was the end result which weighed in.

100th episode wrap party. Left to right: Gaffer Dave Tickell, Louisa, production co-ordinator Anita Truelove, director David Nutter, and construction co-ordinator Rob Maier.

Genny-op Murray Chisolm backstage at GM Place.

In March of 1993, production manager Lisa Richardson, with whom I had worked on several previous shows, hired me to be location manager for the Pilot. None of us knew who Chris was, but when he greeted his new crew for the first time his passion, his kindness, and a suggestion of his perseverance reverberated through everybody.

The script for "The X-Files" was refreshing and innovative. Since the show was presenting new ideas, it was important that we find new locations. We scouted unknown territories within the Lower Mainland and discovered alien worlds. What became the "look" of the show – a mystique associated with the dark, rainy environment – was as much a result of forging ahead at all costs as it was an articulated vision.

Chris had been thrown into an unknown city, and was going to turn its geographical diversity to his advantage, making *The X-Files* a show people would soon be talking about.

– *LG*

Medical doctor Dana Scully is assigned by FBI directors to observe agent Fox Mulder. Scully's first case with Mulder takes her to Oregon, where Mulder believes high school students found dead in the forest are victims of alien abductions.

During filming, our key grip fell into one of the "graves" and broke his leg.

We returned to this location to shoot a cemetery for "Kaddish" (4x12), occupying this portion of the park for nearly three weeks in late November. Special effects spent the entire time draining the grave plot of water.

GRAVEYARD

QUEEN ELIZABETH PARK, CAMBIE ST. AND 33RD AVE., VANCOUVER

The most difficult location to find was the "knoll" setting of a graveyard. After an endless search I suggested the obvious: Queen Elizabeth Park, a large public park in the heart of the city. It was the first time that this park, a prime tourist site, was used for a graveyard and since then, over nineteen graveyard sets have been filmed there.

On the night of shooting, rain towers were positioned on the upper road along with two lighting cranes, creating what are "normal" Vancouver conditions. The numerous takes in the freezing rain soaked Gillian Anderson and chilled her to the bone; a suitable Vancouver baptism for her. On Day Two, it was decided that the semi-truck accident scene could be filmed that night on the road leading to the park. With last minute approval from the City, we were able to pull off the scene.

Exterior shots of the psychiatric hospital were taken at the Westlawn building, which is now condemned due to interior asbestos exposure.

PSYCHIATRIC HOSPITAL

RIVERVIEW HOSPITAL SITE, 500 LOUGHEED HWY., PORT COQUITLAM

This location marked the first meeting with producer Bob Goodwin, who would later become a executive producer and director of *The X-Files*. Crease Clinic, a vacant hospital site at Riverview, offered the best and most practical sets for the interior of the *psychiatric clinic*. Bob had just completed the pilot for *Birdland* (a shortlived ABC series) and was waiting for the producers of that show to hire him for their series. In the interim, he booked Crease Clinic for a year at the price of one Canadian dollar. We approached Bob for use of the space, which we got for $500 a day.

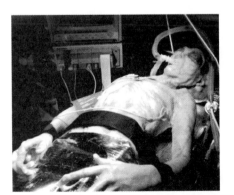

FBI BOARDROOM/PENTAGON WAREHOUSE

KNOWLEDGE NETWORK, 4344 MATHISSI PL., BURNABY

This location was originally scouted for an *FBI head-quarters* which could be filmed during regular work hours. For a price, anything is possible. While touring the site I got sidetracked in the warehouse which housed millions of journals that were organized in racks that were thirty feet high. There was no doubt, we had our *Pentagon files* site.

The warehouse was the focal point, but in order to facilitate filming schedules, the *FBI boardroom* was also created here.

Since we were filming during the regular work day, lights were positioned in and around active workers. One woman was quietly working in her cubicle with equipment clamped everywhere, reflecting light onto her computer screen. When asked if the lights were a problem, she enthusiastically told us that we were no bother.

In following seasons, alternative warehouses were scouted, but none suited Chris' vision, necessitating return visits to the Knowledge Network.

FBI BULLPEN/MULDER'S OFFICE/FBI HALLWAY

CANADIAN BROADCASTING CORP. (CBC), 800 HAMILTON ST., VANCOUVER

The infamous *Washington FBI headquarters*: a nightmare to scout. Every location presented to the producers and directors was somehow inadequate. Photos of the actual interior of the Edgar J. Hoover building were sent to us for comparision.

The open-plan bullpens typically seen in film do not exist today. They have all been converted into semi-private partitioned cubicles, hardwired with complex mazes of wires that cannot be removed.

The CBC television newsroom was the most promising bullpen set but there were compromises, such as only being able to film on Fridays after 10 p.m. To schedule a full day, *Mulder's office* was created in the basement of the CBC building, which was in keeping with the script, and the ground floor hallway became the FBI's.

As soon as they got the word to set up, set decorating scrambled into the CBC newsroom, changed some signage, messed up some desks, disconnected a few computers, and created the *FBI bullpen*. After a few episodes of this hysteria, the CBC newsroom became off-limits.

Eventually the bullpen was built onstage at the North Shore Studios. An expanded version of Mulder's office was also built there.

For the first appearance of the Cigarette Smoking Man, special permission was required to allow "smoking" in a public building.

Many of the names on the desk nameplates in the FBI bullpen are those of crew members.

The most challenging aspect of the new show? Its spelling. For those first seasons, until the show caught on, it was: "X as in 'x' and 'Files' as in 'filing cabinet.'"

Chris wanted his sets and locations to look as normal as possible. That way, the juxtaposition between the normalcy and a slight, even unnoticeable, aberration would create tension. As the show continued, the perception of reality changed. The show became dark and mysterious and its look transformed into the viewer's perception of "mysterious" and "alien."

FOREST

SEYMOUR DEMONSTRATION FOREST, NORTH VANCOUVER

This forest is the mecca of filming in Vancouver: a governed resource fruitful to the film industry. With exemplary guidance, the Greater Vancouver Regional District (GVRD) has sustained forest habitat while still providing a film backlot.

February brings rain in Vancouver – as David Duchovny well knows – so at the request of the GVRD we built platforms at the base of the gully and provided wooden paths with grips for equipment and actor accessibility. This preparation cost about $6,000 for supplies and another $3,000 to provide a plywood base for a crane, which housed a bank of xenon lights.

On the night of filming, the rains – clearly discernible by the cameras – descended. Within five minutes of call time, everyone was drenched. The Vancouver crew was somewhat prepared for the deluge, but supervising producer Daniel Sackheim had not yet become accustomed to Vancouver weather. After an hour of setting up, Dan approached production manager Lisa Richardson and myself and demanded weather cover. At this point in the schedule, our only option was a fast food restaurant that was so far away it would have cost a day's filming.

But Dan's persistence in continuing the shoot culminated in one of the most visually exciting scenes of the Pilot, and established rain as a valuable commodity to the show.

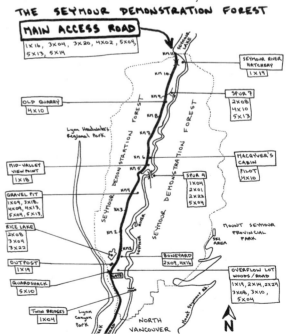

RURAL MOTEL
CEDAR LANE MOTEL, 926-160 ST., WHITE ROCK

Mulder and Scully's first motel stop. The script demanded fire, wind, rain, darkness, and everything else that can be thrown into a night shoot – which made securing a location somewhat difficult.

Cedar Lane was the perfect motel – quaint and well-kept with a retro, nostalgic quality. Everyone loved the motel but the owners decided at the last minute to cancel. Incidents like these devastate a location manager. After I told Lisa of the problem, she looked at me sternly and said, "Offer them more money." It worked.

Fire scenes always require standby municipal firefighters and when possible, those firefighters and fire engines are included in the filming. 160th Street is the border between the cities of White Rock and Surrey and the Cedar Lane Motel is on the Surrey side of the street. Surrey fire engines are green. White Rock fire engines are red. We wanted to use the red fire engines in the filming, but had to have a green fire engine on standy in case of problems. There wasn't enough space to park the camera truck.

It was a big night for special effects co-ordinator Dave Gauthier, who arrived at Cedar Lane with a cube van filled with noisy wind and lightning machines. Dave remained with the show for the entire Vancouver run, but after Season Five, nobody could keep track of the vehicles and equipment associated with his department.

We returned to the Cedar Lane Motel to film "Demons" (4x23).

The truth is outta here

It's official: X-Files creator Chris Carter's leaving Vancouver for L.A., and taking agents

When Chris announced that the X-Files was leaving Vancouver, it was news.

With respect to location managing and specifically, filming on location, there are always bound to be detractors; that is, individuals who either hate the film industry or who appear to tolerate us, so long as we "stay out of their backyard." Over the years — and even on a popular series such as *The X-Files* — we've had our share of NIMBYs voice this exact sentiment. We call it the viewer hypocrisy argument for, in at least fifty percent of these instances, opponents have to admit — when pressed — that they do indeed watch television or go to movies at the cinema. And since everything is shot *somewhere*, it follows that if we all espoused such an attitude, location filming would sooner or later dry up and we'd have no choice but to watch in-studio programming, limiting the range of shows available, not to mention the entertainment value.

The film industry in British Columbia is worth a lot of money in direct trickle-down revenue to a wide array of businesses, from lumberyards to hotels to restaurants and equipment rental companies. Chances are that if you don't benefit directly from revenue film dollars, someone you know does.

Sometime those in the film community can be the biggest problem. When filming "Grotesque" (3x14), the wife of a local producer complained to the Vancouver film liaison that her free parking had been taken up by film trucks, after we had offered her alternative parking. Her free parking space has since been metered.

The X Babies

Not only did the cast and crew of *The X-Files* work long hours to produce a great television series, but many also found time to spawn great progeny.

Piper Anderson (mother Gillian, Dana Scully) Born: 2x07 "Three"

Samuel Bobroff (father Michael, trainee assistant location manager) Borne: 4x24 "Gethsemane"

Baby on location: Francesca Pittson, Christmas 1997.

Dylan Buckmaster (father Richard, gaffer) Conceived: 5x16 "Mind's Eye"

Amber Caughlan (father David, location scout) Conceived: 5x06 "Post Modern Prometheus"

Leora Pearl-Dowler (father Brett, unit manager) Born: 4x21 "Zero-Sum"

Nancy Joan Horsting (father Eric, location production assistant) Conceived: 4x11 "El Mundo Gira"

Quinlan *and* Conner Huff (father Peter, special effects buyer) Born: 4x17 "Tempus Fugit"

Quinn Hunt (father Tom, lead carpenter) Born: 2x21 "The Calusari"

Edin Kane (father Brian, lead set dresser) Born: 5x08 "Kitsunegari"

FBI LOBBY/FBI LABORATORY
B.C. HYDRO HEADQUARTERS, 333 DUNSMUIR ST., VANCOUVER

The *FBI lobby* was first filmed here. During an active work day, a crew and over fifty extras took control of the lobby and two of the elevators. *Scully's lab* was created on the sixth floor of this building. On the day of filming, three other units were parked in close vicinity. One of the streets hadn't been signed for unit parking, which caused huge delays in getting trucks in. As usual, our Teamster captain, Ken Marsden, resolved the situation, and we learned to always check street signage two days prior to filming.

It was outside this location that assistant location manager Rick Fearon and I acknowledged the intrigue of the show and our delight at working on a different and refreshing television concept. We intuitively thought that *The X-Files* had potential for success.

Mulder's office: *a permanent set built on a North Shore Studios soundstage, just prior to being torched for "The End" (5x20).*

EXTERIOR SCULLY'S APARTMENT

610 JERVIS ST., VANCOUVER

This location was *Scully's apartment* used both for the Pilot and "Squeeze" (1x02). The location was later dropped because the reverse angle showed a parking lot and limited the number of shooting angles.

Another apartment – on Pendrell Street, also in Vancouver's West End – was selected. The interior of *Scully's apartment* was a modified set built on a soundstage at the old Molson Brewery facility, which was operated by Aaron Spelling's company. In Season One, when the show moved to North Shore Studios, Spelling wanted over $30,000 for Scully's and Mulder's apartment sets. J.P Finn, production manager at the time, scoffed, and after Spelling relocated, Finn was able to negotiate a new deal for a mere $4,000.

David (at left) takes his lunch at North Shore Studios.

Olivia Kassis (father Bill, best boy) Born: 1x21 "Born Again"

John Kassis (father Bill, best boy) Born: 3x03 "D.P.O"

Emily Kassis (father Bill, best boy) Conceived: 4x04 "Teliko"

Akcinya Kootchin (mother Lisanne, chef) Conceived: 5x17 "All Souls"

Tadeo Labra (father Alexis, location production assistant) Born: 5x05 "Christmas Carol"

Sara Jessica Lieshout (father Peter, lead painter) Born: 5x12 "Bad Blood"

Mackenzie Loewen (father Greg, art director; mother Candace, Second Unit hair stylist) Conceived: 4x06 "Sanguinarium"

Ethan Peverley (father Lance, location production assistant) Born: 5x18 "The Pine Bluff Variant"

Sawyer Scout Pileggi (father Mitch, Assistant Director Skinner) Conceived: 5x01 "Unusual Suspects"

Francesca Pittson (father Todd, location manager) Born: 4x07 "Musings of a Cigarette Smoking Man"

Jack Sandor (mother Joanne Service, assistant to Chris Carter) Conceived: 5x09 "Schizogeny"

Macrae Martin (mother Ainslie S. Wiggs, assistant location manager) Born: 5x20 "The End"

We suspect that six other babies were born during the Canadian run of *The X-Files,* but former crew member parents were unavailable for confirmation.

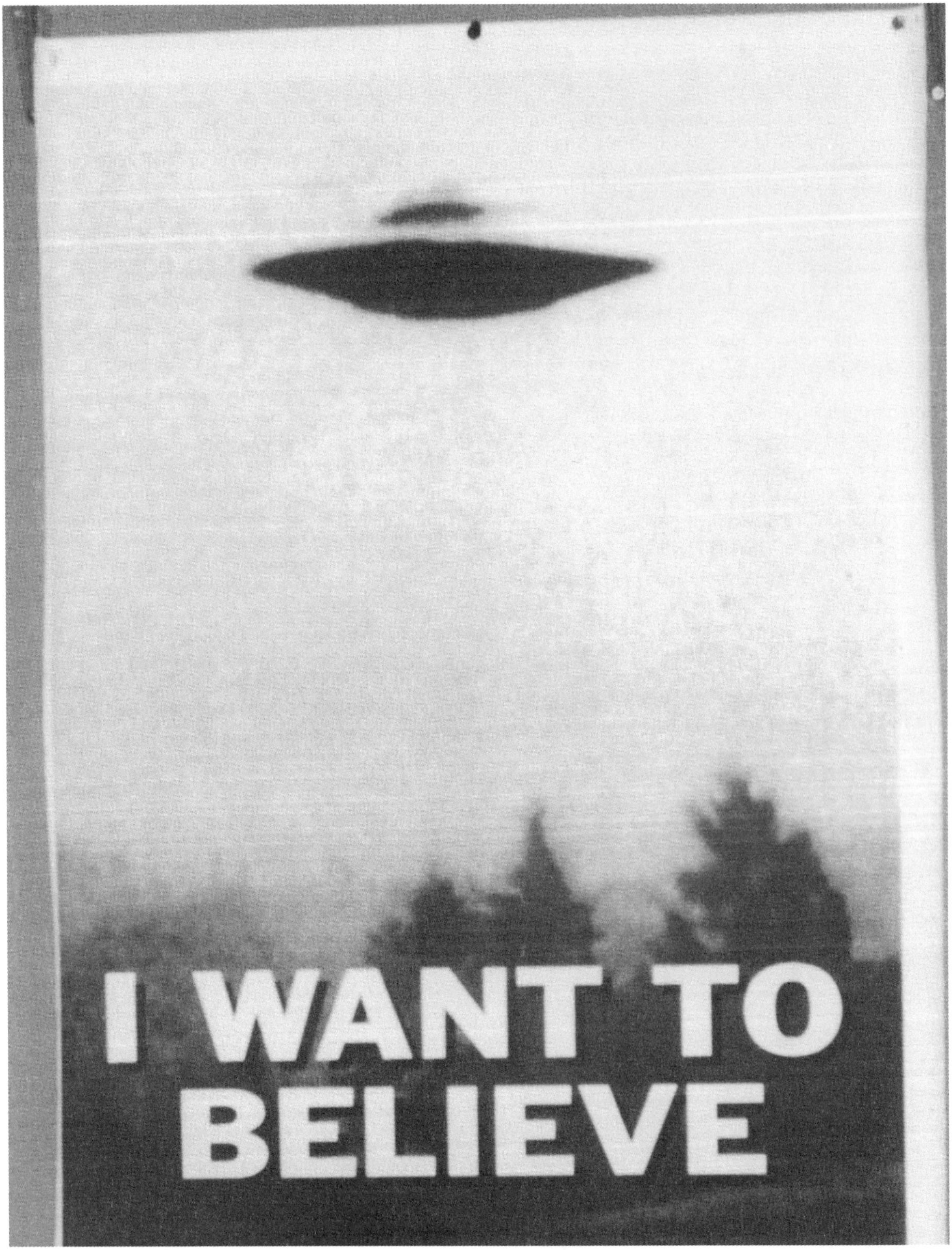
I WANT TO
BELIEVE

For me, it began with a phone call from J.P. Finn, who had just been hired to production manage a new television series called *The X-Files*. It was early June 1993 and film production in Vancouver was already heating up. Good crew would soon be difficult to find.

Asking J.P. what the show was about, he explained that it had "something to do with FBI agents investigating unsolved cases." "Great," I replied, having no idea what I was signing on for. "Probably keep us employed until Christmas," J.P. added. I suspect that was the premise upon which much of the crew was hired. That "Christmas" meant Christmas 1997 plus four months and 116 episodes occurred to no one.

Likewise, names like Chris Carter, Gillian Anderson, and David Duchovny meant nothing to any of us.

But Chris' optimism and passion for the show was infectious. It showed in the eyes of that diverse group of individuals with whom a five-year journey was about to begin. At the first production meeting, I recall doing a quick mental calculation based on the twelve locations required for "Deep Throat" (1x01). Not every episode would be so location-intensive, but even tossing a few hundred out, 1,000 locations over five years seemed very plausible. And that figure did not include the demands of Second Unit which, by Season Three, had become an integral component of the show.

Pondering these numbers, I questioned whether the Lower Mainland could successfully double as so many different regions and states and still retain a sense of newness. Were we destined to become a northern version of Los Angeles, where every possible location had been shot to death over the last forty years, to the point where most locations on most shows were easily recognizable?

Five years is an eternity in the life of a dramatic television series, the only guarantee being the unexpected. Most of us chose to concentrate on the immediate demands of the show and let the future make itself. .

And so it went, episode after episode, year after year. Location after location. By the time "The End" (5x20) finally came in April 1998, we still maintained a respectable list of locations either under-utilized or unused altogether by *The X-Files*. A list which we enigmatically referred to as "Locations We Wished We'd Filmed."

In the end, it was time – and not locations – which ran out for Vancouver and *The X-Files*.

– *TP*

Origins of a Myth

The Season One opener, "Deep Throat," was huge in every way, establishing the show's dynamic from day one. The fabled long days and longer nights for which *The X-Files* quickly gained infamy began here, although it must be said that by the middle of Season Two, a *de facto* Second Unit — operating under the B-Unit moniker — had assumed enough of the workload as to relegate at least a portion of this hardship to crew mythology. Still, the fable persisted, evidenced in the difficulty production sometimes had in finding day-call crew, particularly if there was a lot of other work in town.

The location list for "Deep Throat" speaks for itself, and took us from downtown Vancouver to the furthest reaches of the Lower Mainland: Budahas House, Zoe's House, Ellens Air Base, Perimeter Fence (Air Base),Gateway Motor Lodge, Burger King, Athletic Field, Dunaway's Pub, Flying Saucer Diner, Hague House, McLellan House, Rural Road.

The *Budahas House* was about to receive a facelift when we arrived on the scene. Director Dan Sackheim requested a "hold" be put on further renovations until after filming was completed. Ironically, this home would eventually become a recurring location during the first two seasons of another Carter/Fox series called *Millennium*.

In these early days of the show, it was not uncommon to receive a Sunday afternoon call (we never officially worked weekends) from executive producer Bob Goodwin at his home in Washington State. Typically, he would offer his perspective on a location concern or alert us to potentially tricky location requests in

> Director of photography: responsible for directing the set-up, operation, and movement of the camera; also directs the lighting of the scene. Also called a cinematographer.

1x01	DEEP THROAT	TP

Test pilots at an air base in southwest Idaho disappear, and when they are located they go psychotic. While investigating, Mulder uncovers a top secret facility containing technology recovered from crashed alien spaceships.

ELLENS AIR BASE
BOUNDARY BAY AIRPORT AND VICINITY, DELTA

One of twelve locations called for in the first episode of *The X-Files,* this flat expanse of tarmac, mixed farmland, and lonely country road became our own little Area 51 and a frequent favourite over the years. The airport itself closes to all but emergency air traffic between 11 p.m. and 6 a.m., providing a very narrow "window" within which to complete complicated scenes on the runway. With an average of five hundred take-offs and landings per day (more in summer months), this is a very busy little terminal indeed.

Use of the grand old hangar is contingent upon the co-operation of airport manager Ran Vared and the several tenants occupying the building. They range from private individuals hangaring planes to flight schools and machine shop operators.

This day perhaps set the tone for the large body of show mythology which evolved over the years. It was a sunny Thursday afternoon in July as the crew assembled at the intersection of Airport Road and 80th Street to film scenes at the *Ellens Air Base checkpost,* a structure created by the construction department.

As day turned to night, we moved onto a runway apron and adjacent field, where we continued filming through the night. From the perspective of production, the scene became surreal as cast and crew scrambled to complete the last "night" scene at 6 a.m. the following morning, just as the first rays of sunrise illuminated our hangar deep in the background. By then, everyone was staggering to follow *director of photography* John Bartley's single utterance, "We'll shoot into the western sky . . . that'll buy us a few minutes." Which may in turn have resulted in director Daniel Sackheim's quip: "If suffering were an artform, I'd be Michelangelo."

An adjoining tract of overgrown land once housed married officers' quarters during World War II and doubled as everything from a migrant *Mexican farmworkers' shantytown* in "El Mundo Gira" (4x11) to an *air disaster crash site* in "Max" (4x18) to the bombed-out home of a hacker genius in "Kill Switch" (5x11) to a highway intersection in "D.P.O." (3x03). The attraction to this location was two-fold. A network of paved roads, the legacy of this site's residential heritage, allows for complex night lighting set-ups using *condors* and cranes, as the grid design – separated by stands of deciduous trees and grassy fields – makes for good accessibility for equipment. Similarly, a half-mile stretch of "country road" – complete with a four-way intersection – was ideal for roadwork where total control was necessary. Centre lines were added or erased as per story requirements.

This site came complete with its own folklore. A large earthen cistern rising fifteen feet above the otherwise pancake-flat terrain once served as a water supply for the military residences located here. Neighbours warned us of "strange satanic rituals" being performed atop the cistern late at night, a claim for which no physical evidence was ever found. Nonetheless, the cistern was destroyed by a Transport Canada crew not long after *The X-Files* first filmed here.

"If suffering were an art form, I'd be Michelangelo."
– *Dan Sackheim and a blue-painted figure from "Kitsunegari" (5x08).*

FLYING SAUCER DINER
HILLTOP CAFÉ, 23904 FRASER HWY., LANGLEY

American-style roadside diners – especially those frequented by UFO nuts – are as rare as a full day of sunshine in December in Vancouver. Our establishment, which has seen better days, sits on the side of the highway next to a defunct motel. The selling points here were this location's rustic and isolated-looking appearance and

upcoming scripts. As the show achieved its own rhythm we learned to read each other's minds, and such calls all but ceased. By Season Three, a weekend call from Goodwin meant that either someone had died, the sky was about to fall, or he had a great dining suggestion for our next Technical Survey lunch.

This said, we – as location managers – were extremely fortunate over the five years to have unrestricted access to the writing staff in Los Angeles. Hence, rather than waiting for Day One of prep on a new episode, we were able to discuss in some detail upcoming location requirements days or weeks in advance of prep. This allowed us to sidestep potential problems by either suggesting alternate locations or clarifying the parameters within which a location might be used. This gave both Chris and his staff the opportunity to write to a specific location well in advance of prep, thereby avoiding the messy scramble entailed in adapting scenes or story-points to fit a location once prep had begun.

The Zone

As in other film production centres, a studio zone exists in the Lower Mainland, bounded on the south by the U.S. border, on the west by the Pacific coastline, and ranging for twenty miles north and east of Vancouver. This zone differentiates "local" from "distant" in terms of travel to locations, and was designed to limit excessive travel to and from locations on a daily basis.

Filming outside the studio zone can result in a substantial increased cost to production, as equipment truck drivers incur more hours in reaching distant locations and the mileage costs (crew members are reimbursed a certain amount on a per kilometre basis for each kilometre travelled outside the zone) for a crew of fifty to one hundred people can be significant. Hence this practice is avoided except where deemed absolutely necessary.

Additional Terms (TP)

One of the key points when negotiating for the use of a location is to understand fully your company's location contract, which both location manager and client will be required to sign. Large institutions and corporations such as universities, hospitals, and airports will require you to sign their agreement, a copy of which the location manager must procur and forward to the company's legal representative as early in prep as possible.

In most cases, though, the company agreement will suffice, and while all contracts are not created equal, it is the location manager's responsibility to be prepared to explain fully each article in that agreement. Some articles are self-explanatory, while others are so wrapped in legal jargon that a call to the company's legal representative may be necessary for both clarification and a layperson's interpretation.

The focus of any location agreement are the *hold harmless clause*, the *liability waiver*, and the legal assurance that suitable insurance coverage is in place to protect both parties in the event of mishap. Other clauses stipulate dates and times for prep, filming, and wrap and, of course, the amount to be paid the client (Lessor) for his/her co-operation. A *right of ownership clause* identifies the company (Licensee) as sole owner of all filmed footage and recorded sound taken at a location, reserving the right to use this material in whatever way it wishes.

In "Mind's Eye" (5x16), the Blarney Stone, across the street from the Meat Market, was used as a tavern. The writers liked the named of the pub and changed the script accordingly.

the ability to pull a vehicle up out front. The faded veneer, chrome, formica, and vinyl are reminiscent of the drive-in theatre era.

This day began on a rural road in South Surrey with a chase scene involving Mulder and Scully and some evil guys in black suits and government-issue sedans. Given the distance outside the studio zone (see *The Zone*), production hired a large tour bus to transport crew members to this location. That way, production would not have to reimburse crew for mileage travelled outside the production zone in their personal vehicles, since alternate transport had been provided. It also gave people the opportunity to sleep for the duration of the half-hour ride.

I recall being at the diner when the first crew cars arrived. One by one I counted heads, wondering who could possibly be on the bus, since virtually everyone had arrived by car. When the bus finally pulled up in a cloud of dust, its door swung open and – with a dramatic flourish – the lone occupant, key grip Al Campbell, stepped out. He bowed to the assembled crew, who had gathered to offer a round of applause. With the exception of "Herrenvolk" (4x01), filmed in the Kamloops area, the suggestion to bus crew members to distant locations was never again entertained.

The decision to ferry cast and crew to this location was not without controversy. It was a time-consuming and expensive move. Despite the vintage "look" of this place, we never returned here. When this episode aired, those most opposed to the choice of this location noted that the exterior shot was so tight that we could have shot a diner in downtown Vancouver and made it work.

DUNAWAY'S PUB
THE MEAT MARKET, 1 WEST CORDOVA ST., VANCOUVER

The script called for a wood-panelled, traditional *tavern* which might serve as a watering hole for the Washington political insider crowd. There's a tangible difference between American taverns and most Canadian pubs and bars. Perhaps it's the colourful neon festooning those long, well-stocked bars and the sense of accumulated history etched into the worn wood wainscotting which characterize American taverns and drinking holes and lacking in most Canadian establishments.

In 1986, Vancouver hosted a world's fair – *Expo 86* –

which set off a wave of ill-conceived renovations through the majority of Vancouver's low- and mid-range hotels and bars in an attempt to capitalize on the projected tourist boom. The result was a transformation from "old and well-travelled" (read *character dowdy*) into "generic tasteless tacky."

This location was literally the only one of its kind in the Lower Mainland. Well-travelled without being trendy, the combination of high windows, higher ceilings and a unique arrangement of booths made it the hands-down choice.

> **This location is where Assistant Director Skinner took a bullet in "Piper Maru" (3x15).**

1x02	SQUEEZE	LG

Mulder and Scully pursue Eugene Tooms, an ancient but youthful-looking killer who hibernates and awakens every thirty years to kill and feed on his victims' livers.

CALVERT STREET
1000-BLOCK WEST HASTINGS STREET, VANCOUVER

Tooms made his first appearance in Philadelphia observing his victim through a drainage grate. This location was chosen because of its urban look and the ease of locking off the street for picture purposes. A City Hall maintenance person thought we were crazy spending so much money to film red eyes through a drainage grate. Permission was granted to lock-up the street after 6 p.m. To avoid a lengthy night of filming we began the day in an office dressed by set dec on the fifth floor of a nearby building. Most active offices do not allow filming during work hours. Set dec had to haul thirty desks and associated dressing up to the fifth floor within two days. I have never been forgiven for that location.

On the morning of our arrival not one member of my crew showed up early to cone the streets for unit parking. Luckily our location was situated next to a construction site and with a bribe of coffee and doughnuts, a construction worker guarded the street until assistance arrived.

For the most part, potential clients do not question a well-written contract, provided it has been adequately explained to them. In special cases involving unusual risk (an explosion, a high-fall from a building, the use of a marine vessel or aircraft, for example), contracts may be modified to include specific location concerns as they relate to the nature of these activities.

At the end of most location agreements is a separate article entitled *Additional Terms*, in which these concerns may or may not be addressed. Having said this, requests by the client to include a term are reviewed and granted on an *ad hoc* basis, sometimes with poetic twists.

One of several locations required for "Deep Throat" (1x01) was a motel to play as the *Gateway Motor Lodge* in southwest Idaho. As locations were being "grouped" according to municipality for scheduling and travel purposes, we found ourselves down on 12th Avenue in Tsawwassen at the Beach Grove Motel towards the end of July 1993.

The key elements offered by the Beach Grove were the actual lay-out of the motel: two storeys, an "L" configuration with a parking lot separating the office building from the motel units, and its stand-alone geography on the edge of a neighbourhood of low-slung residences. With a golf course across the street, it exuded a small-town feel.

For filming purposes, access to a motel room, the motel office, and the parking lot would be necessary. Given the time of year, the motel was reasonably quiet. In addition to booking Scully's room (Room 4) for a day on either side of our filming day for set dec purposes, rooms on both sides of Room 4 were booked for the day of filming to ensure a degree of control over extraneous noise. One of these rooms would then be allocated to sound mixer Michael Williamson's sound cart, although his sound van was actually parked on set and is clearly visible in one scene as the *Abramowitz Plumbing van.* The other room was used to store unwanted motel furnishings removed from Room 4. Additional rooms were booked on the day of filming for craft service/first aid and a camera equipment stash since the camera truck was parked some distance from set.

The trickiest point of negotiation involved a small capuccino bar housed in a converted unit close to the road. Not only was it inappropriate for the storyline (although a blessing for a crew fueled by caffeine) but it was directly in the line of fire and would, therefore, have to be "dressed out" to resemble – of all things – a motel unit. This meant not only a separate negotiation for loss of business but additional work for both the construction and set decorating departments, already over-burdened on this episode.

The café operator was enthusiastic although disappointed to learn that her business would not be featured on the show and would be shut down as well. Still, we reached an agreement which I felt worked very much in her favour.

On the day of filming, I arrived on set at about 6:30 a.m. to find my assistant and the locations crew busy preparing for a 7 a.m. crew call. I was standing in the office when I heard shouting from the parking lot. I turned to see, through the gunrack in a truck's rear window, a man arguing with the café operator. Crew members drifted by on their way

---

66 EXETER STREET

**REAR OF IDEAL GIFT AND TOY LTD.,
51-53 WEST HASTINGS ST., VANCOUVER**

The exterior of Tooms' abode was situated in one of the more undesirable areas of the city. Even though there was an attempt to avoid filming on "Welfare Wednesday" (the last Wednesday of each month, when welfare recipients receive their cheques), there was no alternative. The bars were hopping and filming was repeatedly disrupted by outbursts of drunken behaviour. Relief was felt when the crew moved inside an abandoned boarding house above the Meat Market restaurant in Gastown. That was the day I was formally introduced to David Duchovny.

USHER'S UNDERGROUND PARKADE

**VPC PARKADE,
107 EAST CORDOVA ST., VANCOUVER**

This location actually houses the original ventilation system selected by director Harry Longstreet for the scene where Tooms attacks Usher. The system was situated in the upper levels of the parkade and would have necessi-tated a massive *tenting job* to simulate night at huge expense. An exact duplicate was built and assembled in the underground level of the parkade.

1x03   **CONDUIT**   **TP**

After a young girl is abducted by aliens during a family camping trip, Mulder and Scully find that her younger brother may be communicating with the aliens through binary sequences in television static.

1x04   **THE JERSEY DEVIL**   **LG**

Scully and Mulder travel to New Jersey to investigate reports of cannibalized human remains. Evidence suggests that the legendary Jersey Devil is a pre-human evolutionary being.

EXTERIOR VACANT BUILDING/RESTAURANT/PD PARKING LOT

900-BLOCK STATION ST., VANCOUVER

Chris was adament that the she-devil character appear as if she were nude. Hair, makeup, and wardrobe went to work and a nudity suit was devised.

The requirement for the urban component of the show was an assembly of buildings where the she-devil could leap from rooftop to rooftop and we proposed Station Street. The owners of Atlantic Sheet Metals, who owned most of the block, positioned lawn chairs outside of their scrap metal shop during filming. Occasionally I meet one of the owner's in the grocery store and he always says, "Anytime you want to film at my place, let me know."

During prep for this episode, director Joe Napolitano complained about the lack of scouts – who search for potential locations. After this we were allowed to hired scouts.

> We returned to Station Street to film the *bad neighbourhood* scenes for "All Souls" (5x17).

NEW JERSEY WOODS
SEYMOUR DEMONSTRATION FOREST, NORTH VANCOUVER

There are not many accessible caves in the Lower Mainland and the best option for filming is Twin Bridges at the Seymour Demonstration Forest, even though five-tonne trucks are the only vehicles that can negotiate the road, creating a five kilometre run between the *circus* and set. The nudity issue was also a delicate matter given that this location is open to the public. The she-devil was allowed to venture about topless with her hair shielding her breasts. The rest of her was clothed.

INTERIOR TOWNHOUSE/RESTAURANT/ROB'S OFFICE
1451 ANGUS DR., VANCOUVER

All three of these locations were scheduled for one day of shooting. Luckily, we found a mansion diverse enough to make this grouping possible. The dining room was converted into a *restaurant* where Scully would meet a love interest. The den made a fine *office* and the kitchen worked as a *kitchen*. The only problem was municipal time constraints – the curfew between 11 p.m. and 7 a.m. At 10:30 p.m. wrap was called and it was obvious that the set could not be struck by 11:00 p.m. Everyone walked away from set, and the following day wrap was completed. The producers' sensitivity to municipal requirements set a precedent in local filming: don't push the envelope, we're here for awhile. Throughout the entire

to breakfast or the work trucks, but paid scant attention to the drama unfolding. After several minutes of heated mutual accusations, the woman leaned into the cab of the truck, where she was grabbed by the driver and forced to sit. The vehicle then spun around in a cloud of blue smoke and roared out of the motel lot and down the road.

From what we heard, it was evident that we had witnessed a lovers' quarrel in which the boyfriend had arrived back in town only to find a third party involved. Ironically, the passion and intensity of this off-camera melodrama set the tone for Scully's on-camera exchange in the parking lot with Mossinger later in the day.

Returning to the premise of this story and most amusing of all was the additional clause requested by the owner of the motel prior to signing the location contract. It read — and I quote verbatim — "the Company acknowledges that the subject matter of this episode does not contain material which may be construed as damaging to the reputation of the motel." In other words, no on-camera hanky-panky, please. Evidently, this did not apply to motel staff.

A final moment of irony arose a couple of hours after this exchange occurred. Fox's vice-president of production Charlie Goldstein paid a visit to set. His initial comment was something like, "Nice location, how's it going?" Given the day's events so far, I countered with, "Not bad, but if I'm forced to write these guys one more cheque you may as well consider this place Fox real estate." To which Charlie merely looked around, smiled, and — shrugging his shoulders — made a beeline for the camera.

Naked

Location managers and first assistant directors must work closely together, especially during the scheduling of work to be filmed on location. This ensures that a proper understanding exists with regard to what is being filmed when and how, and allows for planned adjustments to be made to the shooting schedule where potential problems could arise with regard to special effects, stunts, and neighbourhood restrictions.

Producer J.P. Finn recalled an incident during the filming of "Shadows" (1x05) in which a lapse occurred:

We were at this house in East Vancouver, *Lauren's house*, I believe it was. Production had been using my car to double the stunt vehicle for the day work and we must have fallen behind schedule, because I remember that at around 10:30 p.m. — as the 11 p.m. curfew drew near — there was a heated discussion between myself, the location manager, and the first assistant director regarding a scene we were about to shoot which involved lightning and wind machines. Ritters, the noisy ones.

Todd was adamant that the scene be scrapped, as it would certainly have taken us past the curfew and, with all that noise, he did not want to assume responsibility for the fall-out. First assistant director Brian Giddens pointed out that the day's work had always been scheduled in this order and that if not for problems with the stunt earlier in the day we would have been home by now.

In any case, it was my responsibility to ensure that we made our day, one way or the other. Back in those days there was no Second Unit to pick up the pieces. The show was in its infancy and money was tight. Everything had to be shot as per schedule.

duration of the show in Vancouver, the producers respected municipal film ordinances, although sometimes reluctantly. When Chris was working on the *Millennium* pilot he personally paid for reshoots on the Burrard Street Bridge, but felt guilty closing down a portion of the bridge for a second time. I told him not to worry because the end result would be good product for the industry in Vancouver.

> We returned here to film exterior scenes for "Fire" (1x11). It doubled as an English country estate.

1x05	SHADOWS	TP

A secretary's murdered boss —from beyond the grave — protects her from danger and uses her to expose the murderer.

1x06	GHOST IN THE MACHINE	LG

A "smart" building's computer system develops a survival instinct.

EURISKO BUILDING
METROTOWER COMPLEX, COMPLEX II, 4720 KINGSWAY, BURNABY

The requirement for this location was an *office tower lobby* during the day. Metrotowers agreed, without knowing the implications or the impact we would have. Our day began on the plaza outside the towers. Filming was taking longer than anticipated so by the time we started filming inside the lobby it was around 6 p.m. and most of the building had been vacated. I was struck with relief when I saw the set-up in the lobby. It would have been impossible for anything else to happen in the lobby. Extras were positioned behind the security counter while lighting equipment consumed the space. The elevator was being pre-rigged with lights and carts of equipment lined the elevator corridor. There was barely enough room for the actors.

Later that evening, the crew went outside and filmed "The Ghost in the Machine," sending a surge of power through each floor of the highrise. The Tower's engineer programmed, by cellular phone, the sequential lighting of each floor.

> The Canadian Security Intelligence Service (CSIS) occupied one of the floors of this building.

1x07	ICE	TP

A group of scientists in Alaska unearth – and become infected by – a worm-like parasite.

DOOLITTLE AIR FIELD

DELTA AIR PARK,
4187 - 104 ST., DELTA

"Ice" was probably the least location-intensive episode of my five-year stint on the show. With the decision to build the interior of the *Icy Cape Research Compound* on one of our soundstages at the old Molson Brewery site, only one location remained on the list.

The primary concern with this location was background, as *Doolittle Air Field* was set in Nome, Alaska, an icier locale than Vancouver. Shooting the principal dialogue scenes inside a hangar looking out limited the exposure to "southern geography," but a flat, treeless landscape would certainly help to sell the location. For this reason, we chose the Delta Air Park with its grass runways and collection of low-slung hangars. It was about as close to the Canada-U.S. border as we could get, which meant a predominantly flat, empty horizon when limited to camera angles from inside the hangar at Nahanni Helicopters.

It was September 29, 1993 and a clear, sunny day as cast assembled in down-filled winterwear and pretended to look cold, although no telltale hint of breath was visible anywhere. What an irony this would prove to be when, almost four years later during the filming of "Gethsemane" (4x24), cast and crew assembled inside an elaborate ice cave set built in a refrigerated building, the temperature on the wall reading -20 degrees Fahrenheit and pretended not to look cold.

This episode marked production designer Graeme Murray's debut on *The X-Files*, his excellent set foreshadowing even greater things to come.

"I could have sworn I parked here." At North Shore Studios' parking lot.

At about 11:50 p.m. we finished blocking and lighting the shot and the Ritter fans were turned on. The racket was considerable, and Todd stormed off set. We rolled camera and cut, preparing for another take. All of a sudden this guy appeared on his porch across the street. He was screaming obscenities at the crew, telling us to go home, that we had no right to be there. But here's the kicker: he was stark naked. He just stood there, in front of the whole shooting crew — men and women — letting it all hang out. We must have got him out of bed or something. Who knows.

Anyway, we ignored him and continued filming. I was determined to get the day and get us out of there as quickly as possible. He blustered on for another minute or so, then gave up. We wrapped around 12:30 a.m. It was one of the most ridiculous on-location moments I can recall during my five years on *The X-Files.*

As a postscript to Finn's commentary, it should be noted that the following morning a written letter of apology was hand-delivered to each resident in that block, along with notification that *The X-Files* was donating $500 to their Neighbourhood Blockwatch program. When we did transgress an understanding or agreement — which was infrequent considering the amount of location filming we did over five years — the company took these issues seriously and sought to make amends in the most socially responsible way possible.

Incidentally, the following morning, the gentleman phoned the production office to apologize for his outburst, and we in turn apologized to him.

1x08	SPACE	LG

A former astronaut is haunted by memories of a spacewalk, and the space shuttle project he is in charge of is sabotaged by an unknown force.

J.S.C. SIMULATOR SHIP CORRIDOR AND HANGAR

CANADIAN AIRLINES OPERATIONS CENTRE, 6001 GRAND McCONACHIE WAY, RICHMOND

Screening Room

During the first season, Fridays meant late-night shooting because *The X-Files* aired at 9 p.m. and David requested a one-hour lunch to correspond with air time. Lunch hour occurs six hours after call time, after which filming resumes for another six hours. Using simple mathematics, the crew determined that wrap hour on Friday nights would be 2 a.m. at the earliest. Fridays were not a favourite night for the crew.

While shooting "Ghost in the Machine" (1x06) one Friday, we began the day filming in Burnaby's Central Park, then moved to film inside the Burnaby Public Library parkade, to be followed by interior scenes inside the Library administration area. The parkade, essentially vacant at the time, provided a perfect venue for "air time" at 9 p.m., but was abandoned in favour of the exterior sidewalk/plaza of the Library where about forty chairs were placed in front of a forty-inch television. Traffic slowed at the sight of forty people watching television outside a library. First assistant director and Lone Gunman Tom Braidwood said it was the most bizarre experience of his film career.

"Space" is one of my favourites; the story was visually challenging, and having Graeme Murray on board helped to turn our ideas into reality.

The locations pertinent to this show led us directly to the airline companies. The Canadian Airlines Operations Centre granted us permission to film during their work day. We required use of the hangar and flight simulator facility. The simulator's operations manager asked if any of the crew would be interested in flying the mock 737s and 747s. I thought he was joking.

On the film day, we ordered four mobile carts to move equipment throughout the hangar area. A fifth was allocated to me as a comp. I arrived on the 4th floor to collect the comp, drove into an elevator, and was transported down to set. Once filming resumed, my cart led me to the simulator. The generator operator, Bill Dawson, was finished his cabling and I told him to come join me. He piloted a trip into Vancouver and I co-piloted a trip out of Hong Kong. During these trips, numerous messages were left on my cell phone to determine my (and the cart's) whereabouts. Word about the simulator got out and before long most of the crew was at the simulator station, forming a lineup. Almost everyone piloted a voyage. Finally, director Billy Graham sought out his opportunity, but production was due to move to another location. The crew was forced to wait for Billy at the new location as he had his turn. Approximately one hour of production time was lost due to "trips abroad," and producer J.P. Finn crashed his "plane" in Calgary.

J.S.C. MISSION CONTROL

ROBSON SQUARE CONFERENCE CENTRE, 600 ROBSON ST., VANCOUVER

One of the most difficult tasks on this episode was to find a *mission control station*. Many locations were presented but none looked like NASA. With a search in progress it was deemed that a space with a sloped floor could provide the basis for rows of "prefab" computer terminals. For this we chose a hidden,

infrequently used ampitheatre in Robson Square Media Centre. Construction ordered over fifty computer terminals prefabricated with plastic and useful for a one-time situation only.

1973 PASADENA BEDROOM
ROOM 1256, SUTTON PLACE HOTEL, VANCOUVER

A "reflective" scene with an encounter from Mars took place at the Sutton Place Hotel, in the room that director Billy Graham was staying in. Billy quite liked the idea that he could walk to work, and at wrap merely take three steps to slumberland. For locations, the hotel was a new venue, as filming is seldom allowed at "Le Grand Residence." After a pitch about the lucrative benefits of the film industry, permission was granted. Every residence was petitioned, and every precaution was taken to ensure minimal disruption to the neighbouring tenants. While shooting at Sutton Place, the Wall Centre, a hotel and office complex then under construction, allowed us to drop a camera from a construction crane to simulate a fall. At the end of the evening The Gerard Lounge – the bar at Sutton Place – provided welcome nightcaps.

1x09	FALLEN ANGEL	TP

On a tip from Deep Throat, Scully and Mulder visit a UFO crash site, and get caught up in the military's hunt for the invisible alien pilot.

WASHINGTON PARK/PLAZA
SIMON FRASER UNIVERSITY, BURNABY

Throughout the course of the show, we worked in almost every office building and public space in the city. Certain architectural styles do not exist in "newer" west coast cities such as Vancouver. Others are simply few and far between, among them the kind of monolithic complexes housing the real powerbrokers in the Canadian government. What was desired here was a large empty plaza surrounded by buildings evocative of the FBI headquarters in Washington, D.C.

Simon Fraser University, designed by well-known local architect Arthur Erickson, provided us with this rather unique location – complete with fountains and ponds – perched high on Burnaby Mountain. The logistics of

Hospital Site

In July 1993, the University Hospital (Shaughnessy Site) began closing wards and offices in preparation for a transfer of ownership to the Children's and Women's Health Centre of British Columbia, a process which was completed by November of that same year. The change of ownership proved fortuitous for the B.C. film industry in general, as the site offered a vacant emergency ward, two vacant fourth floor wards, a vacant sixth floor ward and ICU, an empty building (the Jean Matheson Pavillion), and the Old Stores Building, a wooden structure which sat alone in a parking lot.

The site also offered ample parking for crew and worktrucks alike and, with some restrictions, allowed late-night filming. Under the guiding hand of film liaison co-ordinator Barbara Faerge, the Children's Hospital, as we called it, became a regular location for *The X-Files*. Beginning with "Fallen Angel" (1x09) and culminating with "The Red and the Black" (5x14), we shot scenes for no less than twelve separate episodes on this site.

As a point of interest, the Old Stores Building — most memorable perhaps as *Lee Harvey Oswald's boarding house* and the rat-infested *decaying loft* from which the Cigarette Smoking Man contemplates the assassination of Lone Gunman Frohike in "Musings of a Cigarette Smoking Man" (4x07) — was demolished in March 1999. Executive producer Bob Goodwin purchased timbers from the site to use in building a barn at his Washington State property.

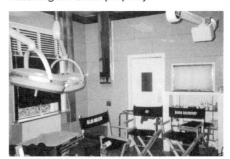

Lunch break at B.C. Children's Hospital.

Also on Burnaby Mountain is the BC Hydro system control centre which played as the *microwave station* in "Fallen Angel" (1x09).

The *flying saucer crash site* was filmed in the Seymour Demonstration Forest's gravel pit. "With all that foam and fire," recalled art director Gary Allen, "it was a wonderful set. We [the art department] cut our chops on that show."

Tenting job: refers to the practice of removing a daylight source from a set, a task performed by grips using black duvetyne material.

Condors: a crane used for elevating lights 60 to 100 feet.

When filming the flying saucer crash for "Fallen Angel" (1x09) at the Seymour Demonstration Forest, co-executive producer Bob Goodwin was caught speeding, and narrowly escaped a permanent ban from the forest. No-one was above the law.

bringing a large film crew to an institution such as this were rivalled only by the bureaucratic process involved in obtaining permission to film on campus during the semester. Parking is restrictive enough for many students, since there is little room for expansion on top of a mountain. It became a real military exercise when parking generators, worktrucks, and trailers *near* access points to locations while ensuring that crew members did not become lost between circus parking and location in the throng of student activity and the vast maze of concrete "ambiguity." Which made Deep Throat's utterance "Keep your friends close, your enemies closer" all the more prophetic.

| 1x10 | EVE | LG |

The daughters of two unrelated men – killed in the same manner – appear to be identical twins. Scully and Mulder discover that the girls are part of an abandoned cloning project subverted by one of the original clones.

LIGHTHOUSE MOTEL/DINER
SEACREST MOTEL, 864 STAYTE AVE. AND WHITE ROCK SUNSET CAFE, 15782 MARINE DR., WHITE ROCK

The most difficult location was the "typical" *roadside diner* with semi-trailers parked outside in the parking lot. Around the Lower Mainland, anyone who owns such prime property near an urban centre certainly would not devote it to non-profitable parking.

After a lengthy search for a diner, I recalled the Old Mill restaurant in White Rock and the café at the rear. The café opened onto a large gravel lot and appeared very rural in its setting.

With great enthusiasm, Graeme designed an awning to complement the exterior. Over ten semis filled the parking lot for a evening of non-stop filming. Many of the drivers were a bit disgruntled by the 4 a.m. wrap time.

| 1x11 | FIRE | TP |

When an "old flame" of Mulder's asks for help in protecting a British diplomat from a kinetic maniac, Mulder has to confront his fear of fire.

VENABLE PLAZA HOTEL
HOTEL VANCOUVER, 900 WEST GEORGIA ST., VANCOUVER

Anyone got a light? This hotel was originally built in 1887 at the corner of Georgia and Granville Streets and consisted of four storeys. It burned down and was rebuilt in 1916 at 710 West Georgia Street. The present structure was constructed at 900 West Georgia Street between 1928 and 1939, taking eleven years to complete. Ironic that our pyrokinetic villain should choose this venue? Actually, the fire which engulfed a room and hallway was filmed on a set built to match the architecture of this hotel. The establishing shot of the hotel was taken from stock footage, whereas the drive-up involved our practical location.

We had initially planned to film the party in a sumptuous ballroom, but due to booking problems, decided to move those scenes into the mezzanine and adjoining hallway. During renovations to the main lobby in 1995-96, the drop ceiling was removed to reveal the original ornately crafted beam ceiling. Another one-of-a-kind Vancouver heritage site.

The 14th floor of the Venable Plaza Hotel is devoted to the lavish and Old World decadent, the various suites bearing the names of English royalty. Assistant Director Skinner spent the night in a suite on this floor in "Avatar" (3x21).

| 1x12 | BEYOND THE SEA | LG |

Mulder and Scully switch roles as Scully becomes the believer and Mulder the skeptic. After her father dies, Scully believes that a death row inmate – who claims to have psychic powers and has offered to help solve a series of couple murders – is able to channel her father's spirit.

OCEANSIDE/BOATHOUSE
GARRY POINT PARK, CHATHAM RD. AND BRITANNIA HERITAGE SHIPYARD, 12451 WESTWATER DR., STEVESTON

On a cold and windy day Scully bids farewell to her father as his ashes are carried out to sea. When filming this scene Gillian stood on the shore of this sandy beach point location. The wind was ruthless, in fact, so much that executive producer Bob Goodwin requested a special warming tent be placed near the set to shelter his wife Sheila Larkin, who plays Scully's mother. It helps to know someone in the business.

Later the company moved to Britannia Heritage Shipyard to resume filming in the blustery cold. Propane heaters were not allowed in the shipyard because of the timber structures and heritage nature of the site. The crew huddled around an old wood-burning stove in a tiny room, telling stories and drinking lots of hot chocolate. The on-site liaison kept the fire ablaze the entire time.

A UFO glinting in the sunshine.

1x13   GENDERBENDER   TP

A rogue member of The Kindred, a reclusive religious sect who can switch gender, is killing city folk using sex as the murder weapon.

THE BRETHREN COMMUNE
ROWLATT HISTORIC FARM, CAMPBELL VALLEY PARK, LANGLEY

When the word *Amish* comes up in conversation, we usually think of barn-raisings and white clapboard buildings, or Harrison Ford and Kelly McGillis – *in Witness* – dressed in somber black and white astride a buckboard somewhere in Pennsylvania. The fictional Brethren of this story needed a turn-of-the-century communal farm to call home. And while the Lower Mainland does boast its share of old farmhouses and barns – from the dilapidated to the fully restored – all but a couple of these stand alone and hence were not suited to the communal look demanded by the story.

Unfortunately, several days of torrential rain wreaked havoc with production. During the winter months, the water table in this area is perilously high. This meant that even the plywood boardwalks we built to keep the crew dry sank into a muddy ooze, making the *grips* and *electrics* especially miserable. Due to the historic nature of our location (circa 1893), we were prevented from altering the appearance of either the clapboard farmhouse (production designer Graeme Murray asked to have it painted white) or the weathered outbuildings for filming purposes. Interiors were built on our soundstages.

LITHIA GENERAL STORE & FEEDSTORE
MARINE GROCERY, 3680 MONCTON ST., STEVESTON

Picture the Brethren on a buckboard urging their horses through a small rural community bustling with activity and you have a pretty accurate vision of what writers Larry and Paul Barber had in mind for Lithia. New England townships and picturesque rural communities are difficult if not impossible to duplicate in this part of the country – let alone in close proximity to Vancouver – since the settlement of the west coast was unique and relatively recent when compared with the histories of central Canada and the eastern United States. Which is why we ended up

---

Electrics: crew members responsible for placing lighting equipment.

Grips: crew members responsible for *shaping* light and making shadows.

Above-the-line: refers to the creative elements (script development, producers, directors, cast) of the show.

Below-the-line: refers to the technical elements of production.

here, a seaside community south of Vancouver doubling for a rural township in Massachusetts.

Urban sprawl and a mounting exodus from the city of Vancouver to outlying communities with affordable real estate and a quieter pace have altered economic prerogatives in those communities. Sadly, the result is – more often than not – either uninspired restoration projects or outright demolition of original architecture.

Near-disaster struck when the old buckboard rented for this scene pulled around a corner and into the main street in front of the *general store,* at which time – and as if on cue – a rear wheel fell off, injuring one of our wranglers, who broke his nose after being thrown into the street.

The X-Files also visited this town when filming "Miracle Man" (1x17).

1x14	LAZARUS	LG

While dying on the operating table, the body of FBI agent Jack Willis, an old boyfriend of Scully's, is inhabited by the consciousness of the bank robber he has been relentlessly pursuing.

BANK
BANK OF MONTREAL, 500-520 GRANVILLE ST., VANCOUVER

This episode was filmed just before Christmas. It took up to an hour to lay cable along the sidewalk leading to the bank due to the maze of pedestrian traffic. At the bank, sec dec had to remove all of the Christmas decorations minutes before filming and then return the items immediately afterwards. The bank robbery scene was alarming – the physical action and Lazarus' aggressive shrill made some people think an actual robbery was taking place.

This was the first episode that did not have Gillian and David in each scene, which meant they got an extra day off. Gillian and David approved, and there was an above-the-line request to create more shows that would give the stars a few extra, and well-deserved, days off.

In the early days at the Molson Brewery offices, the show employed two location managers, two assistant location managers, and production assistants as required. Typically, when filming on our stages, three production assistants were required for sound and traffic lock-ups. When on location, the number of production assistants varied, but there were always at least five. As the show grew in size and complexity, a Second Unit assistant location manager was hired and two full-time location scouts were added. By Season Four, we were usually shooting or prepping three episodes simultaneously; that is, scouting locations for an upcoming episode, managing the episode currently being shot, and "picking up" whatever was left of the previous episode(s).

This situation often created scheduling nightmares and put huge demands on all departments to keep three balls in the air all at once. Last-minute decisions based on weather (did it match with the scene half-shot three weeks earlier in the Seymour Watershed?) and the logistics of transporting David and Gillian from a Main Unit location to a Second Unit location and back again – sometimes taking two or three hours – necessitated that the location department be ready at all times to accommodate production. On studio days – and oh, how we prayed for those rare "studio shots" – there was obviously more time available. But on big days, in sensitive locations or on downtown streets where police officers and a dozen production assistants were needed just to manage traffic, it became very difficult to watch over the Main Unit while organizing or overseeing simultaneous prep and Second Unit.

We are proud to have developed a competent and loyal crew over the years, but this did not come without growing pains. Early in Season One, two production assistants (a man and a woman) had a physical altercation in a stairwell at the brewery. Without getting too specific, the woman felt somehow justified in taking a swing at the man (there were witnesses among the crew) in retaliation for what she perceived to be a physical threat. Two production assistants in a fist-fight on set? After deliberating briefly, Louisa and I decided that the only recourse was to relieve them of their duties. It was a horrible experience with both parties partially at fault, but the argument was far from being black and white. Thankfully, such incidents were never repeated and we, as location managers, learned a valuable lesson with regard to crew compatibility and labour management. By Season Five our department numbered upwards of

fifteen from time to time — each with specific, although overlapping, duties — and it is to the credit of the assistant location managers that, under adverse circumstances, they managed to prevent production assistants from killing each other.

"E.B.E." stands for extraterrestrial biological entity.

Director of photography Joel Ransom (left) and director Bob Goodwin, executive producer and director of "The End" (5x20).

BASEMENT
ORANGE HALL, 341 GORE AVE., VANCOUVER

Orange Hall is an apartment building in the Chinatown area of Vancouver, the majority of whose tenants are Asian. A translator composed a letter informing the tenants of our activity and then spent the day with us on location. We first filmed in the alley, then moved inside to the basement. It became evident that we required an additional police officer for the alley work. We put in a request to Constable Bob Young, special events co-ordinator with the Vancouver Police, and he said he would be on-site in a few minutes or however long it would take to walk twenty feet, since the police station was at the end of the alley. Now that's service.

Filming in the basement proved unpopular. The grips complained about the asbestos-insulated pipes, the electrics were angry because they couldn't clamp lights to the pipes, and everyone griped about the oppressive size of the space.

1x15	YOUNG AT HEART	TP

A bank robber caught by Mulder escapes prison, hooks up with a scientist who has found a way to reverse the aging process, and seeks revenge.

1x16	E.B.E.	LG

Scully and Mulder track a truck transporting an alien salvaged from UFO wreckage in northern Iraq to a secret government facility in Washington state.

POWERTECH
EXTERIOR-TRIUMF, 4004 WESBROOK MALL, UBC AND INTERIOR-POWERTECH, 12388-88 AVE., SURREY

Chris always encouraged us to send photos of interesting locations to the L.A.-based writers, Glen Morgan and James Wong. We sent them a file of the interior of BC Hydro's Powertech, and they agreed the site was a winner. The *lab* where the alien meets his final demise is, in reality, a functional research facility designed for testing different types of electrical current effects. It almost looks like Frankenstein's lab although more colourful. When director of photography John Bartley arrived on location, he was overwhelmed by the massive size of the facility and even more overwhelmed when he realized the number of lights that would be required.

1×17   MIRACLE MAN   TP

Mysterious deaths surround a teenage faith healer and his father's evangelical crusade.

REVEREND HARTLEY'S HOUSE
24990 RIVER RD., FORT LANGLEY

The *reverend's estate* needed to be at least as big as his reputation; large enough, in any case, to park his fleet of Cadillacs in the circular driveway. Set in Tennessee, something approaching a grand Southern look was sought.

Given the nature of our night work at this location – a big night-lighting setup, lightning, and wind machines – I felt our best chance was to stay away from established neighbourhoods. The obvious choices, such as Shaughnessy or South Vancouver, were, at the time, on a *hot list* which precluded night filming. We therefore found ourselves in the Langley area, well outside the city, where a number of large estates offered us more flexibility. The distance factor – which proved considerable – was part of the trade-off.

The home we chose was an interesting one. Situated high on a bluff facing northeast toward the Fraser River, it was self-contained and provided the necessary exterior visual elements. The previous owner had designed his home around a large indoor swimming pool, which could best be viewed from a horseshoe-shaped mezzanine balcony off which the bedrooms were located. The main floor consisted of a spacious foyer, a kitchen, a den, and a study, with the pool as the unifying element.

When the previous owner decided to sell the home, the listing agent convinced him that it would be far easier to market the house without the pool, which was subsequently filled. This created a huge central living room which never quite felt like it belonged, but was great for a film crew.

On the day of filming, I arrived early in the morning to find the property unexpectedly blanketed in snow. The locations, special effects, and greens crews got to work steaming and raking and sweeping snow off the large front lawn, since the first shot was to be a wide *establisher* of the house with the reverend's Cadillac collection lined up in the driveway. Steaming, which was the quick solution, only turned the lawn into mud and had to be abandoned in favour of the more laborious process.

Greensman Frank Haddad was quick to point out that, while there had been no report of snow anywhere in the

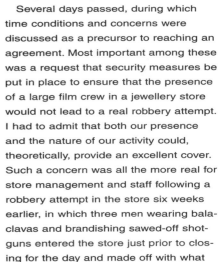

Hot list: When use of a particular location is felt to be heavy, or a major complaint is unresolved, city or municipal film officials place the location on a "hot list" for a pre-determined length of time, and no productions are permitted to film there. We call it "giving the location a rest."

Crime Story (TP)

The truth is indeed stranger than fiction. The *teaser* for "Young at Heart" (1×15) required a high-end *jewellery store* in which to stage the aftermath of a robbery, always a sensitive issue with security-oriented businesses such as this. In the spirit of "starting big," I made an initial inquiry to Henry Birks & Sons – Vancouver's largest and most prestigious jewellery store – and was both surprised and excited to learn that our request for filming was being considered.

Several days passed, during which time conditions and concerns were discussed as a precursor to reaching an agreement. Most important among these was a request that security measures be put in place to ensure that the presence of a large film crew in a jewellery store would not lead to a real robbery attempt. I had to admit that both our presence and the nature of our activity could, theoretically, provide an excellent cover. Such a concern was all the more real for store management and staff following a robbery attempt in the store six weeks earlier, in which three men wearing balaclavas and brandishing sawed-off shotguns entered the store just prior to closing for the day and made off with what

Teaser: The introduction to an episode, an opening scene that sets the premise of the story.

they could, fleeing through the mall and down a street crowded with Christmas shoppers. They were eventually apprehended, but not before scaring the daylights out of both staff and customers. And here I was, proposing a recreation of the aftermath of just such a robbery for an episode of *The X-Files*. The general manager must have thought we were crazy.

The scene opens with Mulder and Scully exiting a car (with the edifice of the "Hudsons Bay Company" — a Canadian department store — clearly visible in the background) and walking towards the front entrance of the store, ducking a ribbon of crime scene tape as they enter. Fake police cruisers — lights blazing — were parked on the plaza as background ambience. Next to them, however, were real Vancouver Police Department officers, who monitored the small crowd which had gathered to watch. Store security guards controlled the back and lower exits to the store, while each crew member wore special identification.

The fact that our story involved a crime scene and not the staging of a crime was very important to both the police and Birks management, as we had agreed that no weapons would be brandished by actors. (On more than one other production, actors have nearly been killed because the safety precautions regulating the use of props, weapons, and firearms had been side-stepped or ignored.) Filming was restricted to non-business hours to avoid disruption of business and to ensure that the most valuable jewellery was removed from the display cases and locked safely away for the night. The evening proved thankfully uneventful for all parties.

Lower Mainland the previous evening, the bluff on which we now stood was a good 200 feet above sea level, which would explain the strange appearance of snow at our location.

| 1x18 | SHAPES | LG |

Scully and Mulder venture to northern Montana to confront a legendary North American wolf-like creature.

RESERVATION
BORDERTOWN, 224TH ST., MAPLE RIDGE

For this episode we travelled to this municipality outside the studio zone. The extra costs made some people grumpy, at least until the result was successfully televised.

The script requirements for a Native *reservation* included interiors for a *police office, morgue, bar/poolhall* plus the exterior of *Ish's house and reservation/town*. Bordertown (a classic western "town" in Maple Ridge that was built specifically for filming), somewhat weathered over time and missing a few buildings that were consumed by fire, offered an interesting cloister of buildings and rustic interiors. Prior to filming, loads of gravel were dumped onto the muddy streets to ensure ease of vehicle, equipment, and people access. It started to rain two days before filming and by the time we arrived on location, the gravel had been absorbed into the mud. The entire crew wore boots; equipment kept getting stuck in the mud, and vehicles couldn't move. It was like filming a scene in a mud bath. The only happy person was first assistant director and Lone Gunman Tom Braidwood, because he lived within a ten-minute drive of Bordertown.

| 1x19 | DARKNESS FALLS | TP |

Prehistoric bugs that have been hiding out in the trunks of ancient trees in a remote forest are released by loggers and swarm their victims when night falls.

LOGGING CAMP/CABIN
LIGHTHOUSE PARK, WEST VANCOUVER

The rains pelted us in horizontal sheets here in the Olympic National Forest for eight days and eight nights, punctuated by only one afternoon of intermittent sunshine. Locating a believable *work camp* in an accessible old-growth forest was as difficult as it was easy to find clearcutting in this part of British Columbia. We ended up in this breathtaking park near the ocean, in an old camp now used as a nature centre.

A collection of rustic cabins arranged in a circular fashion around a small stand of very tall fir trees fit the script well. A dead-end road, permitting single-lane traffic only, offered problematic access to the site, and only essential vehicles (generators, camera truck, first aid/craft service) were allowed on-site. As a consequence, valuable production time was spent shuttling crew and equipment from the public parking lot 200 yards up the trail.

Valuable production time was also spent standing around in the deluge, waiting for the rains to let up long enough for sound mixer Michael Williamson to record essential dialogue, which was being rendered inaudible beneath the intense din of raindrops. This dilemma paled in magnitude when compared to the foul weather which confronted us in the Seymour Demonstration Forest while filming scenes at the *sawmill office* and on the *logging road*. At one point early in the day, the rain was so heavy that filming became impossible. First assistant director Vladimir Stefoff – usually rock-steady and upbeat with his characteristic exhortation, "C'mon, people, we've got to go" – tossed his waterlogged walkie-talkie on the ground in disgust as director and crew huddled in groups trying to figure out exactly *what* we *could* shoot given the conditions.

Key grip Al Campbell – always ready with a story – quipped that "it could be worse . . . we could be out at the Abbotsford Airport." This referred to a show Al and I worked on in 1990 during which a 737 aircraft was chartered for filming. On that day, it rained so hard – horizontal sheets driven by a strong wind – that B.C. Highways posted a vehicle advisory warning motorists to avoid using the freeway between Vancouver and the town of Hope unless absolutely necessary. Director Stuart Gillard – no stranger to filming in inclement weather – got so wet that, warning or no warning, a driver was dispatched to hunt down new raingear and waterproof boots.

The situation in the Seymour Demonstration Forest that day was, in some ways, as bad as that encountered at Abbotsford. At 9 a.m. it was so dark that *day* was effectively rendered *night,* at least where director of photography John Bartley's light meter readings were concerned. Similarly, it is rare – even in the Lower Mainland – to see rain bouncing off a spongy forest floor. Once again, the last word went to Al, who was moved to comment that he

The Silent Scream (TP)

Discord and differences of opinion were as common in the production of *The X-Files* as on any other. For the most part, and considering the 117 stress-fueled episodes during which all manner of conflict had the potential to manifest, such arguments were either privately aired or simply ignored in the daily routine of production. Of note, however, is an altercation which occurred during a technical survey for "Darkness Falls" (1x19). It was about 6:30 p.m. and the survey crew had been on the road since 10 a.m. It was late February and the weather was foul, as were the moods of many of us after having been incarcerated in a bus all day. Darkness had indeed fallen as we parked on an isolated road in the Seymour Demonstration Forest to examine our last location. It was raining heavily as we trudged back and forth on a gravel road while director Joe Napolitano attempted to choose the spot he felt worked best for the scene. After ten minutes, the question arose as to whether, in the darkness of the forest, we really needed to trudge further down a road which looked much the same at the beginning as at the end; it only made accessibility for crew and equipment more difficult. Executive producer Bob Goodwin stood in the pouring rain – caught in the headlights of the bus – arguing forcibly with Joe as we climbed back on the bus, watching, in growing amusement, the silent drama being played out thirty feet away. Mr. Napolitano ultimately lost the battle and, whether by coincidence, mutual agreement, or design, never again graced us with his presence.

As a postscript note, first assistant director Vladimir Stefoff chanced upon Joe emerging from a closed-door meeting with Goodwin later that evening, a glass of wine in hand. Stefoff noted that Joe appeared "as if he had been crying; his eyes were puffy, his face red." Whether it was an allergic reaction to Goodwin's peace offering is unknown, and what was said behind those closed doors remains a mystery.

hoped the weather at least remained consistent, as he and his crew were in no mood to have to match a sunny day to the current dismal weather. For better or worse, he got his wish.

This episode marked the second and final time an increasingly despondent director, Joe Napolitano, would work on *The X-Files* (see *The Silent Scream*).

While filming scenes for "Elegy" in Gastown, a rental car pulled up to the unit park area and a girl photographed the location that doubled for 66 Exeter Street in "Squeeze" (1x02). As it turned out, she had convinced her parents to travel from Australia to Vancouver so she could tour *X-Files* locations. She was invited on set, met David and Gillian, and walked away in disbelief of her chance encounter.

First assistant director Vladimir Stefoff (with the beard) and director Kim Manners (leaning) discuss the blocking of a scene.

1x20	TOOMS	LG

Eugene Tooms, the liver-consuming, hibernating killer, returns.

MALL/FBI PLAZA
CITY SQUARE MALL, 555 WEST 12TH AVE., VANCOUVER

Circus: the "mobile camp" comprising hair and make-up, wardrobe, washrooms, catering, and cast trailers. Together with the work trucks, our "unit" measured about 1500 linear feet.

It didn't take long for Tooms to return as the ratings for his introductory episode expedited a second coming. However, the FBI had become familiar with his traits. Even Mulder became suspicious of heating vents. Tooms' demise in the escalator was a major concern as location production assistants, special effects, and our on-site liaison worked frantically to remove the "blood" from the surface of the escalator. Seepage into the elevator's motors might have caused extensive and expensive damage.

Filming at this location required written approval from all the store owners in the mall, and interior filming was permitted after 6 p.m. only. The *FBI plaza* was filmed on the steps north of City Square.

| 1x21 | BORN AGAIN | TP |

An eight-year-old girl is possessed by the spirit of a dead police officer, who attempts, through her, to exact revenge.

| 1x22 | ROLAND | LG |

A dead scientist, who has cryogenically preserved his brain, psychically uses his autistic brother to continue his research and to get rid of the scientists who were taking credit for his work.

| 1x23 | THE ERLENMEYER FLASK | TP |

Mulder and Scully discover a government research facility in which alien DNA is introduced into human subjects using gene therapy. Mulder's investigation of the X-Files is shut down.

BRIDGE/OVERPASS
VANTERM OVERPASS, CLARK DR., VANCOUVER

Alien nation.

An *X-Files* classic, this episode encompassed ten locations and five large builds on our soundstages which, at that time, was extraordinary for a fledgling television series. The marching orders here were to come up with a *bridge* on which a clandestine exchange could be filmed. It would take place at night and involve three vehicles and gunfire. Complete control of all traffic between the hours of 8 p.m. and dawn was imperative.

Initially, permission was obtained from the City of Vancouver to close the northbound half of the Cambie Street bridge, but director Bob Goodwin was concerned that the actual location appear isolated. Similarly, Bob had planned to shoot a high-angle *master shot* of the entire scene, which necessitated finding another location in close proximity to a very high structure accessible as a camera position.

Another X-Files creature.

The overpass we eventually used served all these needs. A camera position for the high-angle master shot was found atop the adjacent grain elevators at the United Grain Growers facility. Bob, who does not particularly enjoy heights, nonetheless accompanied a small survey as we followed a rather circuitous route of elevators and catwalks up to the roof, where he very quickly chose a camera position, blessed it with the words, "This'll do," turned on his heels, and quickly returned to sea level.

In order to get maximum production value from this

location, director of photography John Bartley requested additional lighting for the grain elevators themselves, a job which required special *HMI lights* with sealed electrical boxes to minimize the risk of highly flammable grain dust coming into contact with a spark or electrical current. A row of lights was positioned at the foot of the elevators to supplement the existent yard lighting and provide depth for several of the reverse shots on the overpass itself.

The only casualty of the evening was a *cameo net* which had been thrown over a railcar parked beneath the overpass to hide its very Canadian markings. Sometime in the early hours of the morning this railcar, and several others, were abruptly shunted down the line, taking the netting with them.

Although we still had studio work on our schedule for this final episode, this was our last location day in Season One, and the crew celebrated with champagne at sunrise.

HMI lights: make use of mercury arc lamps which create light similar to daylight.

Camo net: camouflage netting, usually brown and green, used by the grip and greens departments to hide unwanted visual elements which cannot be easily removed.

MULDER'S APARTMENT

THE WELLINGTON,
2630 YORK ST., VANCOUVER

The interior of *Mulder's apartment* had, like Scully's, already been built on one of our soundstages. So when the time came to establish an exterior with which to pair our set, we surveyed most of the brick apartment blocks in Vancouver. Some were too rundown or otherwise poorly situated to be believable as Washington, D.C., while others incorporated window treatments or other architectural details which did not in any way suggest the interior we had already established.

The location we finally chose was situated in a quiet upper middle-class neighbourhood in the area of Kitsilano, and moreover, the landlord and tenants were amenable to our considerable presence. This feeling of goodwill did not extend to one nearby resident, with whom I had a rather convoluted and unproductive telephone conversation a few days before filming. Not only did he object to the parking arrangements we had made, but he considered the show, "to be the work of the devil and the crew, in doing the devil's bidding, Satan's puppets."

> Had this become a recurring location, it no doubt would have been one of David Duchovny's favourites. It was only a few blocks from the house he rented in Vancouver.

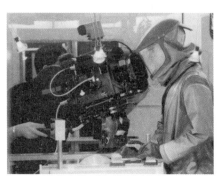

Jaap Broeker standing in for an extreme close-up.

PENTAGON WAREHOUSE
OPEN LEARNING AGENCY, 4355 MATHISSI PL., BURNABY

This location was inherited from the Pilot, when a comprehensive scout of possible locations was conducted by Louisa and her team. The problem which she encountered – and which I would also encounter – concerned scheduling and our desire to shoot these scenes during the regular workday.

This caveat had proven very costly on the Pilot, and in an attempt to save money, another comprehensive scout of warehouses was carried out for this episode. Nothing came even close to matching the thirty-foot-high racks of files and records, meticulously arranged – aisle after aisle – under one vast roof.

We therefore returned to what worked best and after some negotiating, were given a "small break" on the quoted fee. The price still reflected expensive employee buyouts as, once again, we would be filming here during the workday. In this case, the issue was one of dollar-for-dollar production value, and few could disagree that this was a truly unique and impressive location.

The debate, and the return to this location – which was Chris' desire – affirmed for me a notion which was in the process of becoming unspoken *X-Files* law: never settle for second best when second best isn't good enough.

We returned here with Main Unit to shoot scenes for "Redux" (5x02), although a Second Unit booking was cancelled. The fee for the cancelled booking became a charitable donation to the Knowledge Network, a local educational television channel.

Vancouver becomes Los Angeles.

By the halfway point in Season One, *The X-Files* had outgrown the makeshift office and studio facility being leased from Spelling Entertainment at the now-defunct Molson Brewery in Kitsilano.

We moved to North Shore Studios (which became Lions Gate Studios prior to Season Five) and a situation more favourable to our production requirements. We occupied two soundstages – later to be expanded to three – and a lot more office space. The construction and paint departments also moved into a shop from which they were better able to serve the show's demands.

This physical expansion was accompanied by a growth in crew size. In the beginning, we had discussed an ideal production schedule for the show as encompassing an eight-day prep/shoot schedule, with five days to be spent on our soundstages and three days on location. The big advantages of shooting in studio were control of the environment (weather, sound etc.), reduced "travel" costs, comfort level (close to the production office), and savings on location costs (we paid for studio space whether we were on location or not). On the downside, studio work was visually limiting (interiors only) and increasingly expensive for the construction department as sets grew more elaborate.

Conversely, the Lower Mainland offered a huge variety of accessible locations – both exterior and interior – within an hour's drive of the downtown core, one of the principal reasons for bringing a show like *The X-Files* to Vancouver in the first place. And while it was often more practical and cost-effective to "build" a morgue or a motel room or the cabin of an actual airplane than to film on location, building a mansion or a supermarket or a restaurant was cost-prohibitive. In reality, then, we tended to spend more time "out" (on location) than in studio, typically six or seven days on location to one or two days in studio. The size of the location department grew accordingly.

– *TP*

Crazy on You (TP)

Over the course of five seasons on the same show, a certain continuity develops with respect to the location department and location "contacts," who may be defined as everyone from police officers to equipment rental companies to snow removal businesses and restaurant managers. Such relationships have enabled discreet solutions to problems of romantic indiscretion involving certain cast members, excellent last-minute seating arrangements in restaurants for technical surveys, the avoidance of violent confrontations with psychotic citizens attracted by the "aura" of *The X-Files,* and the perceived potential for extortion. It was during the filming of "The Host" (2x02) that a situation arose involving the sub-lessee of a building at 1195 Richards Street and *The X-Files.* We had made a contractual arrangement with the Lessor of the premises to erect a set (a *medical examination room*) in the building. We were scheduled to film on the False Creek seawall near Anderson's Restaurant and needed another location nearby to complete our day's filming.

For the record, the Lessor of the premises had previously moved his business elsewhere and was in no way involved in the activities of the gentleman (let's call him *Mr. B.*) to whom he had sublet the property. At an on-site meeting with both gentlemen, the terms of our rental were discussed and acknowledged. Paperwork changed hands, as did a set of keys and a cheque. The one stipulation was that security procedures be strictly observed, as Mr. B. had some equipment in storage in a back room, which he planned to utilize once he renovated the building into a café and poolhall. Our construction and set dec departments would take two days to complete this set, which meant

 What a difference five years make: crew photos from Season One (top) and Season Five (bottom).

2x01   LITTLE GREEN MEN   LG

Scully is teaching at Quantico and Mulder is running wiretaps. Until he learns of a radar telescope in Puerto Rico that has made contact.

ARECIBO FOREST
SEYMOUR DEMONSTRATION FOREST, NORTH VANCOUVER

The west coast rainforest changes with the seasons, providing different types of vegetation with a variety of green hues. Particularly in the summer, these areas provide cinematic versions of tropical paradises such as the lush landscape of Costa Rica needed for this episode.

The Costa Rican rainforest was duplicated here a second time for "F. Emasculata" (2x22).

FLORIDA AIRPORT
PLAZA OF NATIONS, 770 PACIFIC BLVD. SOUTH, VANCOUVER

This location, a unique building encased in glass, provided an abundance of sunlight, appropriate for conveying a Florida location. The gods were on our side that day, except when the steel drum performers set up for their daily performance on the Plaza outside the building, but they agreed to refrain from playing during takes.

2x02   THE HOST   TP

The flukeman (a humanoid mutation) escapes from the bilge of a Russian freighter and into a New Jersey sewer systems, where it attacks and infects people.

SEWAGE TREATMENT PLANT
IONA ISLAND CAUSEWAY, RICHMOND

"The Host" gave rise to one of the most grotesquely loveable creatures ever seen on the show. From the bilge of a *Russian freighter* to the sedimentation tanks of a fully-functional *sewage treatment facility,* this creature developed a fondness for the sewers of Newark, New Jersey (a truly wonderful setpiece designed by production designer Graeme Murray and built by construction co-ordinator Rob Maier - a.k.a. "Strobie" - and his crew).

Given the odiferous locale, the hot summer weather,

dressers finally finished. She insisted on being left to lock up the premises once she had completed her work.

The following morning I was sitting in my office when the production co-ordinator stormed in, announcing that there was a "fruitcake" on the phone screaming about some stolen video lottery terminals (VLTs) and threatening our company with a lawsuit should we fail to "reimburse" him to the tune of about $8,000. I answered the phone and calmed Mr. B. down enough to hear his story, promising to investigate. I presented my version of the events and asked him if he knew the woman with whom the set dressers had spoken, which he did.

That afternoon, Mr. B. called again and ranted at my assistant for several minutes, threatening to expose the production company as enemies of the small businessman. I had, in the meantime, called the gentleman with whom I had made the original deal and briefed him on the situation. He, in turn, assured me that he would speak with Mr. B. and that I shouldn't worry about it. An hour later, Mr. B. conned his way onto the North Shore Studios lot and entered the front offices of *The X-Files,* where he began screaming at the front office staff and production co-ordinator Anita Truelove. Flailing away, he demanded to see me and again threatened legal action, as he felt he was being "blown off" by big business. He wanted his money now - or else. Truelove was beginning to see a front page headline. As she later mused, "the guy could have had a gym bag with an Uzi in it and mowed us all down. I had to threaten him with a police escort to get him off the lot." During the next week, Mr. B. called the production office several more times (as many as four calls in one morning) in an attempt to surreptitiously secure copies of our insurance policy.

I finally called the Vancouver Police Department and explained the situation to special events co-ordinator Constable Bob Young. He called Mr. B. and told him to leave the production company alone, as we needed adequate time to investigate his claim and resolve the issue. Young also noted that it was now up to Mr. B. to contact his own insurance company after filing a police report. Evidently this did not sink in, because Mr. B. next called the production office and, refusing to identify himself, attempted to get the producers' numbers in Los Angeles. It should be noted here that, given the dates of our contract (which had expired the evening before the VLTs had gone "missing"), my security arrangements and the fact that Mr. B.'s own employee had unwittingly assumed the risk based on her refusal to allow our employees to lock the building, neither myself nor our legal counsel at Fox felt that the production company carried any liability for the purported theft. At this point, we were simply trying to be a good corporate citizen and help this man find out who had taken his VLTs. Another call to Mr. B. from Constable Young resulted in his being informed that he now risked a visit from police officers if he persisted in harassing The X-Files, as the production was considering filingm harassment charges. This prompted Mr. B. to "lose it" as he hurled threats and abuse at Constable Young, who later recounted that this, in itself, seemed to suggest some degree of mental instability. Young informed me of this latest development and of the fact that Mr. B. was no stranger to the criminal justice system in Ontario.

I believe that Mr. B. eventually realized that with our knowledge of his criminal background came certain defeat and the harassment soon ceased. Not coincidentally, the poolhall and café never materialized.

and a 12 noon crew call, crew members were given the choice of opting for the day off or wearing special breathing apparatus (purchased by production at great cost) which filtered out the most offensive odours. Despite the offer, the entire crew reported for work that day, the overwhelming concern being the proximity of the catering truck to the sedimentation tanks. For the record, catering was parked as far away - and upwind - from the facility as the geography would allow.

This was obviously not enough for some crew members; recalling her very first day on The X-Files, second assistant director Michelle Dutka (then a location production assistant) says her most poignant memory is that of an after-lunch vomiting session with unidentified crew members out by the far fence on the perimeter of the property. Key grip Al Campbell later recalled his technique for dealing with the location: "Whenever I began to feel queasy, I'd visit the primary sedimentation tank - the place where the raw, untreated sewage came in. A couple of minutes of *that* and I'd go back to whatever I was doing, feeling relieved and grateful that nothing else was as bad as where I'd just been. For years afterward, no matter how ugly a location was, I'd remind Chris of the sewage treatment plant, pointing out that nothing could ever be as bad as that place. And we *weren't* going back there."

Just before midnight, the plant's emergency alarm system sounded, causing a brief delay in filming. Apparently this happened every couple of years and we were told that The X-Files was in no way responsible. Such "coincidences" were not uncommon to us as the show rolled from season to season.

FREIGHTER/ENGINE ROOM
PORT MANN HYDRO SUBSTATION, 14115 KING ROAD, SURREY

The notion of attempting to film the flukeman's escape from the engine room of a real freighter was entertained only as long as it took to call the Harbourmaster's Office and a couple of large private shipping lines and discover that absolutely nothing was in port and/or available to us. Filming on a real ship - as we would find out soon enough ("Dod Kalm" (2x19) and "Piper Maru" (3x15)) - was certainly not impossible, but it was very restrictive.

If a vessel had been decommissioned, chances were there would have been no heat, no ventilation, and only minimal on-board lighting. If, conversely, a vessel could be found which was on a lay-over for a refit or reloading, then filming had better be completed when the ship set sail. Local film lore includes horror stories of film productions working on cruise ships and freighters which, in port for a day or two, set sail with lights and equipment frantically being thrown ashore as the ship sailed away from the pier. As the Harbourmaster would remind me more than once over the years, "When a ship is loaded, it leaves." It had weather considerations at sea to consider as well as its own shipping schedule. There would be no waiting around for "another take or two."

So the search for an alternative was on; if not a real ship's engine room, then something which looked like it. I was already familiar with an old hydro substation which had been built in the 1950s as a backup power supply in the event of nuclear war and then never used. The owner was in the process of trying to sell off whatever generating equipment he could and the site was available as a location.

Better yet, areas of the facility looked very much like the bowels of a freighter. With the addition of some gauges and piping, and an "aging job" courtesy of head painter Louis Solyom's department, the transformation gave us a very serviceable engine room without the logistical headaches of working on a real boat.

> We returned here three seasons later to again use this location as a ship's boiler room, for "Patient X" (5x13).

2x03	BLOOD	LG

Electronic digital displays send messages to citizens of a small Pennsylvanian farming community, turning them into psychotic killers. An experimental insecticide is determined to be the root of problem.

DEPARTMENT STORE/OFFICE TOWER
ARMY & NAVY, 502 COLUMBIA ST., NEW WESTMINSTER

Army & Navy Boutique is one of Canada's oldest department store chains. Walking through the store is like a walk into the past. While viewing the location during the technical survey, production designer Graeme Murray's hands began to fidget, an important reference for construction co-ordinator Rob Maier and set decorator Shirley Inget (see *Crazy Arms*). By the look of things, Shirley was in trouble. Aisle upon aisle of goods had to be removed and redressed within a two-hour window prior to shooting and early access for set dressing was flatly denied. On the day of filming, waiting for the okay to proceed, Shirley and I lingered about the store, shopping, of course. At around 4 p.m., I asked for an early start.

Crazy Arms

Production designer Graeme Murray possessed a unique language of hand and arm movements which reflected the state of the budgets: hands in his pockets meant he was on track, hands out of his pockets but around hip level meant various departments - specifically construction, set dec, and greens - were at least $2,000 over budget, hands somewhere at chest level meant the department had used up their budget padding for the episode, and arms waving over his head meant more crew members were needed and a budget overage of $10,000 to $20,000 was expected. Department heads would often observe Graeme when wanting to get a sense of the magnitude of a project. Construction co-ordinator Rob Maier once said to greensman Frank Haddad, who had just finished a meeting with Graeme, "I need to know how high his hands went."

Permission was granted, and five set dec crew members quickly descended: goods were boxed and shifted around and gun racks and other items were installed, giving the appearance of some mad holiday shopping frenzy. Customers merely carried on, negotiating through all the ladders, dressing, and tool boxes scattered in the aisles.

Chris with set decorating department head Shirley Inget (left) and Louisa.

Location scouts spent plenty of time in their cars. In four years (Seasons Two through Five), Alan Bartolic logged 52,486 km (32,613 miles) and David Caughlan drove 96,520 km (59,975 miles). The polar circumference of Earth is 39,912 km (24,800 miles).

Blood slabs: portable, translucent pieces of rubber shaped like pools of real blood.

OFFICE TOWER
FIRST CAPITAL BUILDING, NEW WESTMINSTER QUAY

To create a bloody scenario, *blood slabs* were placed on the terra cotta floor of the tower lobby as an alternative to film blood which would have stained the tiles and caused extensive damage. However, no-one had discussed this decision with director David Nutter. I was told that it was my responsibility to inform the director about the blood slabs. Ultimately, the blood slabs worked like a charm. One slab was even permanently mounted on the window of the locations office.

CLOCK TOWER, COLLEGE
UNIVERSITY OF BRITISH COLUMBIA (UBC)

A man wielding a gun in a *campus clock tower*. . . . The script was written with the clock tower at the university in mind; however, guns are not allowed in public view at this location and gunfire was completely out of the question. To effectively portray this scene, part of the clock tower interior was built on stage and while on location, a view of the gun was secretly captured.

AUTO REPAIR SHOP

MAIN SERVICE AUTOMOBILE CENTRE
298 ALEXANDER ST., VANCOUVER

This garage is one of Vancouver's favourite film locations. A very reasonable standard rental fee was established on the basis of previous experience, and for that fee the shop was closed for the day. Film companies often claim half a day's use of a space which in the working world means four hours, but in film terminology means six hours. When set dressing and wrap-out time is added, a half-day can add up to ten to twelve hours. Many businesses in Vancouver, including the Main Service Centre, have been lured by the half-day scenario, but that is now changing.

HOSPITAL

EVELYN SALLER CENTRE,
320 ALEXANDER ST., VANCOUVER

The lawns outside the hospital location were unkempt when originally surveyed. The production designer asked for approval to trim the grass, but on the day of filming, the grass was still long, swaying in the wind. In a state of panic, greensman Frank Haddad raced to the location to save the shot.

"You touch my truck, I break your face."
– Teamster captain Ken Marsden

LOCKERS

OLD YMCA,
6TH ST. AND QUEENS AVE., NEW WESTMINSTER

This location - used several times - became the home of the *police precinct*. While filming, David noticed rows of old lockers, and asked about purchasing a row for his house. Locations arranged for him to have them for a mere $150, much to David's delight.

This location was used as a police station, a coroner's office, a prison, and a medical centre in "Aubrey" (2x12).

Sudden Death Overtime (TP)

Very seldom were we, as location managers, flatly refused the use of a location. And while this had much to do with the growing popularity and success of the show, when that "no" did come, it was usually accompanied by a behind-the-scenes drama rivalling that seen onscreen.

While searching for an eerie construction site in which to introduce a new character, "X," for "Sleepless" (episode 2x04), and espousing the "bigger is better" philosophy, I approached the site manager for the new General Motors Place facility (now home to the NHL's Canucks and the NBA's Grizzlies), at that time little more than a concrete shell with no roof, no floor, and no seats. The initial reaction was positive, given the fact that we wanted access after hours for night filming only. Several meetings and site visits by various department heads ensued, as well as the customary technical survey.

By this point in the schedule, prep had usually reached the point of no return in terms of substantial last-minute changes. Location agreements were signed and insurance certificates issued. Sets were constructed and locations dressed. Moreover, the director had ideally blocked out in his or her mind the staging of dramatic and action sequences given the specific geography of the location.

In this instance, my job was complicated by the fact that I was not dealing directly with the building owners, but with the site office. In location managing, it is always crucial to deal as directly as possible with those with whom final authority rests. However, given the nature of this location and the number of contractors and subcontractors involved, someone in the ownership hierarchy decided that the site manager should act as the intermediary between themselves and the production company. All I could do was comply.

2x04	SLEEPLESS	TP

Mulder is partnered with Alex Krycek to investigate Vietnam vets who were turned into killing machines as a result of a government "sleep eradication" experiment. One of them has acquired the power to kill through his waking dreams.

KAY'S DINER
TWO-JAYS CAFÉ, 81 WEST PENDER ST., VANCOUVER

The script called for a *truckstop* on the edge of town in front of which several large rigs could be parked. The lengthly dialogue scene necessitated traffic control for sound recording. This latter caveat reduced our options to three.

This downtown location was chosen for its great exterior appearance and spacious interior, its lovely vinyl-covered stools and formica countertops being an added bonus. Due to the seedy nature of the area a cleaning crew in special suits was sent in to clean and disinfect the neighbouring streets and alleys.

Although written as Kay's Diner, the real name of this café is featured prominently on screen. Sister Samantha pays Mulder a late-night visit in this diner on "Redux II" (5x03).

BRONX STATION
VIA RAIL TERMINAL, 1150 STATION ST., VANCOUVER

This heritage structure was built between 1917 and 1919 on land reclaimed from False Creek. The building is memorable for its ornate neoclassical style and the old barber shop (and the very elderly barber) is now closed after some forty years of business.

The difficulty in organizing locations such as this rests largely in working around existing train schedules. And while rounding up bands of roving petty-criminals is not an activity usually associated with film crews, this evening proved the exception, as assistant location manager Ainslie Wiggs explained: "It was Friday around 1 a.m. and the entire crew was exhausted after four days of location filming. We had been filming on the platform with seventy extras, when first assistant director Vladimir Stefoff called me over to camera." It seems that a belligerent extra was being particularly unco-operative and Val wanted him removed from set. Ainslie asked him to leave,

Nick Lea out of his Krycek character.

taking him by the arm in an effort to get him moving. "The next thing I knew, " she explained, "he's swinging at me and I'm ducking a punch." At this point, several crew members and the location production assistants intervened, physically marching the man out the main entrance, with security guards bringing up the rear.

"Once outside," Ainslie continued, "the guy taunted the crew about the fact that a *woman* was running the show, before bolting for the park across the street (Thornton Park), where a group of his friends was hanging out." Seeing this, Ainslie dialed *911* and requested police assistance. "I was a little shaken by then and worried that the guy might come back with his friends."

Within minutes, eight police officers arrived on the scene - four men and four women. The female officers began to round up the group, which further angered the man. Another officer explained that they had just come from a nearby Skytrain station, where they'd been watching surveillance camera footage of an act of vandalism that occurred at the station earlier that same evening. Several of the men in the group now being escorted to a paddywagon were identified in the video footage. "Finally," recalls Ainslie, "the paddywagon left, to a round of applause from crew members."

The behind-the-scenes drama had actually begun a little earlier in the evening, when executive producer Bob Goodwin arrived on set and tranformed into his wrathful "Bad Bob" persona. Filming ceased as Bob herded director Rob Bowman into a corner for a rather impassioned oratory on the reality of television production as it pertained to scheduling and the completion of the day's scheduled work in the allotted time. To say that he was displeased with the pace of filming would be a gross understatement.

On the afternoon before we were scheduled to film here, I got a call from a somewhat apologetic (and chagrined) site manager saying simply that there was a "problem" with the location agreement. My jaw hit the desk. The machinery of crisis management was revved up and numerous calls were made. During the course of various conversations, it was even suggested — somewhat tongue in cheek — that Rupert Murdoch (owner of Newscorp and Fox) be asked to call Arthur Griffiths, then owner of the stadium facility, regarding our little dilemma, something which — in retrospect — could have been very entertaining.

In any case, the real "problem" seemed to lie with the specific wording of a couple of clauses in our location agreement. It was 3:30 p.m. I had already called nearby B.C. Place, a nearby stadium, as an emergency backup since we were committed to being in that area of town.

In the meantime, it was suggested that perhaps their company lawyers should speak with our Chief Counsel at Fox, Anatole Klebanow, and let the experts try to settle things. Which is exactly what happened. By 5:30 p.m. the necessary paperwork was in place and sitting on my desk. Filming went ahead as planned.

Or almost as planned. After filming the scheduled scenes and viewing the *dailies*, the decision was made to recast "X" as a man. What eventually appeared on screen was a wide establishing shot of the facility followed by close-ups of the recast "Mr. X" filmed at a later date and on our soundstage.

Dailies: the unedited, processed footage of the day's work, transferred to video for immediate viewing. Also called "rushes."

Augustus Cole's isolation cell was built in a service tunnel as a two-wall set, utilizing the existing walls and ceiling of the tunnel. The set was designed to accommodate the unrestricted access of hospital staff and equipment throughout the day, the back wall and door being placed just prior to filming in the evening.

Walk and talk: a dialogue scene between actors that takes place as they are moving.

By the time this episode rolled around, *The X-Files* had already filmed repeatedly at a number of other hospitals and care facilities, among them Crease Clinic (Riverview Hospital), St. Vincent's Langara, and the University Hospital (soon to become B.C. Childrens' Hospital. See *Hospital Site*).

With the exception of Vancouver General Hospital, which has never really espoused or supported a co-ordinated film policy, accessibility to hospitals for filming has been contingent upon available space. If a hospital had an empty ward - or better yet, an empty floor - chances were good that a deal could be negotiated for filming. Available space was very much a month-to-month phenomenon dependent on the need for beds. It was difficult to predict and very much a coincidence of scheduling which allowed us into some facilities at all.

Writer Howard Gordon wanted a different setting in which to play scenes at a *Vietnam Veterans' hospital* in New Jersey. With space available in the ancient Willow Pavillion, liaison Rick Lowe was anxious to bring *The X-Files* to VGH in an attempt to convince management that filming could be both low-impact and profitable, if properly managed.

While surveying the vacant third-floor ward, we had a discussion about the lengthy *walk and talk* between Mulder, Krycek, and a doctor. Taking Rick aside, I asked him if we might consider the tunnels underneath this Pavillion and, after a brief pause, he agreed. It was definitely love at first sight as we stepped out of the rickety old elevator at basement level and proceeded along one of a series of long service tunnels. The dim neon lighting, low overhead piping and ducting, and glossy stone floors were a perfect fit with the script. Hours of access were the primary restriction. Nothing would happen down here until after the regular dayshift knocked off and, even then, a reduced nightshift would have to be accommodated.

The real problem - and probably the only reason we didn't revisit this location - was the lack of a freight elevator, which meant that construction materials going to both the third floor set and the basement had to be precut to fit the regular elevator or carried up three flights of stairs.

Because of the fragility of the existing elevators, each was operated manually by an attendant. And while we had been warned repeatedly by one of the regular opera-

Stuntman Tony Morelli as an alien for "Jose Chung's 'From Outer Space'" (3x20).

tors not to exceed the posted weight restrictions, we paid her little heed until the first load of crew members - among them myself, producer J.P. Finn, production designer Graeme Murray, and construction co-ordinator Rob Maier - hopped an unpiloted elevator and promptly became stuck between the ground and basement floors. The car descended just far enough that the operator, returning from a bathroom break, could peer at us from shoe level through the small glass window in the elevator door, shaking her finger like a remonstrative school marm as she chided us for disobeying the "rules."

And not unlike the mishap on the Westham Island Bridge years later ("Killswitch," 5x11) involving the technical survey crew and a malfunctioning swingspan, I could only be thankful that it was us and not David or Nick Lea peering up through that window as they received a scolding for disobeying the rules, going nowhere slowly.

Augustus Cole's *isolation cell* was built in a service tunnel as a two-wall set, utilizing the existing walls and ceiling of the tunnel. The set was designed to accommodate the unrestricted access of hospital staff and equipment throughout the day, the back wall and door being placed just prior to filming.

It was during the filming of a stunt sequence on a Gastown street that Robin Williams, in Vancouver for the filming of *Jumanji*, visited the *X-Files* set on his way home from an impromptu stand-up comedy gig at a local club.

| 2x05 | DUANE BARRY | LG |

Former FBI agent, alleged psychotic, and multiple abductee Duane Barry holds people in a travel agency hostage.

AQUATIC CENTRE/HOSPITAL/LAB
AQUATIC CENTRE AND CHEMISTRY BUILDING, UNIVERSITY OF BRITISH COLUMBIA

During Chris' directorial debut we were again on campus at the aquatic centre. David was swimming laps as part of the scene's action, and when he rose up from the pool, his lower extremities also rose up. Calm and composed, David delivered his lines perfectly. Women on set were particularly observant during the filming of this scene.

The generous fans in the chemistry department offered their spectrometer lab for the FBI *office scene*. Another office was used for a *hospital room* for the little aliens.

An autopsy lab for Scully.

The nearby community police office was remade as *Scully's office* ("Duane Barry" (2x05)) on the condition that a police officer (at our expense) had to remain inside during prep, shoot, and wrap. Scores of police officers volunteered for the job.

Picture vehicle: a vehicle featured specifically in a shot.
Hot for picture: anything that will be seen within the camera frame.

A shooting delay at the Treatment Centre ("Duane Barry" (2x05)) was caused when a sign — that Chris specifically requested to read "Please line up quietly," a reference to *One Flew Over the Cuckoo's Nest* — was discovered to have been incorrectly worded. Props quickly composed a new sign.

When Scully is shopping ("Duane Barry" (2x05)), her basket is filled with pickles and ice cream, a subtle hint from the props department that Gillian was pregnant.

COMMAND CENTRE/TRAVEL AGENCY/SCULLY'S OFFICE
WATERFRONT CENTRE HOTEL, 900 CANADA PLACE WAY AND WATERFRONT CENTRE TOWER, 200 BURRARD ST., VANCOUVER

The famous hostage-taking scene required two downtown storefronts situated across the street from each other and complete control of a street for *picture* cars. The two towers at the Waterfront Centre, separated by a fountain plaza, afforded the best visuals. Extras dressed in SWAT uniforms were positioned at the edge of a terraced pool at the hotel with a full view of the travel agency decorated on the lobby level. The final scene was filmed at the end of the "day," fighting the sunrise.

As a token of Chris' appreciation, a crew lunch was held in the grand ballroom of the Waterfront Centre Hotel ballroom, complete with white linen tablecloths and a live string quartet. Thus began the *feast cycle*. Whenever Chris or Bob Goodwin directed an episode, they would supplement the regular catered meal with things like ice sculptures, a sushi chef, and other extravagances.

TREATMENT CENTRE
ST. GEORGE'S SCHOOL, 3851 WEST 29TH AVE., VANCOUVER

In an example of blind optimism, three locations were scheduled for one day: this one as well as a *supermarket* scene and the abduction scene at *Duane Barry's house*. While filming at the school, electrics were prerigging *Duane Barry's house* with 18K lights were rigged in every room of the building facing the street, necessitating fans and special staff to watch for fires. A lighting crane was set up in the alley behind the house and a condor with another 18K was positioned on the street just past the house, lighting up the entire neighbourhood. Local residents brought out lawn chairs and prepared themselves for a evening of entertainment.

With a midnight curfew in residential areas on Friday nights, we asked the police officer on site for an extension to the filming. He denied our request on the basis that it would disrupt the neighbourhood, even though it seemed the entire neighbourhood was watching us film. Fortunately, the abduction scene took only two hours to complete, two hours less than anticipated.

2x06	ASCENSION	TP

Duane Barry kidnaps Scully and takes her to the abduction site. Mulder and Krycek give chase. As Barry hoped, the aliens take Scully instead of him.

SCULLY'S APARTMENT

1419 PENDRELL ST., VANCOUVER

This episode marked Part Two of the first two-part episode; many other two-parters would follow. We'd already established both location and setpiece for *Mulder's apartment*, as well as the setpiece for *Scully's apartment* interior. And not unlike the search for *Mulder's apartment*, the task was to find a suitably modest brick apartment building and match it to the interior setpiece on our soundstage.

We ended up at a smart-looking building in Vancouver's West End, which holds a monopoly on brick architecture in this city. Ironically, the six apartments in this building are all spacious front-to-back units with good natural light. Any one of these would have made a shootable location for *Scully's apartment* had the setpiece not already been built during Season One.

The real challenge here came with parking and night lighting requirements, as this is a neighbourhood of apartment buildings and as such, very densely populated. In order to effectively stage the "crime scene," a location assistant began blitzing apartments and parked cars with filming notices several days in advance to ensure the highest possible degree of co-operation from neighbouring residents.

When filming night sequences at this location, two condors and a scissor lift were standard order, along with a number of smaller lights placed in trees up and down the street. The trick was to light the scene without lighting up half of the adjacent apartments, for which tar-paper and rolls of black plastic became an invaluable asset. Because of the sensitivity of this location, filming curfews (11 p.m. camera wrap on weeknights, midnight on Fridays) were strictly observed, although given the wrap time required for lighting cranes, we always worked backwards from curfew to accommodate the electrics department.

With the exception of the Pilot, we tended to avoid the West End for these reasons, although we did throw a stuntman from the third-floor suite *(Dr. Dickens' apartment)* in an apartment block around the corner at 1091 Broughton Street in "Colony" (2x16). The shooting crew was fond of locations such as this, since the strict observance of curfew with little or no possibility of extensions made for a reasonably "short" night by *X-Files* standards.

Scully's apartment building.

Unlawful Entry

Occasionally, public enthusiasm for the show created very real problems. Such was the case during the filming of scenes for "Red Museum" (2x10) on the street outside Uncle Herbert's Fish and Chips in Ladner.

Doubling as a small Wisconsin town, the production had hired two officers of the Delta Police Department to control vehicular traffic on the street adjacent to our set, as we were filming an exterior scene involving David and Gillian and a group of "townsfolk." At some point in filming, sound mixer Michael Williamson asked assistant location manager Ainslie Wiggs to investigate the source of loud music coming from the second floor of an apartment complex across the street in the next block. Given the nature of the dialogue scene being filmed, he was having a great deal of difficulty recording "clean" lines.

The manager of the complex had introduced himself to Ainslie prior to filming and offered his assistance if necessary. With this in mind, Ainslie, accompanied by a police officer, went in search of the offending party. Unfortunately, the intercom for the complex did not list the manager's number, so it was up to Ainslie and the officer to enter by a common door leading into the courtyard and from there locate the source of the disturbance. At the same time, the remaining officer had thrown a traffic cone onto the balcony of the apartment in an attempt to get the occupant's attention. While the first officer knocked on the door of the apartment, Ainslie left to check on-set activities. She returned to find the apartment door open and the officer entering. In the meantime, the second officer had found a ladder and climbed up onto the balcony.

Over the din of music, the sight of two police officers entering his apartment from opposite directions under-

SKYLAND MOUNTAIN SKYRIDE
GROUSE MOUNTAIN SKYRIDE, NORTH VANCOUVER

Although the North Shore mountains boast three ski facilities, this location was pre-ordained. Again, scheduling is everything. Ski hill operators are not fond of disruptions during the regular ski season and we were fortunate to be here a few weeks before the first snowfall of the year.

We required complete access and control of a lift line for the entire day, not only to feature during filming, but as transport to the mountaintop for crew and equipment. The management dedicated the service gondola lift to our exclusive use, with an agreement that a small camera crew could ride the passenger lift to film pass-bys of our lift. The stunt sequence on the gondola – filmed quickly as the sun was setting on our "day" work – was as hair-raising as it looks, especially for first assistant director Vladimir Stefoff. David insisted on performing his own stunt for this sequence.

The backroad mentioned by the lift operator in the story actually does exist and takes about an hour to drive, although a four-by-four is required as well as special permission. The backroad which Duane Barry drives - as well as the parking lot and chalet at the top of the hill - was filmed on a different day at neighbouring Mt. Seymour.

PARK
ROBSON SQUARE, 800 ROBSON ST., VANCOUVER

"Find a park in the downtown core. It must be visually interesting and within one hundred yards of the Vancouver Art Gallery." These kinds of requests can be a location manager's worst nightmare, as we are tied to a primary location and hence at the mercy of the locale.

Where possible, we choose primary locations with prior knowledge of additional location requirements, but scheduling and availability do not always permit the obvious choice. Fortunately, we found a terraced plaza with a waterfall backdrop around which to play this scene.

To my dismay, a misunderstanding regarding the control of a cascading waterfall during a crucial dialogue scene involving Scully's mother - played by Bob Goodwin's wife Sheila Larkin - and Mulder nearly ended my tenure on *The X-Files*. For while the waterfall can be turned off in an instant, an additional thirty minutes or so are required to drain the pools above and below.

The outcome was a very emotional scene between actors which had to be *looped* afterwards for clarity, attempting to recapture the original intensity of performance as well as the consistency of the thundering background.

> Exterior and interior scenes playing as *Senator Mattheson's office* were shot at the nearby Vancouver Art Gallery.

2x07	3	LG

With Scully still missing, a solo Mulder investigates a series of apparent vampire killings in L.A.

KRISTEN'S HOUSE
2700-BLOCK S.W. MARINE DR., VANCOUVER

Although this location is a private residence, it is worthy of mention, as Pavel Bure, then a Vancouver Canucks hockey star, had just purchased it. Pavel was on-site during filming, and his presence sent a surge of excitement through the crew and office staff. There were more requests for autographs from Pavel than any actor who appeared on the show. Some of the crew attempted to guess the number of women who would be willing to share the pool with Pavel. Pavel told key grip Al Campbell, "Lots."

The local residents had been petitioned for consent to late-night filming at this location. Approval was given by everyone except a next-door neighbour who was away during the petitioning. He called the office and insisted that the unit could not park along the grassy stretch in front of his house. We assured him that the grass would be protected with plywood. But on the second day of filming, he threatened to sue the company and obtain a court injunction to stop filming. After a lengthy conversation, we opted to pay him a fee. Initially a specified amount was to be paid to a charity of my choice, then on the following day, his lawyer called and requested a personal cheque. News of the exorbitant fee spread like wildfire throughout the film community, essentially banning use of that location.

> The quotation inscripted on Scully's tombstone when she is presumed dead ("One Breath" (2x08)) reads: "The Spirit is the Truth."

> David and the actress playing "Kristen" were dating at the time this episode was filmed.

> Looped: technically known as automated dialogue replacement (ADR), voice synchronization by a performer of his/her own on-camera performance (i.e., rerecording dialogue), usually late at night after a long day of shooting.

standably shocked the occupant, who was watching television with his four-year-old son. For the record, the noise was loud enough as to be in violation of local noise by-laws. Which was perhaps the only saving grace in a scenario which resulted in a formal complaint of unlawful entry and harrassment being entered by the resident against both the police department and the production company. The complaint ultimately went nowhere, as the production had no responsibility over the behaviour of police officers, whose first duty — whether in the service of a film company or not — is to uphold the law.

In Cold Blood (TP)

Hell on earth for a vegetarian might suitably be defined as internment in a meat processing plant. In the case of "Red Museum" (episode 2x10), the equivalent was found to be a night of filming at forty degrees Farenheit amongst dangling sides of beef at J & L Beef Ltd., a slaughterhouse and meat packing plant in Cloverdale, south of Vancouver. This is one episode where I was very happy to send out our team of experienced location scouts to investigate all possible options, which included the vilest of poultry processing facilities. In the case of the latter, the mere mention of the words "cameras . . . television show" was met with a sub-zero response, apparently because of the negative press garnered by poultry processors with regard to health standards and working conditions. Regardless, after a preliminary discussion of story requirements and the cost involved in creating our own meat processing plant (complete with rows of "fake" sides of beef on meathooks), the need to find a suitable location became all the more pressing.

J & L Beef was *the* choice. Not only was management amenable to the idea, but the facility was large and clean and, most important, visually suited our needs. Initially squeamish (being a vegetarian) about leading a location survey through the plant, I must say that I was impressed by the operation. On the upside, the cool temperature kept the smell of death in abeyance. Unfortunately, it meant winter parkas and gloves for the shooting crew, who were asked to treat this "interior" location as if it were a winter "exterior" and dress accordingly. Health standards dictated that any meat handled by cast or crew be deemed unfit for resale. For production, this meant "you touch, you buy," which, at $600-$800 per side, had the potential to add up fast.

Care was taken to park the catering truck in the far corner of the yard, well

The town of Ladner was featured extensively in "The Post-Modern Prometheus" (5x06) where a Canada Post Office became a U.S. Post Office. The post office was chosen because of its red brick façade. Later, Chris announced that the episode would be filmed in black and white.

| 2x08 | ONE BREATH | TP |

Scully suddenly returns. While she recovers from a coma, a guilt-ridden Mulder, who is unable to identify those responsible for her condition, resigns.

| 2x09 | FIREWALKER | LG |

A research team at a remote volcano become infected with a parasite that has an Alien-like effect on their bodies.

| FOREST/FIELD BASE |
| SEYMOUR DEMONSTRATION FOREST, NORTH VANCOUVER |

The Cascade Mountain Range is close to Vancouver, but not close enough to actually film there. The compromise was a partial vista of the mountain from "the boneyard" in our favourite forest, useful for scenes like these.

The exterior *Field Base Camp* set was built at this location and then later sold to *The Sentinel* television series. The interior of the *field base* was filmed entirely on location at a vacant BC Hydro substation, which subsequently became a popular location for other production companies.

| 2x10 | RED MUSEUM | TP |

A Wisconsin dairy region is home to a religious cult and adolescents who disappear, then turn up in the woods nearly comotose, wearing only their underwear, and with the words "He/She is one" written on their backs.

| CLAY'S BBQ RESTAURANT |
| UNCLE HERBERT'S FISH AND CHIPS, 4866 DELTA ST., LADNER |

Anyone for bovine growth hormone? This episode was set in the heartland of Wisconsin. After some chilling revelations, Mulder and Scully wander into a restaurant for a meal of – what else? – barbecued ribs. Several street scenes in front of the restaurant necessitated creating the right small-town look, for which existing angle parking in this block was most helpful. A neighbouring barber shop, automotive garage, and heritage building also helped sell this location.

During filming we encountered a "noise problem" emanating from a nearby apartment building. Perhaps it was that bovine growth hormone or just plain zealous enthusiasm for the show, but local authorities found the source of the disturbance by using some rather peculiar methods (see *Unlawful Entry*).

2x11	EXCELSIUS DEI	LG

At a Massachusetts nursing home, seniors whose drug regimen is supplemented by organic mushrooms evidence psychokinetic abilities.

TREATMENT CENTRE
RIVERVIEW (WESTLAWN AND CREASE CLINIC), 500 LOUGHEED HWY., PORT COQUITLAM

This was the first episode to be directed by a Canadian. Steve Surjik, director of *Wayne's World*, offered his services because he was a fan of the show. The script for this episode arrived only two days prior to actual filming. Not having seen the script, we nevertheless secured the Riverview site as the key location. On the Saturday before filming, on a special survey of Riverview, Westlawn's history as an insane asylum asserted itself. While climbing the stairs to the second floor, Steve and I could hear voices. Alarmed, neither of us dared venture into the bowels of the building.

Given one of the most difficult challenges of the second season, Steve's show received ratings equivalent to "Duane Barry" and "F. Emasculata," and better than "Soft Light" and "The Calusari."

2x12	AUBREY	TP

A pregnant detective's nightmares evoke 50-year-old serial killings while also instigating a modern-day imitator in the Missouri heartland.

TIMBERLAND MOTEL
TIMBERLAND MOTEL, 3418 KING GEORGE HWY., SURREY

Rural motels are located on or near major highways for obvious reasons of access and visibility. With most of the "classic-style" motels having disappeared in recent years - the victims of urban sprawl or changing travel patterns - it's not as easy as one might think to find quaint little mom 'n' pop operations in a placid setting.

away from the plant itself and the caterers wisely decided to avoid beef on the lunch menu. Similarly, crew members who — for religious or moral reasons — were uncomfortable with having to work in such surroundings, were offered the day off — unpaid — on compassionate grounds.

Given the scope of work to be done and the fact that we were working between scheduled shifts, Second Unit returned here to film additional footage, at which time employees were used as extras to perform the actual butchering and cleaning duties. If there's a lingering image from that experience, it has to be that of the pet food truck which was parked in a loading bay when we arrived on the morning of the technical survey.

Murphy's Law (TP)

Murphy's Law dictates that if some thing can happen — no matter how improbable it may seem — it will happen. To this dictum I would add only that it will happen on a film set. The storyline for "Red Museum" (2x10) involved, in part, the crash of a small plane and the subsequent discovery of a mysterious briefcase among the wreckage.

The fiery crash was to be played as an "effect" at night. What was required was a location in which the wreckage could be strewn along a simulated crash path. A grove of trees at the edge of a pasture or field would do nicely, so long as some sort of natural path or clearing existed in the grove in which to create a scorched crash site.

The geography required by the script — rural Wisconsin — matched that of the Delta area, which is where we would find our barn and small town. It therefore made production sense to locate this scene in that area as well. A good location was found on the perimeter of Burns Bog, on agricultural land owned by a local farmer. Access to the pasture was good, if not a little muddy. More important, a natural swath occurred in the

Hero: a featured prop or location.

Props guy Don McGill and . . . a prop.

stand of trees adjoining the pasture. A bark mulch road ran along the back end of this grove, allowing access for lighting cranes and support vehicles.

Arrangements were made with the Delta Fire Department's Fire Prevention unit to accommodate an explosion using napthalene, gasoline, and black powder which would produce a fireball rising one hundred feet in the air. A full fire crew with a pumper truck would be on-site for the duration of the explosion. On our previous location surveys to this site, I had noted a small wooden shed at the side of the access road leading into the pasture. A hand-painted sign saying "Danger . . . Keep Out" was posted on the structure along with an emergency phone number. Parking for work trucks was problematic in this location and we wanted to park several vehicles around the shed for quick access. I left a message to this effect at the listed number, but my call was not returned.

On our final technical survey, we arrived to find a pick-up truck at the shed. A guy was loading boxes into the back of the truck. I hurried inside with the intention of not only explaining our presence, but of making a deal to park vehi-

Our requirement here was for a row or more of detached bungalow-style units with as classic a look as possible. The Timberland's management was very helpful, but warned us of one rather "odd" individual who declined to even talk to us. Because the scenes being shot were night exterior scenes, we needed all porch lights on units except our *hero* unit be turned off to indicate the late hour. Having been down the road of non-co-operation before, we (cleverly) asked this individual to kindly leave her light *on*. Of course, when she promptly turned it off in protest, we rolled film.

THE COKELY HOUSE
13275 COLEBROOK RD., SURREY

This house was a gem of a location, set alone beside a treed windbreak on the flats below Panorama Ridge. A long rutted driveway ran from the main road across several sets of railway tracks and over a drainage ditch to the house. Untouched for years, it retained much of its original weatherworn turn-of-the-century character, while offering a large filmable interior layout.

What many of the crew members remember, however, is the fierce November cold. While filming exhumation scenes in an adjoining pasture at night, the mercury dropped so low that frost actually formed on the backs and shoulders of crew members clad in winter parkas. Similarly, the greens crew had pre-dug the site and the art department had placed a pattern of human remains, but with the ground frozen solid, it was very difficult for the actors to *actually* dig.

This location was so good that we had to return here one other time for what would become the most infamous of all *X-Files*. It played "Home" to the most unusual family of Peacocks (4x03).

2x13	IRRESISTIBLE	LG

Mulder and Scully investigate a series of gravesite desecrations in which the hair and fingernails of young female corpses are being removed.

2x14	DIE HAND DIE VERLETZT	TP

The devil-worshipping faculty at a New Hampshire high school are put in their place by a true demon: a substitute science teacher.

2x15   FRESH BONES   LG

A "processing centre" for Haitian refugees in North Carolina is the site of military-perpetrated human rights abuses, which lead to revenge, voodoo-style.

FOLKSTONE PROCESSING
VERSATILE SHIPYARD,
109 EAST ESPLANADE, NORTH VANCOUVER

The script called for a *Haitian refugee camp* in the middle of winter in the middle of Vancouver. As a compromise to a completely outdoor setting, a derelict, partially covered building at Versatile offered the look of an oppressive camp setting while keeping out the cold. The makeshift camp set had to be completed before the Christmas hiatus to ensure it was ready for filming on the first day back in January. This necessitated twenty-four hour security during the holiday.

EXTERIOR CEMETERY
NORTH SHORE CEMETERY,
LILLOOET RD., NORTH VANCOUVER

During this episode, we discovered the rainy winter months of Vancouver are not the best time to dig graves. We located the site for a grave in an unused section of this old graveyard in North Vancouver. The grave was excavated while the January rains descended and special effects had to be called to location to deal with the influx of water. Sump pumps were in full force and crews were hand-bailing water. When director Rob Bowman arrived on site, he was expecting the worst, and he got it. The water level in the grave rose even between takes, making continuity almost impossible.

2x16   COLONY   TP

An Alien Bounty Hunter kills a number of physically identical (i.e., cloned) abortion doctors as Mulder and Scully give chase.

MULDER'S FATHER'S HOUSE
6476 BLENHEIM ST., VANCOUVER

While *Scully's mother's house* actually "moved" a couple of times over the years, *Bill Mulder's house* established itself as a recurring location, inasmuch as we visited this

Production co-ordinator Anita Truelove and the snake used in "Die Hand Die Verletzt" (2x14).

cles. What I saw stopped me cold. The room was piled high with crates of dynamite, which he subsequently informed me were "perfectly harmless" without the blasting caps. "They're in the next room," he said matter-of-factly, gesturing with a finger. The horrible irony of our situation struck me. Not only were we to park and work in the immediate vicinity of an explosives storage facility, but we planned to stage an explosion of considerable magnitude within 300 feet of several tons of dynamite. Moreover, in terms of production, we had reached the point of no return.

An alternate office number was proffered as I hastily made two calls, one to the Delta Fire Department and one to the explosives company. The end result, to my relief, was a stern warning to refrain from smoking anywhere near the building and an assurance that our explosion — as described — was perfectly safe given its proximity to the storage facility. So why was I still nervous?

As it was, filming went off without a hitch. Well, almost. It seems that, after being warned by both the locations and transportation departments to keep their *full* pumper truck off the soft access road at the back of the property — it had no business being there — the fire crew decided to take the vehicle four-wheeling. Within three minutes, it sank in the soft bog, woefully stuck. If that wasn't enough, some weeks later I received an invoice from the Delta Fire Department for the towing costs associated with extricating the vehicle from the mess.

Here Comes the Rain Again

The Lions Gate Travel Lodge provided the backdrop for a Season Four interview with David, an interview he consented to after weeks of negative media coverage about his "rain" comments. Fortunately it was a sunny day when David apologized to Vancouver. But David restated that Vancouver is a place of much rain. David is right. Rain, rain, and more rain. Film crews detest working twelve-hour shifts in the rain, and time and money lost because of it.

Savage Love (TP)

Shows involving exotic animals engender certain "technical" problems peculiar in themselves. For "Fearful Symmetry" (2x18), an elephant named Bubbles was trucked in from California. Daily reports, peppered with amusing expletives, on Bubbles' progress and health were issued by production co-ordinator Anita Truelove. For my part, I learned something about municipal by-laws and the appearance of circus animals on public property. As scripted, Bubbles runs down a road and narrowly avoids a collision with a tractor-trailer. Most municipalities in the Lower Mainland now have bylaws in place prohibiting the use or appearance of circus or show animals on public streets or property, meant ostensibly to protect such creatures from exploitation and inhumane treatment. For this

home on three separate occasions. The script placed this house on Martha's Vineyard, Massachusetts, which is where executive producer Bob Goodwin wished it to remain. Moreover, having vacationed at Martha's Vineyard on at least one occasion, Bob had a very particular idea of what this house should look like.

As noted elsewhere, recreating New England in southwestern British Columbia is a stretch to say the least. Faithful examples of New England or Cape Cod-style architecture are scarce, but the house we finally found could have been a New England transplant. Located on a sloping corner lot, this white clapboard structure occupied the uphill portion of the property. And while the house itself resembled a large beachhouse, the spacious grass lawns and high cedar hedge gave it a substantial presence. The real selling point was the wrap-around veranda.

'11 x 15'3   Family Room. 21 x 16

hlands Landmark! Everyone's favourite home - a classic farmhou sited to catch South & West sun overlooking exceptionally p try estates. **Featured 'Cape Cod' house on the X-Files series.** S er levels feature family room, three bedrooms and games are ed sunroom, lacquered woodburning stove in family room & t

Chris at Mulder's father's house, which was put up for sale in 1997.

| 2x17 | END GAME | LG |

The Alien Bounty Hunter trades Scully for Mulder's "sister" Samantha, who is subsequently killed. The Alien Bounty Hunter, with Mulder in pursuit, travels to the Arctic and escapes.

MOTORLODGE
LIONS GATE TRAVEL LODGE, 2060 MARINE DR., NORTH VANCOUVER

The X-Files should have permanently rented rooms 224 and 226 given the number of times this motel was used for filming. Each time the motel's name above the lobby was changed. Eventually construction co-ordinator Rob Maier could prep the location within two hours.

The X-Files used this location on at least ten occasions.

2x18	FEARFUL SYMMETRY	TP

Aliens are abducting zoo animals in Idaho, in an attempt to ensure the survival of the species.

2x19	DOD KALM	LG

The crew of a Navy destroyer succumbs to an illness that causes them to age rapidly and die.

U.S.S. ARDENT
H.M.C.S. MACKENZIE, BARRY POINT TERMINAL, PENZANCE ST., BURNABY

Most of this episode was spent in the bowels of the *H.M.C.S. Mackenzie* (a former destroyer) inhaling the dregs of kerosene and freshly painted sets. Unfortunately, there is no ventilation on these old ships, other than a trip to the deck.

The ship was initially moored at New Westminster Quay but relocated to Barry Point, a more remote site, upon Chris' request to avoid urban ambient light while filming night exterior scenes, which was done at the cost of a mere $10,000. Given that the ship was to portray an abandoned vessel, production designer Graeme Murray requested the ship be "paint-aged" then repainted back to its original colour after filming. Barges were dispatched along with paint crews and spray guns.

On the second day of shooting inside the overheated vessel, the crew surfaced on deck, only to be blinded by a snowstorm. The ship was moored at a dock situated at the base of a steep hill. The Teamsters, anticipating that many of the crew vehicles might get stranded, managed

It was while filming at this location that the show won its first Golden Globe Award, for best dramatic series.

reason, we ended up on a quiet country road in South Surrey, the only municipality in the Lower Mainland that would allow such an activity at that time. The road was barricaded and filming proceeded.

Bubbles, I must say, was a true professional, hitting her marks with as much accuracy — and with more consistency — than many actors. Unfortunately, the same cannot be said for the driver of the tractor-trailer who, in overshooting his mark by a couple of feet, collided with Bubbles. Both elephant and truck were at a near-standstill at the time, but the force of impact with a creature the size of a Volkswagon beetle was enough to shatter the truck's windshield. Bubbles merely surveyed the damage, turned to her handler, and began the slow trudge back to her "first position."

As a sidenote, Bubbles not only consumed mass quantities of fruits and straw, but evacuated similarly massive quantities of waste, something which left the location production assistants very nervous when it came time to clean up. To this end, it can be said that the handlers were also, thankfully, professional and managed to contain this potential problem with practiced skill and very large shovels.

A tiger also appeared in this episode. It prowls through the bowels of a construction site at night, where it is

The H.M.C.S. Mackenzie *is now an artifical reef at the bottom of the Georgia Strait ("Dod Kalm" (2x19)).*

73

eventually cornered and "shot." For obvious reasons, this location had to be safe for both crew and creature, and containable in the event that the tiger got spooked and made a run for it in downtown Vancouver. For those now living in the then-half-completed east tower at 555 Jervis Street, it might be amusing to know that the upper level of the underground parkade was employed as a location. The biggest issue here became one of keeping the tiger calm and warm, since it was February and very cold in the unheated underground parkade in the middle of the night.

Florida North

"Humbug" (2x20) was a dark comedic episode written around circus freaks. Jim Rose and The Enigma of the Jim Rose Travelling Circus Sideshow were cast as Dr. Blockhead and The Conundrum. A funeral involving the recently departed Gerald Glazebrook and the grandstanding Dr. Blockhead, who tears his way out from beneath the turf under Glazebrook's coffin, required that we "dress" our own cemetery at Semiahmoo Park in White Rock.

This location was convenient and in some ways ideal, as it was close to the trailer park — a key location — and it also held a commanding view of the ocean. Headstones and grave markers were trucked in and a hole very carefully dug and concealed for Dr. Blockhead's "entrance." As we were on Semiahmoo Band land, there was some concern that we might unearth either relics or human remains.

The night before filming, it snowed lightly for several hours. By calltime the next morning, our "Florida cemetery" was blanketed with an inch of snow. We had to shoot, so everyone pitched in. The special effects boys grabbed tiger torches while the greensmen and loca-

to move them to the top of the hill. After a long search, a snowplough was located, thanks to a nearby oil refinery.

INTERIOR ICU AND INTERIOR GILDESKALBAR
JERICHO SAILING CLUB, 1300 DISCOVERY ST., VANCOUVER

The two other locations scheduled for this episode were a *hospital* and *Norwegian bar*. We wanted to find one site where we could film both, even though the combination of the rustic bar and an austere hospital ward seemed a nearly impossible task. The Jericho Sailing Club fit the bill. The fact that the dark, dingy *bar* setting was only a few steps from the bright, stark *ICU unit* set was amazing to the crew.

While we were waiting for the trucks to arrive at Jericho, David and his dog Blue jogged by. David rarely arrived on location early. The close proximity to his home had not gone unnoticed. On the following day, the producers approached locations and requested that locations close to David's home be found for future filming.

The bartender in this episode and in "Never Again" (4x13) was Barry (Bear) Hortin, a Teamster who was responsible for pulling Gillian's trailer.

2x20	HUMBUG	TP

A trailer park populated by ex- and aging circus freaks is plagued by a series of bizarre murders.

TRAILER PARK
MEMORIAL CAMP, 16327 BEACH RD., WHITE ROCK

There are a few geographies which are difficult, if not impossible, to duplicate in the Lower Mainland. Among them, Florida stands out. That said, a script set in Florida arrived and called for, among other things, a trailer park known as *The Gulf Breeze*. Aside from the obvious problem with climate – it was late February – we needed to avoid coniferous trees.

We found our location close to the ocean, at a trailer park so near the Canada-U.S. border that if you missed the turn-off, you'd end up at Duty Free Shopping. The site itself was managed by the Royal Canadian Legion and home to a vast array of trailers, from the funky rustic to the modern state-of-the-art. Its denizens were primarily retirees who spent the warm summer months here, treating the camp much as one might treat a lakeside cabin or retreat. On a sunny day, the unobstructed view of the ocean across the road was spectacular.

Aside from relocating a troupe of Brownies, who were scheduled to camp over for the weekend in the dormitory, the park was still closed for the winter. Filming here in July would have been unthinkable.

Even the vegetation worked, although not without the addition of several truckloads of trees by greensman Frank Haddad and his crew to make the site look smaller than it actually was. The weather was thankfully unseasonably mild and sunny, with one chilling exception (see *Florida North*).

Shooting a scene at the trailer park for "Humbug" (2x20).

Down the road from the trailer park was the tidal waterway in which Mulder, out for a jog, spots the emerging tattooed Conundrum clutching a salmon in his teeth. For the record, The Conundrum is known in real life as The Enigma (affectionately Niggy), who planned to use some of his earnings from this show to get more tattoos. Standing there in his loincloth, I wondered just where he intended to put more tattoos. If you ever meet Jim Rose of the Jim Rose Travelling Circus Sideshow, ask for a demonstration of "organ origami."

> Contary to rumour, Gillian did not eat the bug Jim Rose's Dr. Blockhead offered her. She did, however, put it in her mouth.

2x21	THE CALUSARI	LG

An old-country Romanian grandmother tries to save her grandson, who has been possessed by "the howling heart of evil."

tions crew used rakes and brooms to clear a section of the cemetery large enough to stage the sequence without snow being visible.

As a postscript note, our production company usually housed out-of-town talent at the Sutton Place Hotel (a five-star facility). In this case, the Jim Rose entourage requested lodging at a hotel located just off the far-from-exclusive Granville strip. As production co-ordinator Anita Truelove recalled, "We offered them the Sutton Place and they requested this place they'd stayed in before. I guess it made them feel more comfortable. Anyway, it had gone downhill since their last visit, to the point where they'd no sooner moved in than they wanted to move to the Sutton Place."

Organ Origami

Organ Origami refers to a "sideshow" created by Jim Rose to more fully utilize the potential of the male genitalia, which he believes is generally underused 75-80 percent of the time.

While in a special effects make-up meeting for "Humbug" (2x20) — a meeting which included Chris, Bob Goodwin, J.P. Finn, Joanne Service, and Anita Truelove — Rose gave an impromptu demonstration of this routine (he had a somewhat hideous make-up application covering his chest). He proceeded to drop his skin-tight leather pants and twist his member into what very closely resembled a *Flying Squirrel*, much to the intrigue of his "audience." Ever the showman, Rose then turned his back and, reinventing himself, turned around to reveal first a *Wrist Watch* and then a *Windsurfer*.

Inspired by this feat, Bob suggested he attempt *Three Midgets Fighting Under A Blanket*. It was, Joanne recalled, "one of those unbelievable, very special *X-Files* moments."

The Invisible Location (TP)

Sometimes the pain and hardship endured in finding a location *so* explicit to a storyline that it just *has* to be this or that hardly seems justified by the two seconds of soft-focus screentime it ultimately receives. And while we would be wise to remember that this is the nature of the medium — which is *television* — such an explanation does little to soothe the final frustration of the *invisible location*.

A large number of options were discussed in the search for Gerald Glazebrook's backyard pool in "Humbug" (2x20). Below-ground pools either failed to provide the necessary height for camera positions or the houses to which they were attached were deemed unsuitable. Running out of time (we had already begun to film this episode in White Rock), it was finally decided that an above-ground pool would be rented and installed in the backyard of a suitable house.

Given the Florida setting, director Kim Manners was adamant that the house be of a two-storey woodframe design. If existing landscaping offered some visual interest — perhaps by way of gnarly old trees or bushes — so much the better. The scenes, which would document Glazebrook's untimely demise, were to be shot at night to add to the sense of campy horror.

The house we finally chose was an old two-storey clapboard structure painted a soft yellow. Located at 1120 Harold Street in North Vancouver, the backyard was large and empty, with several old fruit trees standing to one side of the property. And while there was plenty of room for the pool, the ground sloped from east to west, which meant that the greens crew would be performing a major excavation to level the site: a hole twenty-four feet long, twelve feet wide, and four feet deep. Nonetheless, a deal was made with the owner whereby a nicely landscaped

| 2x22 | F. EMASCULATA | TP |

A deadly tropical parasite is introduced into a Virginia prison population. When two infected cons make a break, Mulder and Scully race the clock to prevent an outbreak.

RURAL GAS STATION
DELTAPORT FARM MARKET, 2757-52ND ST., DELTA

Rural gas stations are not unlike rural motels in that they're invariably located on busy highways. Similarly, many have fallen prey to oil company monopolies and been driven out of business.

Besides the visual component of the story, this location had to accommodate the safe landing of a helicopter, for which pilot involvement was necessary early in the scouting process. This requirement precluded the use of any existing gas station in the Lower Mainland, for either aesthetic or logistical reasons. Typically, a week to ten days is required for regulatory approval of flight paths and associated activities.

In this case, let's just say that the locations and art departments got together and created a piece of movie magic, transforming a fruit and vegetable market in Delta into the desired location. Sitting on a large corner lot, the market itself was fronted by a dirt parking lot and offered good rural backgrounds and reverse angles. The proximity of agricultural lands on all sides gave the pilot the clear flight path necessary in case of an emergency landing.

Just as important was the lone hydro line servicing the market, which could easily be temporarily removed without the need to remove power poles. This provided the helicopter with an uncluttered landing area just a few feet from the building. Gas pumps, an office, a washroom, a telephone booth, and signage were added to affect the makeover, which fooled at least one passing motorist who stopped for gas.

In the evacuation scene from the "washroom," the quarantine gurney never actually exits the washroom (as was written) on its way to the waiting chopper. Through an unfortunate error in measurement, the washroom doorway was built too narrow to accommodate the bubble.

Gas . . . food . . . quarantine. The rural gas station *for "F. Emasculata" (2x22).*

BUS STATION
DENNISON DODGE/CHRYSLER, HWY. 17 AT VASSEY RD., DELTA

The prospect of occupying a fully operational bus station was never considered beyond a quick survey of available locations for the sake of curiosity. Neither the Vancouver nor the New Westminster depots were attractive enough to fuel a debate, so the scout for a space in which to create our own Greyhound bus station began.

The way this episode had *boarded out,* first assistant director Vladimir Stefoff was pushing for a location to be found in the Delta area, where we were already committed to a day's worth of work at the *rural gas station.* He also hoped that there would be some way to put several Greyhound cruisers inside whatever facility we chose, as the weather forecast was bad. Because the scenes involving the buses themselves were to take place at night, an interior would provide the ability to shoot this work *day for night* before moving to the main passenger waiting area.

It so happened that a car dealership and showroom sat vacant just off the freeway and immediately south of the Deas Island Tunnel on the Delta border. Not only was it situated on an acre of parking lot, but the structure itself contained a large glassed-in showroom with a mezzanine and a larger shop area with enough service bays to park several buses. The owners had moved to a new facility in Richmond and were in the process of selling this one. They were, in the true spirit of their profession, more than happy to turn a buck from our location rental.

With a little signage from the art department, a few benches from set dec, and a contingent of extras, this venue was transformed into a smart-looking bus station. Several Greyhound buses were angle-parked in the service bays to complete the illusion.

An incident of sorts occurred in the parking lot during

patio would be left once the pool was removed.

A pool company was hired to assemble and fill a pool on the prepared site and a canvas of the neighbourhood undertaken, as we were prepared for an all-night shoot. In the end, Manners and the Second Unit crew wrapped things up at around 3 a.m.

Watching the dailies, I was appalled by how little of anything had been recorded by the camera. The house was all but invisible and the trees — the spooky old trees — were nowhere to be seen. The action sequences in the pool were, however, great. Which is ultimately what counts, although I joked afterwards that the pool could easily have been placed on the grass at North Shore Studios and the same effect achieved for a lot less. A whole lot less.

Boarded out: refers to the first assistant director's production board, on which each scene in a script is carefully laid out and scheduled.

Day for night: the practice of shooting during the day, but making the scene look as though it is taking place at night.

"Whatever you do, don't swallow . . ." (TP)

"I cannot believe the conversation I just had." These were my words to location scout David Caughlan as I hung up the phone after a rather convoluted discussion with a Richmond city official in early April 1995. After a thorough scout of the Lower Mainland for a stream or waterway in which to drive a truck loaded with chickens (actually, chicken feathers), we had come upon a suitable location at a rural junction in Richmond.

As is typical of this area of Richmond, irrigation ditches or sloughs separate agricultural lands from a network of rural roads. The script requirements for "Our Town" (2x24) with respect to this location were three-fold: (1) come up with a country road adjacent to a waterway into which a vehicle could be safely driven into the ditch and partially submerged, (2) cover a portion of the surface of this waterway with a solution consisting of environmentally-friendly red food colour and cooking oil (a special effect), and (3) locate an easy access point to this waterway — preferably nearby — from which a "dragging operation" would discover human remains.

I had learned years earlier, while scouting locations for the Paramount feature *Intersection*, how difficult this first requirement could be. Assuming a road in correct proximity to a waterway could be found, chances are that any waterway in the Lower Mainland would be fish-bearing, in which case the Department of Fisheries was unlikely to issue a thumbs-up. We had, nonetheless, found a waterway seemingly devoid of fish, and with modifications to the flatbed we were intending to use (with the engine, crankcase, and oilpan removed and the brakelines drained), had come to an agreement on this point with the necessary departments at City Hall. A stuntperson/driver would simply sit in the cab of the stripped-down truck and be catapulted into the Woodward Slough.

the afternoon while the shooting crew was at work inside. Transportation co-captain Baba Ram and one of his hair & make-up trailer drivers became involved in an emotional debate over some contentious issue. Unable to agree, they decided to settle the issue with a fifty-yard sprint through the parking lot. The winner would also receive a ten-dollar cash "prize." Neither contestant could be characterized as athletic, but Baba was younger and carrying far less excess weight than his opponent. He also confided in me that he'd been a sprinter as a kid in Fiji. In one of those moments which can only be called surreal, and with arms and little legs a-pumping, Baba breasted the tape far ahead of his Teamster brother, thereby settling the argument. As one spectating crew member noted, this was, "one very sick remake of *Chariots of Fire.*"

2x23	SOFT LIGHT	LG

A physicist's botched experiments into dark matter leave him with a lethal shadow.

TRAIN STATION/PLATFORM-AM BUILDING
VIA RAIL, 1150 STATION ST., REAR OF 48 WEST HASTINGS ST., VANCOUVER, AND PACIFIC MARINE TRAINING INSTITUTE, 265 WEST ESPLANADE, NORTH VANCOUVER

This was Vince Gilligan's first script, which he wrote because he was a huge fan of the show. During filming, we noticed a very quiet man carrying a camera kept showing up at all the locations, hovering around the periphery of the set. It turned out to be Vince, who financed his own trip to Vancouver to observe the making of his episode. Vince would later write other episodes and, unlike many writers, his scripts (and those of the Glen Morgan and James Wong) were not subjected to the same degree of revisions by Chris. Their scripts meant that "real" prep could commence immediately.

The train station and platform are exactly what they are. The Pacific Marine Institute permitted filming after 5 p.m. only; this time constraint hampered the expectation for a relatively early night wrap and a relaxation of the rule was warranted. I spent an hour in the Dean's office; just to get rid of me, he approved our request to start filming at 2 p.m.

2x24	OUR TOWN	TP

An Arkansas town with a thriving poultry business must account for the disappearance of an FDA inspector and several citizens.

THE CHACO MANSION

1388 THE CRESCENT, VANCOUVER

Eerily prescient of "mad cow" disease, this episode called for a grand *Southern residence* in which the bizarre chicken magnate Mr. Chaco could reside. Our west coast concept of a mansion usually has little in common with the corresponding American vision of California's Hearst Castle or the lavish estates built by the Vanderbilts and Astors around Newport, Rhode Island at the end of the 19th century.

We chose The Hollies, as this estate is known. Sitting on a 2.2-acre lot in the heart of Shaughnessy Heights, it was built in 1912 for Pacific Great Eastern Railway mogul George MacDonald.

This mansion features nine bedrooms, twelve bathrooms, five fireplaces, and a grand entrance hall complete with carved wood staircase, and a marble floor. An addition to this home features an Arthur Erickson-designed glass conservatory and pool. And while it's not the largest home in the city, from the street it instantly conveys both the grandeur and faded glory of the deep South.

Script approval and deep pockets are tantamount to filming in this mansion. Out of respect for the owner's religious beliefs, scenes involving death or bad omens (fire, etc.) may not be filmed here. As a result, the shot depicting the shrunken heads in the armoir was filmed elsewhere and edited into the existing sequence.

Coincidental to our story, a previous owner of this property died in the library wing of the house. The new owner had the wing demolished and the original stonework buried beneath the considerable grounds should future owners wish to rebuild. Ironically, the

As for the final requirement, we were lucky. A resident living across the road (we would ultimately use part of his property to park worktrucks) had built a small, Huck Finn-style dock on the slough about a hundred yards from our intersection. This would become the location from which the dragging team would operate.

The contentious issue — the source of my disbelief — was the city of Richmond's refusal to grant us permission to put the special effects solution into the water. In the course of petitioning local residents and informing them of our intended activities, location scout David Caughlan had learned some interesting things.

The junction in the road we had chosen to drive the truck into the slough was, it seems, a natural choice. Residents across the road confirmed that, over the years, several vehicles — usually travelling too fast at night — had missed the turn and ended up precisely where we intended to jump our truck. Any incredulity on behalf of the neighbours was not aimed at our choice of location, but at our intention to send a human being into the drink with the vehicle.

A couple of years earlier, the driver of a car which had dunked into the slough had consumed large amounts of water. His injuries were apparently minor, but a few months later he began to complain of acute chest and stomach pains. He was admitted to hospital, where he died shortly thereafter, apparently from toxic poisoning associated with the bacterial composition of the sloughwater itself. The waterways and sloughs bordering this farmland form drainage ditches for the adjacent farm fields. Pesticides used on the crops drain into the ditches, along with all manner of feces. As one resident put it, "tell your stuntman that, whatever he does, he'd better not swallow."

Hearing this, I became concerned for the health of stuntman Ken Kirsinger and hired a local lab to test a water sample from the slough. Given what the local

The flatbed truck comes to a stop ("Our Town" (2x24)).

residents were saying, I found City Hall's intransigence puzzling, to say the least. The results of the test were predictably horrifying. Little wonder this slough would not support fishlife. I then broke the news to Ken who, like a true professional, gritted his teeth in firm, if not utter, resolve. As it was, this issue would subside a few days before filming commenced as another alarming discovery was made.

In the three weeks leading up to our shoot, I had had several conversations with both concerned department managers at Richmond City Hall and residents along our hero road. At no time in any of these conversations had the word "tidal" been uttered by anyone. Similarly, I had been on at least two location scouts with department heads to this location prior to our technical survey, and had noticed nothing unusual. However, on the day of our technical survey, twenty of us arrived at the slough to find the water level at least five feet lower than it had previously been. That meant that the deepest part of the ditch was now about four feet.

"Of course these sloughs are tidal. There's a sluice gate where this one flows into the Fraser River, a couple of miles down the road. Didn't anyone tell you?" This was the substance of my next conversation with Richmond City Hall, as the technical survey stood at the edge of the slough trying to figure out how to remedy the situation.

A number of solutions were advanced before it was finally decided to "shoot with the tides." A line of dialogue was added to the scene in which the sheriff's crew reveal human skeletal remains to Mulder and Scully, to the effect that "we closed the spillway and the water level dropped. . . ." This explained away the fact that the water level was dropping significantly as the day progressed.

Which led to one final discovery. Filming lurched to a halt briefly while director Rob Bowman waded into the ditch in an attempt to herd a couple of fish into deeper water. Contrary to all

owner chooses to live in a large coachhouse in back of the property, furnishing the mansion as needed for parties and other social events.

> The current owner of The Hollies bought the property in October 1991 for a then-record $8.1 million. He subsequently had the address changed from 1350 The Crescent to 1388 The Crescent, the pair of eights symbolizing prosperity within the Chinese culture. In 1996 it was again listed for sale for $12 million.

2×25	ANASAZI	LG

An anarchist hacker delivers to Mulder a digital tape with evidence that proves the government's knowledge of UFOs since the late forties. Mulder's investigation takes him to New Mexico, and into a boxcar buried in the sand, where Cigarette Smoking Man appears to kill him. Scully, in the meantime, tries to keep the FBI brass – who want to know just where Mulder is – at bay.

RED ROCK QUARRY
4892 QUARRY RD., COQUITLAM

The request for Arizona desert almost seemed laughable until the serious expression on executive producer and director Bob Goodwin's face suggested otherwise. Desert means sand and rock, not rainforest. The scouts were dispersed to sandpits and quarries which were all active and restrictive, until I recalled a derelict rock quarry where the desert idea could be realized. There was one major problem: the colour. Head painter Louis Solyom and his crew meticulously applied red paint to the quarry's rock walls while propped on a crane. The weather co-operated while painting the quarry; however, on the first day of filming, the rains descended. Filming was postponed, but as time began to run out, Bob decided to go. That night the clouds receded and by morning there was a brilliant sun overhead. That glorious day came to be known as an "X-Files Day" and was from then on used to describe any day when the production was blessed with luck.

> The buried train car necessitated blasting a hole in the rock to create a depression and the removal of thirty-two dumptrucks worth of boulders. The exterior rock faces were sandblasted to provide a clean surface for painting. Over 1,000 gallons of red paint were required to create the Arizona desert.

How to get to "Arizona"

- FOLLOW HWY 1 ACROSS 2nd NARROWS, EAST BOUND ALL THE WAY TO EXIT #44
- EXIT ONTO LEFT LANE & FOLLOW SIGNS "PORT COQUITLAM ⑦ EAST" UNTIL YOU REACH THE INTERSECTION OF HWY ⑦ & ⑦A THEN TURN RIGHT ONTO HWY ⑦ (LOUGHEED) & PROCEED EAST TO COAST MERIDIAN THEN TURN LEFT (NORTH) ONTO COAST MERIDIAN & PROCEED TO APEL, VEER RIGHT & GO TO VICTORIA DR. & TURN RIGHT ONTO VICTORIA THEN LEFT ONTO VICTORIA & PROCEED EAST ALONG. VICTORIA / QUARRY ROAD (GRAVEL)
  - FOLLOW QUARRY RD. TO THE SPUR ROAD ON THE RIGHT
  - FOLLOW SPUR RD. TO QUARRY LOCATION

4892 QUARRY ROAD, COQUITLAM

2X25 'ANASAZI'

MAP NOT TO SCALE

QUARRY IS 8.7 Km from Coast Meridien

Painting the quarry required the permission of various environmental groups and the owner of the site. The owner was having a leisurely lunch at Swan-E-Set golf course, which is directly across from the quarry, when his partner remarked upon the colour of his property. Shocked by what he saw, the owner called immediately and questioned the extent of the paint job, even though he had been completely informed about the task at hand. With further assurances, the owner endorsed and later became the proud owner of the desert transformation.

> Two years later, you could still see the "painted desert" from the clubhouse lounge at Swan-E-Set Golf Course in Pitt Meadows.

> David Duchovny received a story credit for this episode.

Head painter Louis Solyom creating the Arizona desert for "Anasazi" (2x25).

reports, *The X-Files* discovered fish in a slough in which it was widely believed no fish could survive.

One other problem was actually solved as a result of the tides. Special effects co-ordinator Dave Gauthier expressed doubt — given the current in the ditch resulting from tidal flow — that any solution he could place in the water would remain in one place long enough to be captured on film. Hence we abandoned this idea although, on film, the natural "sheen" on the water — and for this we were blessed with a couple of days of flawless weather — would seem to indicate otherwise.

And when that truck did narrowly miss Mulder and Scully's fast-approaching sedan, swerving off the road and over the dyke into the ditch (where it submerged up to the base of the front windshield), we never saw anyone get out of a wreck so fast as stuntman Ken Kirsinger.

Whatever you do, don't swallow ("Our Town" (2x24)).

These are the results of the sample received April 12.

Product Sampled: One water sample was received in the laboratory for analysis.

Tests Performed:	X Files Productions; Woodward Slough Intersection No. 4 Rd. and Finn Rd.: April 12/95
Standard Plate Count:	1,080
Total Coliforms:	23×10^3
Fecal Coliforms:	11×10^3
Salmonella species:	Negative
Staphylococcus aureus:	<1
Pseudomonas aeruginosa:	<1
Streptococcus faecium:	130

After two years, the crew was exhausted. Halfway into the season, most department heads were uttering the same off-the-record statement: "I just can't live through another season." But in the final weeks, as people reflected on the year's accomplishments – and with a holiday in sight – all thoughts of the difficulties subsided and pride took over. There was no doubt then. "I'll be back."

This led to the final task of the season: the visit to the "principal's office." Everyone wanted to negotiate their deal for the upcoming season with producer J.P. Finn before the hiatus.

The ambitious ending to Season Two set a precedent for Season Three. The creative and technical requirements of the show mushroomed to equate that of feature filmmaking. As director Kim Manners said in a 1998 interview: "This is not episodic TV. This is what I call event TV."

A full-time Second Unit was established to shadow Main Unit, and was also given the task of filming the teaser. More sets were built, which required a third soundstage, and like with feature films, it was taking longer to film a simple scene.

– *LG*

Paint touch-ups for "The Blessing Way" (3x01).

Chris (in the hat) and Rob Bowman (with the rolled-up sleeves) shooting in the red rock quarry *("Anasazi" (2x25), "The Blessing Way" (3x01)).*

The Cigarette Smoking Man arrives ("Anasazi" (2x25), "The Blessing Way" (3x01)).

CGI: computer generated imaging.

| 3x01 | THE BLESSING WAY | TP |

Scully is suspended from the FBI for not disclosing Mulder's whereabouts. While Mulder recovers in New Mexico, Scully discovers a computer chip implanted under the skin at the base of her skull.

RED ROCK QUARRY

4892 QUARRY RD., COQUITLAM

This is a location which virtually everyone remembers. The Red Rock Quarry evolved from the final cliffhanger episode of Season Two. With the story set in the Sedona area of Arizona, it was decided to shoot everything but wide establishing shots here. The task of matching colour and aerial spraying was a once-in-a-career opportunity for head painter Louis Solyom. It also presented an environmental challenge in that the paint used had to be environmentally friendly and water-soluble over time.

| 3x02 | PAPER CLIP | LG |

A reunited Mulder and Scully are taken to an abandoned coal mine where they find medical records and tissue samples of nearly everyone born in the U.S. since the fifties. Skinner uses the digital tape (from "Anasazi") to bargain for Mulder and Scully's jobs (and safety).

MINE

BRITANNIA MUSEUM OF MINING, BRITANNIA BEACH

During the production of "Anasazi" (2x25), while filming the *Arizona tract housing,* Chris toured the adjacent abandoned copper mine. Within a few months, an episode was written for the mine location, but with a few additions. The mine tunnel was to house hundreds of thousands of filing cabinets; *CGI* would take care of the thousands, but the art department had to create the hundreds. Construction installed the cabinets (most of them had false fronts) while set dec gathered and attached the brass hardware to the fronts. The first of three days of shooting at the mine was scheduled in the tunnel, and on the following day construction was given approval to wrap the filing cabinet façades. However, it was noon before first assistant director and Lone Gunman Tom Braidwood – having arrived home at 5 a.m. - surfaced from slumber and alerted the office about an uncompleted tunnel scene. Construction co-ordinator Rob Maier, quick on the draw, stopped his boys from wrapping, and the set was reassembled and salvaged for the impending night of shooting. The search for someone to blame for the foul up became imminent.

A corrugated metal façade was constructed beside the main shaft so Mulder could look up and view the ascending flying saucer at night. A musco light crane with nine 4K HMIs – essential to create the overall lighting effect – was brought in from L.A. and special effects developed a special truss for mounting lights. Best Boy Bill Kassis was delegated the job of building the UFO lighting effect which would engulf the mine. Working from a design based on Chris Carter's vision and gaffer Dave Tickell's technical requirements, Kassis later recalled that this was the single biggest lighting effect he'd ever been involved in creating.

Using an eighty-foot truss suspended from a 200-foot-high construction crane, Kassis spent a week on the North Shore Studios lot configuring and reconfiguring a variety of lights in an attempt to generate the maximum amount of light given the weight restrictions of both truss and crane. After "flying" the rigged truss for Chris and others - and making adjustments as requested - and getting a final thumbs-up, the truss was derigged, disassembled, transported to the mine, then mounted on a crane to ultimately create the illusion of a flying saucer rising overhead. The mine interior glowed while the musco light, not required after all, was relegated to lighting the catering truck, providing one of the most well-lit meals we ever had on the show.

In total, the rigged truss produced more than 100,000 watts of light for the effect. The intensity was such that a vehicle advisory warning was issued for those driving along the Squamish Highway.

DINER
TEA SHOPPE, BRITANNIA BEACH

While the 99er Diner was the original choice for the *diner*, once the magnitude of filming at the mine site became apparent, an alternative location had to be found, largely to avoid the time it would have taken to move the work trucks the two hundred yards to the 99er. At this point, the 99er had already posted notices for closure on the specified filming day. As a result, compensation for inconvenience and potential loss of business was provid-

Disassembling the lighting truss to travel to Britannia Mine to shoot "Paper Clip" (3x02).

The mine was closed to the public for seven days to accommodate filming.

Rigging the lights.

ed. This incident certainly didn't stop the crew from eating there. The wooden trellis and walkway that construction built to lead to the Tea Shoppe remained part of the façade treatment.

ORCHID HOT HOUSE
SOUTHLANDS NURSERY, 6550 BALACLAVA ST., VANCOUVER

The script called for an *orchid nursery*. Director Rob Bowman and the producers agreed that the main retail/gardening building at Southlands met the script requirements. On the day of the technical survey – with only two days of prep remaining – Chris inquired about an alternative to the main complex at Southlands. Everyone listened while Chris explained that the structure should be more intimate. I asked florist Thomas Hobbs to tour us through other facilities. We walked through a simple and very typical dome-shaped fiberglass hothouse, which Chris consented to. The department heads worked feverishly to organize what would be a hasty prep. Set decorator Shirley Inget pounced on Hobbs for assistance, as it was apparent that all the bedding plants in the hothouse had to be relocated and replaced with row upon row of orchids. Fortunately, we were filming at a nursery and had access to all the plants we needed.

3x03	D.P.O.	TP

A trouble-making teenager who can summon lightning takes his schoolteacher crush too far.

OSWALD HOUSE/PASTURE
JACKSON HOMESTEAD, 24554-102 AVE., ALBION

"Find me an old farmhouse and a pasture where I can nuke these cows." This was roughly the sentiment expressed by director Kim Manners with regard to the location which would play as *Darin's house* in Connerville, Oklahoma.

Several good options in Delta and South Surrey came to mind, but Manners was not yet done. "And this pasture . . . needs to have some sort of a rolling hill or gully in it . . . to help me reveal Darin in a low-angle shot when he turns into a human lightning rod." He made his trademark "V" with his index and middle fingers to illustrate the direction of the camera. So much for pancake-flat Delta and South Surrey.

Director Kim Manners and steady-cam operator Marty McInally in full flight.

I recalled only one location matching this requirement. The good news was that it was owned by an old gentleman who, in the past, had been very accommodating to film companies. The bad news was that this turn-of-the-century farmhouse was way out of the studio zone and would therefore not be an accountant's first choice.

Given the politics and hierarchy of the show, I grappled with posing the suggestion, knowing that it would be a popular creative choice but murder from a budget perspective. Fortunately, Manners unwittingly solved the dilemma for me. He seemed to "recall an old farmhouse with rolling fields" from some show he'd done years previously. He remembered it being "way out there hell and gone but a great location." Could he see some photos?

Which is how we ended up in Albion at 94-year-old Vin Jackson's place. Mr. Jackson - who has since passed away - helped settle the area and build the first roads. His farmhouse was a set decorator's dream, complete with original linoleum and fixtures. The decor appeared as though it hadn't changed in sixty years.

Mr. Jackson enjoyed a good yarn and if you happened to arrive at breakfast time, you could always be assured of a place-setting. In the past, he had entertained movie shoots such as *Jennifer 8* and *Jumanji,* and seemed both puzzled and amused by the time and effort production companies devoted to recreating reality.

When I asked him if we could use his small herd of cattle as background action in the pasture on the day of filming - for which I had been instructed to offer him $5-$10 per cow - he laughed and shook his head as if to say "Don't worry about the money," adding, "Sure, why not - they're there anyway."

3x04	CLYDE BRUCKMAN'S FINAL REPOSE	LG

A reluctant psychic who can foresee people's deaths helps Scully and Mulder track a serial murderer who is killing the psychics of St. Paul.

STREET/CONVENIENCE AND LIQUOR STORE
3500-BLOCK COMMERCIAL ST. AND ERNIE'S GROCERY, 3599 COMMERCIAL ST., VANCOUVER

This street - a hidden gem for filming - is composed of a mix of unimposing residential and commercial buildings. This film experience was essentially a neighbourhood party. The police officers closed down the street for the exterior scenes and the locals milled around set to satisfy their curiosity. Clyde Bruckman, our hero, spent the day in fictional torment wandering the street, in

Louisa held the location department record for the most expensive monthly cellular phone bill: over $1,200. Todd preferred the land line.

Field of Tulips

Production designer Graeme Murray requested real flowers to create the field of tulips on which Clyde lies ("Clyde Bruckman's Final Repose" (3x04)). Two days before filming, over 200 tulips were imported from Holland, only to be rejected on aesthetic grounds because they looked too "real." This ordeal only cost $250, but the real costs had yet to surface.

The greens department ended up stapling 450 silk tulips onto a large elevated platform built by the construction department. Filming the scene took two seventeen hour days because each time actor Peter Boyle moved out of the tulip bed, he altered the original arrangement, and the silk tulips had to be meticulously repositioned for the next take.

Body Double

During the technical survey for "2Shy" (3x06), clutching our coffees as we made our way back to the van, I saw David Duchovny's identical twin crossing the street. I pointed him out to the team, noting that even his walk was similar to David's. Director David Nutter asked driver Ken Marsden to give chase. We sped across the street, stopped abruptly, and, in a fury, Nutter, Tom Braidwood, and I leaped out of the van to chase the Duchovny look-alike. When we caught up to him, the young man backed away - he later told us he thought we were trying to sell him stolen stereos. But we insisted he take one of our *X-Files* business cards. He looked it over and then offered his phone number. Within a couple of months, Steve Kiziak's electrician apprenticeship was over. He had become David Duchovny's number one photo double. When the show moved to L.A., so did Steve. He even made a guest appearance on Jay Leno's *Tonight Show* in February 1999.

David Duchovny's photo double Steve Kiziak.

search of his curse at the *convenience store* and at an artist's studio on the block which was decorated as both the *Tarot Dealership* and *Palm Reader Shop*.

> Two Emmys were collected in 1996 for this episode: writer Darin Morgan won for Writing and Peter Boyle won for Guest Actor in a Drama Series for his performance as the title character.

3x05	THE LIST	TP

An executed murderer returns from the dead to seek revenge by killing five people.

3x06	2SHY	LG

In Cleveland, a man's genetic mutation requires that he consume the fat of other people in order to survive.

VIRGIL'S APARTMENT/ELLEN'S CONDO
2500-2600-BLOCK, QUEBEC ST., VANCOUVER

With these locations only a block apart, *Virgil's apartment* and *Ellen's condo* were filmed on the same night. While David and Gillian were filming in the alley at the rear, their doubles were being filmed entering from the front. Appropriate arrangements had been made with the respective owners for this brief scene and after director David Nutter staged the scene, second assistant director Collin Leadlay and the doubles got to work.

> Steve Kiziak, David's new double, started his new job at this location. When asked about his fondest memory he recalled coming face to face with his mirror image for the first time.

In the episode, Scully and Mulder are seen from the street bursting through the front door. In reality, it was the doubles doing the bursting. After five takes, the shot was complete, and the crew moved on. The next day a woman called, wanting to know why her dinner party had been interrupted. As it turned out, the doubles had been directed to barge through the wrong door.

As *Ellen's condo* was being illuminated by condors and an 18K, another condor lit up the adjoining block to establish the exterior of *Virgil's apartment* at night. The bright lights were visible more than twenty blocks away.

3x07   THE WALK   TP

Scully and Mulder investigate a series of killings at a veterans hospital, where a multiple amputee Gulf War vet uses astral projection to taking revenge on his former superiors.

INTERROGATION ROOM/HALLWAY/DETENTION CENTRE/ROACH'S CELL
BLAKE HALL, JUSTICE INSTITUTE OF B.C., 4180 WEST 4TH AVE., VANCOUVER

With one notable exception – the Callahan House at 3638 Osler Street – this episode was written around *psychiatric hospitals, jails,* and a *swimming pool.* And while old standby Riverview Hospital may have seemed like the logical choice to accommodate most of the sixteen-odd sets required for this episode, production (and locations) was now in the position of respecting David's fervent desire that he not be put in a position to visit the Riverview site again for a very long time, the distance (a forty-minute drive from his home) being the primary reason.

The task of finding locations closer to Vancouver to satisfy this new edict therefore became a priority for the locations department. Several sets for were already being built and dressed at the Jean Matheson Pavilion on the B.C. Children's Hospital site *(psych ward isolation room, hallway, elevator* and *stairwell)* and in the Old Nurses Residence at Vancouver General Hospital *(Callahan's office, observation room* and *hallway).*

The former site of the Justice Institute of British Columbia had been vacated in the summer of 1995 as the Institute moved to its new facility in New Westminster. What remained – the gym and pool facility, the administrative and catering buildings, and a school – had just come under the new ownership of the West Point Grey Community Centre, located a few blocks away at Aberthau Manor.

We looked at Blake Hall – the former administrative building – as a location for the long hallway scenes leading to the *interrogation room, detention centre,* and *Roach's*

The scenes in the swimming pool and locker room were filmed at the pool facility next door. We had been looking for a pool without all the lines and markings associated with a public recreational facility. Similarly, these day scenes would be better served if the facility had windows through which supplemental lighting could be added. Both conditions were ideally served by this location.

The Justice Institute's catering building was used as the site of the Chaco chicken plant in "Our Town" (2x24). The large industrial kitchen was stripped of much of its defining hardware and our own set dressing brought in to create the look of a processing plant without the smell.

One big lab at the Justice Institute.

Money-Back Guarantee (TP)

In the location managing end of this business, it is not customary for an individual or a business to actually offer to return monies (damage and security deposits excepted) to the production company. Quite the opposite is usually true. However, rare exceptions do exist.

The list of locations required for "Nisei" (3x09) was not lengthy by *X-Files* standards (eight locations over eight days), but it was somewhat eclectic and included a *small ship* (of the 100-foot-plus variety), a *dock facility* at which to berth this ship, a *railyard* and *train station*, a *Coast Guard headquarters* (view of the water preferred), a *harbourmaster's office* (view of a very large ship loading/unloading preferred), a *police station parking lot*, an *embassy*, and two *houses* (one an "eyesore," the other a modest fifties-style bungalow).

The modest house (*Betsy Hagopian's house* in the script) was found on Grand Boulevard in North Vancouver, owner-occupied by a very friendly senior citizen. Great care was taken to explain to Mrs. M. exactly what was required of her property and what this would mean to her. A full dress was required, which meant that she was given the option of a hotel or a couple of nights with relatives. She decided to stay with relatives. We came, we filmed, we left.

Three months later I called Mrs. M. to inform her that the episode was to air the following weekend, thinking that she might get a kick out of seeing her house on network television. She thanked me and then asked if it was alright to cash the cheque. I drew a temporary blank. "What cheque would that be?" I asked. "The cheque you gave me for filming at my house," she replied. "I've been carrying it around in my purse ever since." The cheque, incidentally, was worth about $3,000. "Of course you can cash it. It's your money. The show's about to be on television." To which she sweetly added, "I just wanted to make sure that every-

cellblock. This building, which would be demolished within six months, gave us the latitude to paint and build without concern for costs associated with restoration.

The hallway walls were soft yellow tile and the floors had been carpeted throughout, hiding the lovely masonry. A sub-contractor was hired to remove both carpet and adhesive residue, which was considerable and extremely stubborn. It's no exaggeration to say that they worked day and night – experimenting with different chemical agents – in an attempt to remove every trace of the black goo which had been used to firmly affix carpet to floor.

An industrial cleaning company followed closely, bringing the stone floors and tiled walls to the desired reflective sheen. By the time *The X-Files* returned to this site in February 1996 to film scenes for "Pusher" (3x17) in the recently-vacated McDonald Building *(FBI firing range* and *hearing room/hallway),* all that remained of Blake Hall was a gravel parking lot and a vast expanse of lawn.

| 3x08 | OUBLIETTE | LG |

A kidnap survivor simultaneously manifests the experiences of her abductor's latest victim. Mulder uses her as a road map, Scully thinks she is an accomplice.

WADE'S HOUSE
MOUNT SEYMOUR LODGE, SEYMOUR MOUNTAIN

The script called for a house in the middle of nowhere, but the notion of "remote" to some producers often means somewhere close to the studio. Even though the Lower Mainland appears to offer remote dwellings, fields, and roads, there are very few isolated houses easily accessible to a film unit. When needing to accommodate 1,500 linear feet of work trucks and sixty crew cars, "remote" suggests areas that could appear rustic while being next to a parking lot.

This remote dwelling was in reality a log house situated near a parking lot at the top of Seymour Mountain. The ski lift, however, was a visual impediment to the setting. Frank Haddad and his team were instructed to conceal the lift with a bank of trees. Hundreds of trees. On a Friday afternoon, during the Tech Survey, the schedule was changed and access to the Mountain on the following Monday for three days of intensive prep was required. Greens estimated a minimum five-day prep for their department.

The contract with Provincial Parks had not yet been approved and Parks requires one week notice prior to any film activity whether it be prep, shoot, or wrap. Cellular phones are godsends. When we finally reached the Parks representative, we were promised that the utmost effort would be expended to approve the request on Monday so prep could begin, but were warned not to begin prep without a signed contract. While waiting for the decision and realizing the magnitude of greens work, Frank began to secretly haul truckloads of trees up the mountain. Little did we know that the Parks officials could see the trucks roaring past their office. When the trucks reached the summit, feeling rather smug about the clandestine activity, the Parks representative called and yelled, "Stop that truck." We were caught. By noon, approval to begin prep was given and the truckloads resumed.

> To create the appearance of seclusion, 350 trees were brought in to dress the set.

RIVERBANK

SEYMOUR RIVERBANK, SQUAMISH NATION
PROPERTY, 320 SEYMOUR BLVD., NORTH VANCOUVER

This episode prompted a survey of all the local rivers in wilderness settings. Capilano River and Lynn Headwaters were too shallow and ultimately the Seymour River near Twin Bridges was selected because the high water table offered "jeopardy," but was safe for actors. The location was scheduled for the eighth day of shooting. Then the rains came.

On day six, Kelly Mortensen, the Greater Vancouver Regional District representative, informed us that the Seymour River had risen a foot and was rising still. It became evident that all of the rivers were too high and dangerous for the scene. Director Kim Manners demanded a new location, and the portion of the Seymour River near its mouth proved to be, at least on the Friday, the shallowest body of water to be found locally. The scene was scheduled for filming on the following Monday. Frank spent his weekend hauling truckloads of trees to camouflage the houses opposite the chosen riverbank. Locations spent the weekend one step ahead of Frank, getting approval from home owners to place trees on their properties. By Monday morning the river was ten inches higher, but despite the persistent deluge, a persistent Kim Manners kept filming. By noon the entire crew was water-logged and Kim's director's chair, originally positioned on a gravel bed on the bank, rested in a foot of water. When asked about the day he merely responded, "It couldn't be fucking worse."

> The greens department used more than 1,000 trees to hide the houses along the riverbank.

thing was okay and that you were happy with everything and that you didn't need to do reshoots."

The story does not end here. Flash forward two years and three months to "Memento Mori" (4x15). Scully is again required to visit the *MUFON* (mutual UFO network of abductees) *house*. By then, Mrs. M. was an old pro at location filming. She was also eager to be of assistance. The necessary arrangements were made and her house was again committed to celluloid.

Several weeks later I received a letter at the production office. The return address listed Mrs. M. as the sender. I opened the envelope to find a brief hand-written note and a cheque equalling the amount agreed upon as reimbursement for hotel expenses. Mrs. M. explained in the note that, since the prep crew left her bedroom intact, she returned home the night before filming and sweet-talked our security guard into allowing her inside because she wanted to sleep in her own bed. She therefore felt it only right that the money should be returned to us. And that is a rare occurence indeed.

March 19, 1998

Dear Resident:

On Wednesday, March 25, Thursday, March 26 and Friday, March 27, X-F Productions Inc. of North Vancouver will be filming scenes for an episode of "The X-Files" at 522 East 12th Street.

This dramatic series deals with paranormal events and unexplained phenomena within the realm of extreme possibility.

Filming will take place between the hours of 7am and 5pm approximately on Wednesday only, between 8:30am and 11pm on Thursday, and between 9am and 12 midnight on Friday. Wednesday's work will involve interior filming only, while Thursday's and Friday's work will involve interior filming during the day and exterior filming on both nights.

Parking restrictions will be as follows:
1) Wednesday only (7am and 5pm)
   - north/south sides of East 12th from Moody Ave. to Grand Blvd.
   - east side of Moody from East 12th to East 13th Streets
   - east side of Grand Blvd. from East 11th to East 13th Street
   - north side of East 11th Ave. between Grand Blvd. east and west

2) Thursday (7am) to Saturday (8am)
   - east side of Grand Blvd. between 11th and 13th Streets
   - north side of East 11th Street between Grand Blvd. east and west
   - north/south sides of East 12th between Grand Blvd. and Moody Ave.
   - east side of Moody Ave. between East 11th and East 13th Streets.

On all these days, crew vehicles will park in the parking lot at Moody and East 13th Street.

Please expect a complete closure of the 500 block of East 12th Ave. on Thursday and Friday (local traffic exempted) between the hours of 1pm and 11pm respectively.

Please note that on Thursday and Friday nights, we will be using lighting cranes and lightning machines. The lightning machines are very bright. Please do not stare directly at the flashes, as this could cause temporary altered vision.

Chicken (TP)

The onset of Season Three saw the creation of an official Second Unit crew, whose responsibility it would be to shoot all inserts, time-consuming stuntwork, and special effects shots not involving principal cast, and additional footage or reshoots as required by the producers, director, or editors.

Very quickly, Second Unit also took responsibility for episode teasers as well as work involving both principal cast members. Expectations grew with each new episode. A scene would be reshot until it was deemed good enough. If an episode was found to be lacking, additional scenes were added to bring it up to snuff.

This created a number of scheduling problems when trying to accommodate Second Unit work within the Main Unit schedule, particularly when David and Gillian were needed for both shoots. For the locations department, it meant being in a continual state of readiness to accommodate, as Second Unit schedules and demands were often not decided until two or three days before prospective shoot dates.

Robert Murdoch was hired as the Second Unit assistant location manager, the theory being that Louisa and I would organize and negotiate the location requirements for Second Unit while Murdoch took care of the nuts and bolts (parking, maps, resident notification, etc.) and provided a physical presence on set. As many of the locations required by Second Unit were repeat locations used by Main Unit (hence they'd already been scouted and deals negotiated), it was not felt that a Second Unit location manager position was justifiable. Experience would subsequently prove this to be a half-truth at best as episodes ballooned in size and degree of difficulty, with Second Unit often cleaning up

| 3x09 | NISEI | TP |

A suspiciously realistic alien autopsy videotape puts Mulder on the trail of a salvaged alien spacecraft, a group of Japanese doctors who are experimenting on alien life-forms, and a mysterious train on which the experiments take place.

| COAST GUARD HQ/HARBOURMASTER'S OFFICE |
| BALLANTYNE PIER, VANCOUVER |

Neither the Canadian Coast Guard nor the Vancouver Port Authority offices commanded the kind of views of the harbour required by us for this episode. Not only did director David Nutter want ships and harbour in the background, but he wanted them as close as possible.

Ballantyne Pier and cruise ship facility was chosen because it was, literally, on the water and because there was vacant space in which to create our own offices. The companionway on the east side of the facility (with a panoramic view to the northeast) was chosen to house the *Harbourmaster's office* set, while the opposite companionway to the west (with a view to the northwest) would serve as the hallway leading to *Coast Guard HQ* in which the walk-and-talk was staged.

Shipping companies offer no guarantees when it comes to scheduling, but with the help of the management at neighbouring Casco Terminals, we best-guessed a scheduled arrival and plugged that day into our shooting schedule. As luck – and the weather at sea – would have it, we were fortunate enough to have a large freighter off-loading within fifty feet of our set.

| EDWARDS TERMINAL, QUEENSGATE, OHIO |
| BC RAIL STATION, NORTH VANCOUVER |

This episode and "731" (3x10) are known in *X-Files* mythology as the "train shows." Not only did we commandeer a passenger train and travel up coast with it, but we purchased an old daycar and blew it up in a spectacular explosion on a siding at Porteau Cove, B.C. The gutted wreck was subsequently returned to BC Rail for scrap.

All this required a huge plan to circumvent logistical problems, among them the weather and existing train schedules using the same set of track. Our rail terminal was actually the departure point for all trains heading north on this line. These scenes were filmed between morning passenger departures and late afternoon arrivals, with some surprised looks from terminal staff and travellers.

Scenes involving the arrival of the scientists, Mulder's surveillance from the roof of the locomotive shed, and the departure of "731" on its clandestine journey were filmed in the adjoining railyard.

The Budd car explodes ("731" (3x10)).

ALICE STREET OVERPASS
26TH ST. AND BELLEVUE, WEST VANCOUVER

Five words came up during a preliminary script discussion which carried both a sense of excitement and foreboding: *Mulder . . . jumps . . . onto . . . moving train*. Fine. An old wooden pedestrian overpass did exist on the rail line we would be using with "our" train, but questions of safety and liability required a quick redress.

Similarly, its location in West Vancouver was a factor, as many residents of this lovely enclave would just as soon raise the drawbridge as let a film company into their neighbourhood. A structural engineer examined the overpass and gave us the green light, at which point some municipal goodwill (were they fans?) kicked in, granting all but one of our requests, which involved night filming after 5 p.m.

A piece of the overpass was recreated on the lot at North Shore Studios to accommodate low angle shots of David moments before his decision to jump onto the roof of the moving train, a cleverly-executed stunt staged almost entirely on location with both actor and stuntman.

A West Vancouver by-law restricts filming and the moving of trucks and trailers to between the hours of 7 a.m. and 5 p.m. No night filming or extensions are allowed unless approved by city council. On the day of filming I arrived just before 7 a.m. to find a noisy construction company at work on a residential site no more than 200 yards from set.

work from two — and sometimes three — previous shows simultaneously. This provided Rob with many challenges, many headaches, and a measure of responsibility which sometimes exceeded both his title and job description.

A scene in "Nisei" (3x09) required a location to play as the *Japanese Embassy* in Washington, D.C. A quick internet search confirmed that Embassy Row in D.C. consisted of several old mansions and estates converted into diplomat headquarters. Conversely, the Japanese Embassy in Vancouver was housed in a very modern black glass and tile highrise in the downtown core, austere and visually uninteresting. The University Women's Club of Vancouver at Hycroft in Shaughnessy would be our replacement. Given our research, it seemed like the logical choice.

Built in an Italianate villa style, the house comprises 15,000 square feet on three floors and includes a ballroom, lounge, and wine cellar on the ground level floor. Hycroft originally sat on a 5.2-acre parcel of land which included a stable, greenhouses, tennis courts, and a tiled swimming pool. All but the pool were eventually demolished and the property subdivided, leaving two acres of grounds around the house.

With its grand Edwardian architecture, Italian tiled roof, and ornate Grecian Corinthian columned entrances, very little set dressing was needed. A Japanese flag was hung, greens and vines were added to the pillars, and white parking lines were temporarily removed. As this scene was written for night, calltime was set for 4 p.m. Filming at Hycroft has always been more about getting worktrucks, equipment, and personnel in and out of this very sensitive neighbourhood by 11 p.m. than about the craft of movie-making. Add to this the logistics of lighting a night exterior in which a lighting crane had to be parked out on the street, and both Rob and director Kim Manners had their work cut out for them. After all, a neighbour (and long time film industry NIMBY) would be watching and waiting, his hand on the City Hall hotline.

At about 9 p.m. Rob called from set. He was worried. The overhead crane shot of the Japanese diplomat being garroted in the back seat of the limosine was taking forever to set up and he was concerned that Kim would not finish shooting in time to be loaded up and gone by 11 p.m.

Kim, a veteran director with a lot of prior production experience in Vancouver, was well aware of the situation and trying hard to wrap things up. Unfortunately, problems with the *Swiss Jib* and reflections in the limosine sunroof had slowed the pace and there were only so many shortcuts he could take. I urged Rob to remind Kim of the deadline and call me with an update at 9:45 p.m.

When my phone rang again, the desperation in Rob's voice told the story. We would, he reported, be lucky to be finished filming by 10:30 p.m., an unacceptable scenario. "Well, if that's the case," I began, "I hope you're ready to pull the plug. You are my representative on set and Kim knows the drill. I'm not about to burn this location. That just won't happen." There was a long pause on the other end of the line.

A remote control camera on a Swiss Jib.

DRYDOCK/TALAPUS
PIER 94/VANCOUVER SHIPYARDS, NORTH VANCOUVER

Here's a classic example of creative geography. Mulder leaves the Coast Guard HQ at Ballantyne Pier on the Vancouver side of the harbour, disappearing amidst a sea of containers. Moments later, he emerges in a North Vancouver shipyard and ascends three storeys onto a submersible drydock facility, where he spots our hero scow – the Talapus – moored nearby.

As serendipity would have it, the ship (it really was called the Talapus) was located – already berthed – at Pier 94 in North Vancouver. Pier 94 is adjacent to Vancouver Shipyards' massive floating drydock, which was subsequently written into the script and added to the location list as an afterthought because a) it was there, b) it was visually very cool, and c) the operators were enthusiastic to play host to the show.

David's photo double Steve Kiziak split the on-camera duties with David in traversing the overhead catwalk, which had an unnerving habit of swinging in the wind and bouncing uncontrollably under the weight of scurrying footsteps.

3x10	731	LG

In one of the secret railcars Mulder discovers that the experiments are on alien-human hybrids while Scully, at a West Virginia research centre, discovers open graves filled with hybrid bodies.

TRAIN EXPLOSION
PORTEAU COVE, SQUAMISH HWY.

The alien's transcontinental rail trip essentially covered thirty kilometres of BC Rail's line with one stop at the overpass in West Vancouver, terminating with an explosive finale at Porteau Cove. Film schedules had to be tight and shots had to be confirmed. With regular trains travelling the single track line, there was no time to spare. The actual explosion necessitated co-ordination with the railway and Squamish Highway officials. Traffic along the highway was closed during each attempt to explode the rail car.

Special effects needed ten days to prep the railcar and three days to pack it with explosives. After the set went hot, a seaplane buzzed the set at an altitude of only 200 feet. As the explosives were to be detonated by radio control, the seaplane and its instruments jeopardized the entire crew.

This Budd's for you: (l-r) BC Rail's Mike Zalecki, Brett Dowler, Rob Bowman, and a special effects crew member prep the explosion for "731" (3x10).

The train explosion for "731" (3x10).

As a continuation of "Nisei" (3x09), this episode required a separate track along the train line to rig and explode the train. In other words, an inactive line where special effects could rig explosives, and the actual explosion wouldn't impede or impair regular rail schedules. In order to find the ultimate location, art director Greg Loewen and I scouted the entire rail line by Hi-Railer - a jeep fitted with rail grabs to drive on either the rail track or off-road. The $1,000 trip afforded us a spectacular view of the ocean and the thrill of riding above the sculpted canyons of Garibaldi Pass. Off-road excursions for breakfast and lunch enabled us to scout some of the finer culinary delights enroute.

At the beginning of prep, a great deal of time, energy, and creative talent was devoted to the aesthetic of the alien's railcar (a BC23-Budd car) and its position in the line of railcars. After lengthy discussions, the alien car was placed at the end of the train. Several weeks of prep later, we learned that a Budd car cannot safely leave the station at the end of a train. The alien car was then designated second to the end. The picture locomotive, Engine 756, was painted with removable stripping for the lineup and the roofs of all of the cars were painted with non-skid paint to ensure David's safety when he jumped onto the moving train.

Gusts of wind off the ocean peaked at 50 kilometres per hour while filming at this location.

"Pull the plug on Kim. . ." Rob's voice trailed off. "Yes," I replied. "I did it to Wes Craven once. It wasn't very pleasant, and I almost got fired. But I was right, and I knew it. And what's more important, he knew it." Somehow Rob seemed less than convinced by my example.

The toe-to-toe which ensued was, by all accounts, one for the books. Rob began by standing next to Kim and looking pensively at his watch in an attempt to get his attention. "Sir," Rob began, "I'm afraid we're going to have to wrap things up. We're out of time." Kim seemed to ignore the suggestion. "Kim," Rob repeated, every inch the gentleman, "I'm going to have to pull the plug." To which Kim wheeled around to face Rob and, poking him in the chest with his finger, launched into a tirade. "Wait a minute," Kim began. "You're shutting me down . . . you . . . you're shutting me down?"

"At that point," Rob later recalled, "all the crew slowly began to back up around us. As Kim became more agitated, that lovely midwestern drawl of his became more pronounced, too."

"You're . . . you're shutting me down," Kim continued. "Let me get this straight. You're shutting me . . . down." To which Rob replied, "Yes, that is correct."

The exchange went on for some minutes before Kim calmed down and realized that Rob was only doing his job which, at this time of the night, meant protecting both the location and the neighbourhood. Miraculously, the Second Unit crew wrapped at 10:05 p.m. and were gone by 11 p.m. No complaints.

For two seasons, Kim had exhibited a predilection for a certain fast-food fried chicken. He occasionally treated his Second Unit crew to a few buckets at wrap, this night being no exception.

Second Unit assistant location manager Robert Murdoch.

Fans often surrounded the set hoping for autographs. Production assistant Woody Morrison recalled that during the filming of "War of the Coprophages," a young fan waited all night hoping to catch a glimpse of David. As David was heading to set at 7 a.m., he stopped by to say hello, sign an autograph, and get his picture taken with the awestruck girl.

Producer J.P. Finn knew the property manager of the location to be used for the *methane plant* exterior. Although we anticipated no problems negotiating a satisfactory arrangement, the manager insisted on an exorbitant fee. Unfortunately, J.P. was unable to reduce the fee, and we had run out of time and options. Sometimes "who you know" doesn't help.

Six German cockroaches escaped the sets at North Shore Studios.

| 3x11 | REVELATIONS | TP |

Scully questions her own faith while she protects a boy who exhibits stigmata, and who is being pursued by a serial killer.

| 3x12 | WAR OF THE COPROPHAGES | LG |

Roaches appear to be overrunning a Massachusetts town.

| INTERIOR METHANE PLANT |
| CRANE CANADA, 225 NORTH RD., COQUITLAM |

No matter how subtly the subject of cockroaches is introduced, there are no warm welcomes. I explained to the producers that at most practical locations, the idea of having German cockroaches infiltrate private homes and businesses would not be entertained. Imagine the ramifications if some of the insects ventured off set. It was expected, however, that the question be posed at the location of the interior methane plant. To deal with the issue tactfully and expediently, it was broached with the manager while discussing the massive paint job required to effectively portray a lab. While the manager was considering the paint issue, he turned to us and remarked, "Cockroaches skirting around here would be fun." There was complete silence from the survey team. Painting and filming took place at this location without a single cockroach escapee.

The exterior of the Crane Canada building was not visually interesting enough for our exterior filming needs, so another nearby warehouse was selected. It had numerous windows and glass loading bay doors through which tons of debris could escape after the explosion of the *methane plant*. To minimize the damage associated with the explosion, special effects sealed the office. Too well. When the explosion occurred, the office imploded. Entire walls ballooned out into the corridors although staying intact. Special effects spent several days cleaning up the mess, and construction added an entire build to their list of things to do for this episode.

| MINI MART |
| PETRO CANADA, 489 NORTH DOLLARTON HWY., NORTH VANCOUVER |

This location was scheduled for a Friday night shoot and in expectation of a late night, the neighbouring residences were petitioned for permission to shoot until 2 a.m. Saturday. The Dollarton Mall businesses were also petitioned for the use of nineteen parking stalls for work truck parking behind the location. The *mini mart* location was chosen for its small town setting and convenience store/gas station combination. The scene depicts Scully arriving at the pumps, only to be hemmed in by frantic locals who are buying everything in the store. It was expected that this scene would take the crew well into the night, but due to inclement weather, and a growing intolerance of the rain, director Kim Manners called an early wrap.

EXTERIOR HOSPITAL
CLAIRMONT CAMERA, NORTH SHORE STUDIOS, NORTH VANCOUVER

When Lions Gate Studios was developed, hideous false storefront facades were built in front of some of the stages. These storefronts gave a new definition to "fake," and are only used when desperate. Really desperate. The Clairmont building, adorned with mirrored glass, could conceivably be found in the "real" world, and as an exterior location close to our stages, it suitably depicted a modern *small-town hospital*.

3x13	SYZYGY	TP

A strange planetary alignment sends everything out of wack. Everything's off-kilter including Mulder, who is guzzling vodka, and Scully, who is chain-smoking on cigarettes.

CLEARING IN WOODS/CLIFF
OLD CYPRESS MOUNTAIN QUARRY, CYPRESS MOUNTAIN, WEST VANCOUVER

The teaser for this episode called for a clearing around a cliff face where police discover the body of a teenage boy dangling from above. This type of location is always problematic when it comes to access for equipment and crew. Safety issues were also a big concern; natural locations are almost always dangerous or inaccessible. The *desert quarry* used in episodes 2x04 and 3x01 was ruled out as it was still red.

The discovery of this location came about as the recollection of a crew member who seemed to recall "a cliff and a bunch of boulders" from some other show he'd worked on. He thought it was "somewhere in West Vancouver."

Calls were made to West Vancouver and it was soon

Sifted Evidence (TP)

The West Coast rains were not the only culprit to wreak havoc on production. During the filming of scenes for "Syzygy" (3x13) at the Boundary Bay Airport, strong winds blew a large propane heater into the wall of our 20' x 20' extras holding tent, causing the tent to catch fire and melt within minutes. Fortunately, all extras were on set during the accident, but many had left changes of clothing and personals in the tent. I later received a lengthy list of damaged or destroyed items from extras casting, and was both shocked and amused to note the number of expensive designer suits, handbags, Italian shoes, and custom eyewear which had gone up in flames. Given that the scenes we were filming involved a crowd of townsfolk from a small rural community and that this was a night shoot, I was further puzzled. I asked that the claimants bring in the charred remains of their belongings for verification pending replacement. Virtually nothing materialized at the production office.

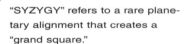

"SYZYGY" refers to a rare planetary alignment that creates a "grand square."

Burning a location: actions by a production that lead to complaints severe enough that a location is immediately placed on the hot list.

A Lesson in Manners (LG)

Location scout Alan Bartolic had been assigned the task of scouting North Vancouver for a creepy-looking alley as one of the locations in "Grotesque" (3x14). It had to be there for scheduling reasons, although we all knew that North Vancouver was the wrong place to be looking and that *anything* he came up with would be less than perfect.

When the time came to review the photofiles with director Kim Manners, I suggested Alan take care of it since he hadn't yet worked directly with Kim and was looking forward to inching a little closer to the creative core of the show. Alan later recalled his meeting with Kim:

When I arrived at Kim's office door I think he'd just heard some bad news. Perhaps that he was expected to film a creepy alley scene in North Vancouver. He knew as well as we did that this was the wrong place to be and any choice would mean creative compromise.

What I was about to learn was Kim's method of expressing his frustrations. "How the fuck am I supposed to shoot a fucking monster attack in this mother-fucking alley!" he exclaimed as I attempted to lay the photofiles out on the desk in front of him. "We may as well shoot this in a parking lot. Hell, why don't we just use fucking stock footage from an Ed Wood flick, for chrissakes." Words to that effect.

To say I feared for my life would be to understate the range of emotions I felt at that moment. I had stared into the abyss and the message staring me back seemed to be saying "We won't be needing you tomorrow." I do not recall the walk back to the locations office. I do remember not being able to feel my legs.

When Kim got wind of my reaction to his blustering, he came down to the locations office. "Sorry about that, bud," he said. "It wasn't about you. It was about that motherfucking alley!"

established that an old quarry did exist on the road up to Cypress Mountain.

The property belonged to a development company and was in the rezoning process but we were - in the meantime - welcome to film there.

This location proved ideal for director Rob Bowman. Not only could the top of the cliff be easily accessed by road and path, but there was room enough for him to stage the complicated crane shots he envisioned.

The entire site was accessible by a servicable road, although the lack of flat ground to park work trucks was problematic. Fortunately, this would be a Second Unit shoot, which meant "less" of everything. The concern that did finally arise was the possibility of snow, as filming was scheduled for December 12, 1995, and we were, technically, at altitude. As luck would have it, we avoided the first snowfall of the year by a week.

3x14	GROTESQUE	LG

A long-time detractor of Mulder's asks for help in catching a murderous gargoyle.

ART STUDIO/HISTORICAL BUILDING
HERITAGE HALL, 3102 MAIN ST., VANCOUVER

Although this location had been booked for several weeks, only four days prior to filming we noticed that the exterior sidewalk was under major construction. A call to the City was imminent. The construction crew reassured us that the work would be completed by the film day, and it was, only two hours before the trucks moved in. Prep of the exterior of this building involved positioning a gargoyle on the rooftop with special bracing to avoid any damage to the heritage structure.

Heritage Hall is a fairly popular filming location, and over the years there have been numerous parking complaints from neighbours. In response to the complaints, the City requested that we park our trucks a block further away. Several months later a rumour - that *The X-Files* was responsible for *burning this location* - surfaced. Even now, similar myths abound in the the film community. In reality, *The X-Files'* locations team paved the way to scores of new locations in the Lower Mainland, and we were often shadowed by other companies.

DARK ALLEY
ALLEY AT BONANZA MEAT MARKET, 1ST ST. AND LONSDALE AVE., NORTH VANCOUVER

The alley was scheduled on the same day as a studio shoot and therefore had to be found in nearby North Vancouver, while reflecting the exterior sandstone block facade of Heritage Hall. Our only option did not match, but production designer Graeme Murray resolved the problem by suggesting that we paint the walls on one entire side of the alley to look like Heritage Hall. The walls had to be painted back after filming.

Wrapping the gargoyle for "Grotesque" (3x14).

3x15	PIPER MARU	TP

A French salvage ship arrives in San Diego with its crew dying of radiation burns, victims of an alien form that enters and leaves humans as an oily film.

CHINESE RESTAURANT (HONG KONG)
THE HO-HO CHOP SUEY HOUSE, 102 EAST PENDER ST., VANCOUVER

When searching for scripted locations, the most logical candidates do not always make the cut. Availability or scheduling concerns sometimes intervene to force other choices. Not so this time around. Hong Kong was on the locations menu and we were fortunate in finding a neglected old Chinese restaurant beneath a rooming house on the edge of Vancouver's Chinatown.

The edge of Chinatown made the difference here, as filming in Chinatown is at best extremely expensive, for what is gained in production value and at worst a locations nightmare. Most merchants resented our presence, but tolerated us as long as they got a piece of the action.

When the prep crew arrived on January 8, 1996, the Ho-Ho had already been out of business for some time. Several inches of grease coated every surface in the well-worn kitchen. The interior, however, remained fully intact. Furniture, appliances, cooking utensils - even calendars and wall ornaments - had not been disturbed since the day the restaurant closed its doors. It was a good fit for us as we required a spacious booth-style seating arrangement and four days to clean and prep the set. The cleaners alone took two full days to scour and disinfect the kitchen so that the crew could access the location from the back alley.

A vacant restaurant meant no buyouts for loss of business and the chance to hold our set for several days after

While filming, director Kim Manners wanted more blood on the razor, the gargoyle's murderous weapon. Props informed him that a severed throat would not produce much blood, so having more blood would not reflect reality. Kim, rather stunned by the response, looked up and said, "A gargoyle killing people isn't reality either, so give me some more damned blood."

一月五日一九九六年

致全體商人和租戶：

在本星期五，一月十二日，北岸之光怪陸離 X-Files制片商將會在好好抖擻飯鋪 Ho-Ho Chop Suey Restaurant。120 東片打衡拍攝電視連續集 - 光怪陸離 X-Files 之影片。

這項拍攝將會排定在本星期五下午二時至星期六早上二時，而這拍的攝將會分為兩部分其一者會從下午二時至晚上九時 在室內拍攝，而戶外的拍攝是 從晚上九時後才開始。

對於戶外之拍攝過程中，本光怪陸離 X-Files 之制片商在東片打衡100號的東片打衡之全部商店將關的廣告屏障會在夜間點著至早上二時，因為我們將需要備裝事情在香港發生。

在同時間裡，溫哥華市政局將會在東片打衡100號地上，不允許泊車，的路牌。（有效期將會在午後六時至星期六早上二時）。在拍攝期間警察部門也將會分派人手在拍攝範圍巡邏及指導公共汽車繞道路線。

在這兩天期間，本光怪陸離 X-Files 之制片商的華人聯絡員將會在唐人街地區向各商人分發及解釋這封信的內容。以及代表各位傳達問題及意見給本人參考。

本光怪陸離 X-Files 之制片商將會捐獻一套捐款於中華義協會以表謝意。如果您有任何意見或問題的話，請致電：983-5391或試聯絡本制片商之華人代表。

對於各位的充份合作，本人在此表十二分之謝意。

光怪陸離 X-Files 之制片商
TODD PITTSON。地點經理啓

We revisited the Ho-Ho (why not, we cleaned it up the first time around) later in Season Three during the Chinatown-featured episode "Hell Money" (3x19).

filming if necessary. This latter practice had become increasingly important to the scouting and negotiation process by Season Three, as scenes grew more complicated and ambitious in their execution and therefore more time-consuming to film.

This place was once a mainstay of the Chinatown restaurant scene, the ornate neon sign featuring prominently in virtually any Chinatown street scene. The neon sign still hung from the building, but was beyond repair and subsequently removed by 1997. The exterior night footage depicting a very vibrant Chinatown represents stock footage taken elsewhere.

The sniper from "The End" (5x20).

Wild walls: moveable walls.

MIRIMAR NAVAL AIR BASE

ORTONA CRES., DEPARTMENT OF NATIONAL DEFENCE (DND) JERICHO BASE, VANCOUVER

There was only one military base of any consequence in the Lower Mainland, so when an initial discussion of locations was held for this episode, the Jericho Base was the one and only suggestion presented. With its tree-lined streets of cookie-cutter-style base housing, aging barracks, and parade grounds, this became *Miramar Naval Air Base.* We had simply to pick *Commander Johansen's house* and install the requisite *checkposts* and *sentry huts* on the adjacent streets.

With the permit process uncomfortably drawn out for an episodic television schedule - final approval rested with the Department of National Defence (DND) in Ottawa - we were fortunate in having fans in high places who were willing to grant verbal permission by telephone and "worry about the paperwork later." First assistant director and Lone Gunman Tom Braidwood simply remarked, "When in Rome. . . ."

We returned here to film scenes involving the young Cigarette Smoking Man (circa 1962) at his Fort Bragg, North Carolina barracks, this just before the barracks were officially demolished by a wrecking crew.

A standing set designed on DND Jericho Base housing was constructed for "Christmas Carol" (5x05) and "Emily" (5x07). Playing as *Bill Scully Jr.'s San Diego Naval Station home*, it made production sense to film these lengthy scenes on a soundstage, where a larger version of the original interior - complete with *wild walls* - offered advantages not available to us in the cramped practical location.

Cigarette Smoking Man: now and then.

KALLENCHUCK'S OFFICE
AJATAN STUDIOS, RAILWAY ST., NORTH VANCOUVER

As this was very much an episode about "the deep blue sea," we tried hard to come up with a harbour view setting for salvage broker *Jeraldine Kallenchuk's office*. Having been through a major scout for similar office settings on "Nisei" (3x09), I thought we had the territory covered until one of our scouts showed me pictures of a shop and studio under the north end of the Second Narrows Bridge.

A long, narrow office space above the shop offered a breathtaking view of the bridge structure and waterway. The owner was in the process of turning this space into his own office, so with some paint and lumber, the construction department helped him along and gave us a great salvage office.

GAUTHIER'S APARTMENT
3215 VICTORIA DR., VANCOUVER

At the concept meeting for this episode, a house was described which sounded very familiar. We were looking for a San Francisco-style *row house* or *apartment* (the only exterior consisted of Mulder knocking at the front door) with a large open floorplan and some brick detail.

I recall going home that night and fixating on the ground floor of my house which, while too confining for a film crew, offered certain characteristics common to our discussion earlier in the day. Within moments, I was on the phone to my next-door neighbour, whose home was almost identical to mine but had been recently renovated. Walls had been knocked out to expose a central brick fireplace and create an open floorplan. After a quick pitch, my neighbour was more than happy to comply.

The large Trout Lake Park and Community Centre parking lot across the street offered ample parking for crew and circus, while I was happy to watch the proceedings from my kitchen window next door. Ironically, my neighbour - a local actor - had appeared in "Miracle Man" (1x17). At the time of filming, she ran the ground level of her home as a bed and breakfast.

Location managers cannot be in every place at every time. Luckily, some people actually had a sense of humour. During Season Four, when *The X-Files'* popularity had been confirmed, one man had been waiting for some time to move his car, which was blocked by a set decorating truck. When the Teamster driver finally returned, the man asked for an explanation. "Don't you watch television?" the driver asked. "What does that have to do with anything?" the man wanted to know. "Haven't you heard?" the driver returned. "*The X-Files* has been given the keys to the city." The inconvenienced man simply laughed, and drove away. Luckily he was Second Unit location manager Rob Murdoch's friend.

The budget for raw 35mm film stock was pegged at 12,000 feet per day for two cameras. On more than one occassion, veteran director Rob Bowman came close to using 20,000 feet per day, with the other veteran director, Kim Manners, not far behind. In contrast, Chris — as a relative neophyte to directing — tended to take much more time setting up and shooting a scene, and never came close to shooting 20,000 feet of film in one day.

On "Piper Maru" (3x15), the interior of Ballantyne Pier doubled as two international airports — Hong Kong and San Francisco — while simultaneously hosting the assault of a military hazmat team on a salvage vessel (the *Piper Maru*) docked outside.

Wide establishing stock shots of a vessel, very similar to the *Charlotte Explorer* but anchored far out at sea, arrived courtesy of co-producer Paul Rabwin to complete the illusion.

While trying to secure permission to place an 18K light on the roof of the Eaton's building, location scout Alan Bartolic and Louisa sat, anxiously, in an office for nearly an entire day — the day before the shoot — waiting for a representative to return to the office to sign the location contract.

The Lone Gunmen: (left to right) Langly (Dean Hagland), Frohike (Tom Braidwood), Byers (Bruce Harwood).

PIPER MARU
CHARLOTTE EXPLORER

An episode named after a ship named after Gillian Anderson's daughter needed a hero vessel to call its own. After a number of calls to local shippers and marinas, we chose the 190-foot *Charlotte Explorer*, a converted seismographic vessel originally built for an oil company.

Owned by Sewell's Marine Group of West Vancouver, it had been refitted for use as a luxury fishing lodge. Not only did this vessel look deep sea-worthy, but it also had a large fantail rear deck, which was to prove very useful to the handlers of the Newtsuit, a 900-pound deep sea diving apparatus developed and built in North Vancouver.

The *Charlotte Explorer* was moored on the waterfront in East Vancouver, which was convenient to our first location, Ballantyne Pier. The ship would be berthed for a day of filming and two days of prep and wrap before being moved to Berry Point - where underwater visibility was much better - for all scenes involving the diver's submersion in the Newtsuit. Here the vessel would remain for an additional three days of work.

Budgetary concerns (yes, after renting a vessel of this size for six days, we remained very cost-conscious) dictated that all vessel movements and spottings were carefully planned and orchestrated, as *The X-Files* was paying for fuel as well as the wages of the captain, a chief, an assistant engineer, and a deckhand. The last thing we wanted to see was a lengthy docking process needlessly repeated because the vessel had been berthed incorrectly to camera.

3x16	APOCRYPHA	LG

Mulder, who has captured Krycek, travels to a missile silo in the northern U.S. to reveal an alien craft. Scully and Mulder get as far as the door, while Krycek gets left behind with the black oil.

SKATING RINK/STREET/ALLEY
ROBSON SQUARE SKATING RINK, 600 ROBSON ST., VANCOUVER

This episode required thirteen practical locations and ten sets. The Lone Gunmen were to go ice skating, but all the skating rinks in the Lower Mainland were booked at this time of the year (January). The optimal compromise - which ultimately was more visually interesting - was the open-air rink at Robson Square. Tom Braidwood is a natural on skates. It was seldom that *The X-Files* stars were in full daylight view in the downtown core, so the Lone Gunmen's walk across Howe Street to Mulder's car attracted unprecedented crowds.

CEMETERY
STANLEY PARK, VANCOUVER

The cemetery was created near the Rose Garden in Stanley Park. The Park's representative noticed David's dog, Blue, frolicking without a leash. A tethered Blue was an unlikely scenario and, to avoid any conflict, an unsuspecting Jaap Broeker, David's stand-in and one of Blue's best friends, was reprimanded for Blue's actions.

A dog named Blue: one of David's best friends.

Stanley Park was used as a location more than six times while *The X-Files* was produced in Vancouver.

3x17	PUSHER	TP

Scully and Mulder struggle to arrest and convict a felon, Robert Modell, who can make people see anything he wants them to see.

DRIVING RANGE
TAKAYA GOLF CENTRE, 700 APEX AVE., NORTH VANCOUVER

Originally scripted as a golf course, the concept changed somewhat when a huge snowfall failed to dissipate before filming began in late January, leaving most local courses blanketed in snow. The placement of camouflaged SWAT members and a camera position on the treed perimeter were also important considerations in choosing this particular driving range. Not only did a forest abruptly begin where the range ended, but an access road skirted the entire perimeter.

Given these considerations, setting these scenes at a driving range rather than a golf course was both more believable and more visually appealing in the dead of winter. It also gave the hard-working crew an opportunity to brush up on their swing over lunch break.

Explaining a $12 petty cash receipt for clubs and a bucket of golf balls while scouting golf courses with director Rob Bowman and producer J.P. Finn resulted in a rather awkward call from production accountant Angela Will.

Celebrities often visited The X-Files *set. Pictured here are David and the Smashing Pumpkins.*

Foo Fighters' Dave Grohl and his wife had walk-on roles on "Pusher" (3x17), having been invited to set by Gillian.

Dirty (TP)

Very few production office staff or crew members worked longer hours than our dedicated core group of location production assistants. With a fifteen-hour workday allowable under the Directors Guild of Canada contract, this entry-level position is the lowest-paid — yet arguably the most versatile — in production.

Along with the assistant location manager, production assistants are almost always first on location and last to leave, "parking" the catering truck in the morning and ending their day only after the last truck in the unit (usually the camera truck) has shown its taillights. Theirs is a largely thankless training position with a steep learning curve for the bright and ambitious. What they learn has often as much to do with public relations and social work as it does with the mechanics of making a movie or television show.

Such was the case when we found ourselves on the edge of Vancouver's Skid Row during the filming of scenes for "Hell Money" (3x19). We had been filming at the defunct Ho Ho Chop Suey Restaurant and up and down the 100-block of East Pender Street. With parking at a premium in Chinatown, most of our vehicles had been left in a public lot two blocks away, with only essential worktrucks parked nearby.

It was late in the afternoon when I was called to the electrics trailer by a rather distraught production assistant. The trailer was parked at the mouth of one of Vancouver's most disreputable alleys and, while unclear, the message relayed over the walkie seemed to indicate that an altercation had occured between production assistant Rob Chalmers and a resident of the 'hood.

SUPERMARKET
FALSE CREEK GROCERY, 760 WEST 6TH AVE., VANCOUVER

Here we had to come up with the *Mt. Foodmore Supermarket* in Loudon County, Virginia. If you need a supermarket for a day or two of filming, round up all interested candidates (many have no interest in disrupting the shopping habits of long-term clientele) and decide what the budget will allow. As of January 31, 1996 (the day of filming), this meant anywhere from $7,000 to $18,000 per day of closure, depending on the time and day.

For our purposes, only supermarkets with three or more shopping aisles and at least three check-out carousels were considered, since Rob wanted a full-size, full-service store.

Our final choice was based as much on these requirements as on budgetary concerns. The owner required that filming be completed on one of his quieter days, to minimize the inconvenience to his regular customers.

Meat and produce deliveries were re-scheduled to avoid the deterioration of fresh stock which, after twenty-four hours or more on the shelves, would have been rendered unfit for resale. This, in turn, would have resulted in a rather large grocery bill for *The X-Files*.

Similarly, restocking shelves with "fake" or "cleared" product - to avoid copyright infringement - can be a time-consuming process. In this case, a full set dec crew descended on the supermarket at 6 a.m. in order to be camera-ready by 9 a.m.

Night filming, which is a less costly option when using locations such as this, became a scheduling impossibility when it became necessary to add several exterior night scenes to the end of this day's call sheet. That aside, a storypoint in the teaser involves Modell's view of a police cruiser pulling into the parking lot out front. Written as a day scene, subsequent day scenes in the teaser would not have worked for the story, even if scheduling could have accommodated a switch to night. We therefore completed our work at the supermarket and, as darkness fell, moved across the street to a parking lot owned by the City of Vancouver. This parking lot became the *Beltway Commuter Lot* in Falls Church, Virginia, where Mulder and Scully spend half the night staking out a pay telephone.

FBI LOBBY
GRANVILLE SQUARE, 200 GRANVILLE ST., VANCOUVER

This was a challenge, since the real J. Edgar Hoover Building in Washington, D.C. bears no resemblance to anything in downtown Vancouver. While there are no shortage of office buildings of all colours and stripes, most lobbies are either cramped or poorly laid out for filming purposes. The architectural term is *sense of entry*, which is what this location demanded as we were recreating an existing location built on a monumental scale.

The building we finally chose, while much smaller in scale than the real thing, offered a believable sense of entry when viewed from certain angles. At the time, Granville Square housed a number of high-profile tenants, but we were fortunate that the ground floor offices - now occupied by Pacific Press - were vacant and accessible to our art and lighting departments.

Daytime pedestrian traffic through the lobby was, however, very heavy and precluded any notion of filming here during office hours. Some signage and minor set dressing was allowed on the morning of filming, but most of the art department's set-up had to wait until 5:30 p.m. A piano mover was hired to remove a grand piano and a local art gallery contracted to remove a large piece of textile art hanging on the wall. Similarly, my deal with the company managing the property stipulated that the lobby be returned to its original configuration by 7 a.m. the following morning.

The FBI lobby.

Contrary to what may have appeared in print elsewhere, Granville Square — not Simon Fraser University — appeared twice in the series as the FBI headquarters, in this episode and in "Talitha Cumi" (3x24).

I arrived to find Rob pacing the sidewalk, shaking his head in disbelief. He had been assigned the task of guarding the van from intruders and would-be thieves, having been shown a position on the sidewalk at the alley's entrance from which he could watch both the van and a generator parked beside it.

"This is pathetic and disgusting," he began. "Do I have to put up with this kind of abuse?" He gestured down the alley where a man sat in a wheelchair, his back to us. As the man glanced back over his shoulder, a woman's face suddenly peered out from in front of the wheelchair. She proceeded to direct a barrage of colourful expletives at us. The image may have caught me off guard, but the message was loud and clear. In the best gutter English, we were told to "get the fuck away . . . can't you see you're making this guy nervous . . . I just want to get this guy off so I can get my fucking money and buy my fucking drugs."

A hooker, on her knees, servicing a guy in a wheelchair in an alley strewn with spent syringes and garbage? "Welcome to Skid Row," I said to Rob. "C'mon, let's just leave them alone and move a few feet this way, out of sight. They'll be gone in five minutes."

I then explained that, while he had certainly done the right thing by calling

Riverview was still being used as a facility for mental patients. One day, as Gillian was headed for her trailer, a young man, being chased by production assistant Woody Morrison, ran up to her. Unruffled, Gillian simply smiled as he took her picture.

my attention to the situation, his prescribed position was always subject to adjustment. "This is a very tough neighbourhood. Most of the residents down here see film crews as a nuisance and big inconvenience. Just use common sense, which is sometimes not so common. Give them their space."

Another production assistant came face to face with a different sort of problem while filming scenes for "Genderbender" (1x13) at the Rowlatt Historic Farm in Campbell Valley Park. Given the wet weather and the poor condition of the lane providing sole access to the site, shuttle vans had been used to ferry cast and crew from the circus — in a parking lot a quarter of a mile away — to the commune. It was late in the afternoon and getting dark

Left to right: Gaffer Dave Tickell with stand-ins Bonnie Hay and Jaap Broeker.

| 3x18 | TESO DOS BICHOS | LG |

A vengeful jaguar spirit that is released when an Ecuadorean shaman's remains are unearthed wreaks havoc in a Boston museum.

| MUSEUM/MORGUE/GRAD OFFICE/PARKING LOT |
| RIVERVIEW SITE, 500 LOUGHEED HWY., COQUITLAM |

With the exception of two private residences, most of the locations for this episode were contained on the Riverview site. Construction co-ordinator Rob Maier was challenged with the construction of eleven sets, the most extensive of which was a maze of six tunnels constructed to house the feline horror. Special effects make-up artist Toby Lindala created a "fake" cat and attached it to a stick to complete a close-up of Scully being attacked by the creature. During the first few takes, Gillian couldn't stop laughing. Neither could the crew. Director Kim Manners remarked that, "No matter what I do, kitty cats are not fucking scary."

After a few weeks of feline presence at the studio, a special cleaning crew was recruited to rid the place of the pungent smell and repugnant leftovers.

| 3x19 | HELL MONEY | TP |

Mulder and Scully discover a link between a sinister lottery and the blackmarket for human body parts.

W.I.S.E. Hall set to become Asian gambling parlour

The W.I.S.E. Hall is celebrating its 60th anniversary with a major face-lift, courtesy of the film-set cosmeticians from The X-Files. The East Vancouver venue (which has

Georgia Straight

| 3x20 | JOSE CHUNG'S 'FROM OUTER SPACE' | LG |

The story of an alien visitation is told through flashbacks as novelist Jose Chung conducts interviews to learn the whole truth.

DINER
OVALTINE CAFÉ, 251 EAST HASTINGS ST., VANCOUVER

An all-time favourite episode. The *diner* was scheduled as the second location of the day and involved a unit move from a nearby residence. This, of course, takes time, but the move to the *diner* was exceptionally expedient. Not expecting this, director Rob Bowman, had returned to his hotel for a massage. The crew spent an hour drinking coffee awaiting Rob.

The Ovaltine and its famous neon sign was one of the very few locations which required almost no prep. Set dec and construction were relieved of their duties and props had only to place edible pies in the racks.

HOSPITAL/AUTOPSY ROOM/MOTEL ROOM/COMMUNITY CENTRE/MEDICAL OFFICE/MILITARY ROOM/HAROLD'S CAR
WOODLANDS HOSPITAL SITE, CENTRE BUILDING, 9 EAST COLUMBIA ST., NEW WESTMINSTER

In previous years the Centre Building had been used quite extensively by film groups. This was evident by the amount of film garbage (old flats, garbage, missing doors and door hardware, etc.) spread throughout the building. Once the heating had been disconnected, interest in the site waned. Wading through the maze of junk, the potential for filming numerous scenes became apparent. With a healthy budget in mind, and production designer Graeme Murray at my side, the opportunity to clean the facility surfaced. The trash was labelled and removed, and the floor scoured. Within days, the facility was returned to some semblance of its original derelict state. The old kitchen was painted grey and the tiles were whitewashed, contributing to the sanitary look of a morgue. The hallway was also painted and a small room off the hallway was revitalized to pose as a motel room.

While filming, the two site commissionaires informed us that many of the other buildings would soon become vacant, thus opening up more filming opportunities. This was an *X-Files* locations secret, and in Season Four the site was exclusively and repeatedly frequented by us. Woodlands was eventually referred to as Studio 4 and, surprisingly, the film community-at-large incorrectly assumed we possessed exclusive rights to the entire site. In due time, *Millennium* found out where we had been hiding.

As buildings were vacated, we occupied them, careful to adhere to the stipulations that the structural integrity of the buildings not be altered and changes could be

when a production assistant summoned assistant location manager Ainslie Wiggs on her walkie. There was a problem at the shuttle van parked at the end of the lane.

The story subsequently related involved a crew member who had requested that the shuttle come down to set to take him back to the circus. For some reason, the day-call driver failed to answer his walkie and a production assistant was dispatched to relay the message. Approaching the van, she was shocked to discover the driver engaged in what looked to her like an act of masturbation. He sat in the driver seat illuminated only by an overhead light. The production assistant made no attempt to interfere. She simply walked away.

It was my job to broach this subject with the transportation co-ordinator, who appeared dumbfounded as he listened to the story. He promised to make a discreet inquiry, and by late the following morning, was able to offer a very different explanation.

Evidently what the production assistant had witnessed was not a lewd act after all. The combination of poor lighting and the practiced motion of the driver's hands working methodically in his lap had only left this briefest of impressions. The driver — who suffered from some form of cancer — had really been rolling a marijuana cigarette, a palliative for his condition.

I couldn't decide if this was better or worse than the first scenario. I could only suggest that drivers on the show shouldn't be smoking pot for any reason, certainly not while on the job. I was then assured that the driver would not be invited back and that no prior knowledge of his condition had been noted or he would not have been hired in the first place.

Mitch Pileggi as Assistant Director Skinner.

Celtic Roulette (TP)

Preliminary discussions surrounding "Hell Money" (3x19) suggested a hellish episode for the locations team. Not only was it a *fait accompli* that Vancouver's Chinatown would stand in for its much larger San Francisco cousin, but that locations would have to be found in which to construct seven standing sets (Crease Clinic on the Riverview Hospital site was used) and create an ornate *gaming room.*

A dozen local halls and performance venues were considered before choosing the W.I.S.E. (Welsh Irish Scottish English) Hall on Vancouver's East Side. Its intermediate size was appealing, as was the *faux* balcony which ran the length of the east wall of the building. For the sake of visual interest and depth, this offered the art department something to work with. Still, the art and construction departments were faced with transforming a hall used by ballroom dancers and folk singers into a Chinese gaming den.

The transformation was realized by building a second balcony along the west wall to mirror the original. The two were

made only if the buildings were restored to their original state. The commissionaires guarded our sets, inspected the wrap-out, and developed many friendships with crew members. They were so integral to filming at Woodlands that when the site was almost completely vacant and their on-site jobs were threatened, they were placed on *The X-Files* payroll in case we needed the facility at a moment's notice.

> More than twenty-one episodes were filmed at the Woodlands site.

3x21	AVATAR	TP

Cigarette Smoking Man tries to discredit Assistant Director Skinner and frame him for murder by exploiting Skinner's nightmare of a hag-like succubus.

CHESAPEAKE LOUNGE
THE GERARD LOUNGE, SUTTON PLACE HOTEL, 845 BURRARD ST., VANCOUVER

Upscale. Dark. Dignified. Wood-panelled. During the concept meeting for this episode, these words summarized the requirement for this location. Lounges and bars are a dime a dozen in Vancouver, but finding just the right establishment for these scenes left few choices. As luck would have it, other factors came into play, leading us in one direction very quickly.

I had already booked a suite of rooms on the opulent fourteenth floor of the Hotel Vancouver as the place in which Skinner awakens to make a rather unnerving discovery regarding the evils of casual sex. As a point of interest, when a film crew uses a room on this floor, it must reserve the entire floor for filming days. Given the rental cost of some of these suites, hotel management feels it unfair that guests be subjected to the bustle of a film crew outside their door. Fair enough, but we had to be prepared to write a large cheque.

The shooting schedule dictated that the *Ambassador Hotel lounge* scenes be shot at the beginning of our day, followed by a late-morning move to the Hotel Vancouver. This was in accordance with the wishes of the Sutton Place Hotel, who are ever-supportive of the film industry (and for good reason since many productions in Vancouver use the Sutton Place to house their out-of-town talent and crew) but not at the expense of guest comfort. Ironically, none of the three lounges in the Hotel

Vancouver were suitable for the scripted lounge scenes and we were fortunate that The Gerard Lounge is only a block away from the Hotel Vancouver.

We were also fortunate to have more than one *in* with this establishment, as both first assistant director Vladimir Stefoff and cast driver Baba Ram spent a great deal of off-set time here over the years.

> Many visiting film stars hang out at The Gerard, so a visit will invariably be rewarded with a brush with fame. Or infamy.

3x22	QUAGMIRE	LG

Scully and Mulder go in search of a legendary prehistoric lake monster.

FISHING DOCK/TED'S BAIT AND TACKLE/LAKEFRONT/QUAGMIRE
PITT LAKE, PITT MEADOWS

Three lake locations were selected to fulfill the script requirements demanded by this episode. The *fishing dock* and exterior *Ted's Bait and Tackle Shop* were combined at Pitt Lake. The lakeside trailer was outfitted with Graeme's design, and the fishing dock was filmed as is. The Scully/Mulder driving scene was actually filmed on Neaves Road which leads to the fishing dock.

ROCKY LAKEFRONT, QUAGMIRE REEDS, RV PARK
BUNTZEN LAKE, PORT MOODY

Buntzen Lake accommodates almost as much filming as the Seymour Demonstration Forest and some of the forest areas have been eroded by film crews. As a result, locations are somewhat limited, depending on the time of year and extent of public use, and environmental guidelines are strictly enforced. Speeding crew vehicles have been the bane of site liaisons at most Park facilities.

The location for the quagmire reeds was granted on the basis that only essential crew enter the forest area, a walking trail be clearly be marked with flagging tape, and any equipment on the side of the road outside the trail be placed on plywood. This particular forest area is blanketed by a spectacular species of moss which takes up to a hundred years to regenerate. Moss hung off the trees and formed webs between branches. The crew completed the

then connected overhead by a series of ornately carved Chinese screens or lattices, thereby creating a more intimate space. A number of pillars supported these screens at regular intervals. The stage was plugged and the gymnasium-style hardwood floor treated. Last was a thorough paint job.

Before any of this could begin, however, negotiations and arrangement had to be made with the handful of renter-users of the facility to compensate or relocate for the two-week duration of our activities.

The big challenge lay in negotiating a deal with Rogue Folk Club organizers, who had booked a Celtic Mini Festival for the weekend prior to filming. With no suitable alternate venue available, and musicians flying in from as far away as Ireland, it was not an event which could be cancelled.

The overriding concern was the fact that the Celtic musicians would be performing on a movie set, completely altering the configuration of the performance space. A portable stage would be required for the performers, since the existing stage would be inaccessible. Similarly, the placement of pillars dictated that the new stage be placed along a side wall, which would alter both existing sound and lighting arrangements. A deal was struck whereby *The X-Files* would cover these costs, which were minimal when compared with the cost of the set itself.

A pay-or-play deal of sorts was negotiated wherein the Rogue Folk Club would receive a calculated lump sum based on nightly attendance figures from previous Celtic Festivals at the W.I.S.E. Hall, regardless of attendance figures at this festival. Patrons and musicians alike would either love the new venue or hate it, and vote with their feet.

I recall sitting in the audience on opening night and counting the empty seats which, by curtain time, I could do on one hand. The audience, for the most part, seemed appreciative of the sublime irony, and with the revamped sound system working well, the musicians seemed happy to have a venue and an enthusiastic audience. Period.

Throughout the weekend, references to *The X-Files* and the transformation of the hall, which has to number among our top ten sets for creative use of a location, were made. Upon completion of filming, W.I.S.E. Hall management requested that the new balcony be left in place for aesthetic reasons. It was, finally, a huge endeavor for one day's worth of filming, but not uncommon on a show willing and able to go that extra mile. And an effort not lost on local viewers and fellow industry workers alike who, for months afterward, requested the address of "that great Chinese den. Like, where did you guys film that, anyway?"

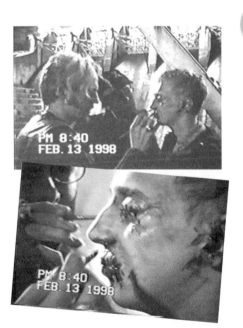

"Don't try this at home."
– *special efffects makeup artist Toby Lindala working on "Patient X" (5x13) and "The Red and the Black" (5x14).*

filming without any damage, and only one crew member was reprimanded for speeding. He didn't notice the production assistant hiding in the forest armed with a pen and paper, writing down the license plate numbers of offending drivers.

Part of the quagmire reeds set was duplicated at the studio. When greensman Frank Haddad arrived on set, he knew his crew had done a good job creating a forest. Frank called it his most memorable experience on the show. "It even smelled like a forest," he recalled.

LAKE
RICE LAKE, SEYMOUR DEMONSTRATION FOREST, NORTH VANCOUVER

We concluded at Rice Lake. In addition to the "missing limbs" and alligator required for the episode, special effects makeup artist Toby Lindala was expected to create an Ogopogo-type monster whose eel-like body would glide on the surface of the water forming a series of arches. The monster's first movement had the entire crew and director Kim Manners speechless, silent, and disappointed. It appeared as if a giant snake had just ingested fifty rats, then awkwardly wobbled across the surface of the water. The final image of the monster was a product of CGI.

ROCKY ISLAND SET
B.C. RESEARCH WAVE TANK, 3650 WESBROOK MALL, UBC

The rock island where Scully and Mulder are stranded was a set constructed at a wave tank - a special indoor pool where miniature boats undergo hydrodynamic testing. The pool was initially emptied to enable construction to erect a platform to position and brace the rocky island.

On the day before filming, water was released onto the set to submerge the platform and expose only the rocky island, but the platform began to float like a barge. An emergency crew of carpenters, attired in hipwaders, worked furiously through the night to secure the structure. Not only did they have to solve the problem, but they had to be finished with enough time to allow for the water to flow onto the set. The entire set was intact with only hours to spare, but when Kim arrived at the wave tank, he saw a twelve-foot island in the middle of a 100-foot wave tank. A dot in the middle of nowhere. In total disbelief, Kim said, "You've got to be kidding." Access to the rock was impossible without hipwaders, so Gillian and David were piggybacked to set.

| 3x23 | WETWIRED | TP |

A sabotaged television signal imparts subliminal suggestions, turning people's into anxious murderers.

| MIRADOR MOTEL |
| 2400 COURT MOTEL, 2400 KINGSWAY, VANCOUVER |

It took the better part of three seasons to get to our favourite motel in the entire Lower Mainland, but we finally made it here for the penultimate episode of Season Three. This collection of meticulously maintained white and green bungalows lays out in a 3.5-acre "U" around inner-facing grass courtyards and a centrally-located motel office.

Originally built for army housing during the Second World War, the site was converted into an autocourt in 1946. The sixty-odd units constitute a true gem, from original linoleum floors to chrome-and-formica dinette sets, and vintage Kirby vacuum cleaners. A bold neon sign, featured twice in this episode, proclaims both lineage and location. The words "2400 Court" also appear on a book of matches from which Mulder takes a phone number.

Several rooms were reserved for four nights, allowing both set decorating and construction departments to settle in. The amount and nature of the work to be filmed in Scully's room dictated that a replica of this room be created on our soundstage. Scenes in which day and night motel interiors were physically tied to motel exteriors were shot on location. If an exterior was revealed from inside Scully's room, or a scene played as a continuous shot from the interior to the exterior, it had to be shot on location. For this reason, a breakaway door was added to the rear of Scully's unit, while the front door was replaced with our own rigged version, which would later sustain several rounds of gunfire. Scully's room - 274 - was also redressed. Mulder checked in to room 127.

We were fortunate that it was late April, for Easter was over and the summer tourist season had not yet begun. This enabled us to pick whatever rooms we wished, although filming activity was confined to the west half of the motel grounds and new guests given rooms in the "east wing." Night scenes in the parking lot were lit from the roof of an adjacent apartment complex and with the help of two condors placed around the corner and across the street.

On location at 2400 Motel, Vancouver

We revisited the 2400 Court Motel late in Season Five to film scenes for "The Pine Bluff Variant" (5x18), at which time Chris Carter sadly announced the move to L.A. to assembled crew members.

The Truth About Poles (TP)

"So this is an episode about telephone poles. Is that what you're telling us?" Location scouts Alan Bartolic and David Caughlan stood indignantly in my office, a banker's box of rejected photofiles in front of them. Given the fact that the script for "Wetwired" (3x23) involved no less than twelve very specific locations, I understood their frustration. Moreover, I understood the prep schedule, with a locations technical survey just four days away.

Five houses were required for this episode. Two of these – the *safe house* and *Mrs. Scully's house* – had been relatively easy finds. The *safe house*, located at 6120 MacDonald Street, was actually a stately home on an acreage in South Vancouver. It was slated for redevelopment and, in its vacant condition, had been used by several film crews in the past. It was storybook-perfect, being empty and overgrown. A circular driveway offered Mulder a clear point of view of the ubiquitous cable van as it pulled into the yard.

This was one of the very few locations in which we virtually walked in and shot as is. The greens crew thinned out some shrubbery next to the front door, giving Mulder a place to hide when he saw the van. The construction department installed a breakaway back door — which Mulder kicked in to gain access — and temporarily removed a large development permit application sign from the front yard. With no furniture to relocate, set dec simply removed a developer's model of the property and dressed in a table and a couple of chairs.

This was the final night of Main Unit location filming for the season for both director Rob Bowman and odd episode designates. Wrap was called just before 11 p.m., and once equipment had been stored in the work trucks, several crew members took advantage of our room reservations to host a private party.

Several weeks later, a photograph of David and Gillian taken by stills photographer Ken Staniforth and donated to the 2400 Court Motel disappeared from its position behind the front desk, evidently the object of a souvenir-hunting guest. It was later replaced by *The X-Files*.

TREE FARM
HAZELGROVE FARM, FORT LANGLEY

Orchards are not usually associated with the Lower Mainland and for good reason. Anything approaching the large commercial variety simply does not exist here. The Okanagan – a four-hour drive due east – is true orchard country, but too far to travel crew and equipment for a single day of filming.

Several weeks before prep began on this episode, writer Mat Beck (who was also visual effects supervisor on *The X-Files* during Seasons One to Three) asked to see photofiles of all the orchards in the Lower Mainland. He was visualizing macabre night scenes shot amidst row after row of cultivated trees. Needless to say, a very small collection of photofiles went south very quickly.

The choice – if you can call it that – was between a small apple orchard in Delta (young trees with a maximum height of eight feet) and a private hazelnut orchard just outside Fort Langley. I had been intrigued by the latter ever since my days working on The Black Stallion, which was filmed almost exclusively in this area. Hazelnut trees, which typically stand twenty to thirty-feet high, have a rather unique appearance, with very little trunk and a wide mushroom-like crown. It was early enough in the spring that no leaves had yet appeared, lending a visual starkness to those perfectly straight rows. When lit for night filming, they exuded an eeriness befitting the show. Ideal silent witnesses to a clandestine burial.

Having just wrapped the Main Unit portion of his last episode, director Rob Bowman was thrilled to pull an all-nighter out here with the Second Unit crew.

We returned to this orchard for "Schizogeny" (5x09).

RIDDOCK'S HOUSE/LANE
3792 WEST 1ST AVE., VANCOUVER

Given the subject matter of this episode, a very specific requirement was essential for both the *Riddock* and *Patnik houses*: a clear sightline from the living or dining room to a back alley where a utility pole had to be visible.

With regard to the *Riddock house*, an unobstructed view of the neighbours' backyard was also required to stage the scene in which Riddock's wife hallucinates her husband and another woman in each other's arms on a hammock. A total of five houses played in this episode (these two as well as the *suburban house* next door, a safe house, and *Mrs. Scully's house*), and production designer Graeme Murray wanted each home to be distinctly different in appearance.

Riddock's house was conceived of as lower middle-class suburban and both the house next door and the immediate neighbourhood had to reflect this. Similarly, interiors had to be large enough to accommodate a film crew.

The house we chose fit the above requirements. It was also the home of one of our two full-time location scouts, David Caughlan.

Mrs. Scully's house was found a few blocks away. The owners had constructed a beautiful Cape Cod replica which worked very well for the scripted scenes.

The problem facing the scouts had more to do with the views required from the living/dining rooms of both these homes than with actual architecture, although production designer Graeme Murray felt that, given the number of houses in this show, each should be of a contrasting style. *Patnik's house* should be a moderately large, two-storey wood-frame structure located in an older, upscale neighbourhood. *Riddock's house* was to have a more suburban character, a modest, single-storey home in a similar neighbourhood. *The suburban house*, which - as a storypoint - had to be located next door to Riddock's, was to be of similar design and from the same era.

As Alan and David pointed out, these combined requirements eliminated two-thirds of the homes in Vancouver. If the architecture and interior layout worked for story, a tree or garage obscured the view to the back alley, although in some cases there simply was *no* back alley. The opposite was just as often true — the telephone pole in the alley was clearly visible from the kitchen or the bathroom.

At this point in prep, and with the pressures of production mounting, good location scouts show their real value. Not only is a constantly-revised knowledge of the city invaluable, but so too is the

On Vancouver's downtown streets for "The Pine Bluff Variant" (5x18).

ability to visualize and interpret script requirements (technically the location manager's job) on the fly. By Season Five, if a scout presented a less-than-ideal location file, he also presented a sketch of the location as he had scouted it with notes on camera angles and blockings which might make it workable in the event that nothing better was found. This, in turn, helped the director to decide which locations were worth his time to survey.

In this case, we sat down with a map of the city and reviewed suitable neighbourhoods, eliminating those without alleys. Rejected files were re-examined for their shortfalls and the territory once again divided up equally between scouts. At one point in our discussion, David abruptly stood up and walked out of the office. For a moment, I thought he had quit in disgust. Two minutes later he reappeared and, with a devilish grin, tossed a photofile on my desk. "This one will work perfectly," he said confidently, before walking me through the geography of the location.

Thumbing through the file, I had to agree with him. Flipping back to the file cover, I noted the address and contact name, which listed the resident's name: David Caughlan. "Will anyone have a problem with this?" he asked. "Your wife?" I joked, then added, "Not if it works. Same deal as anyone else gets." So much for *Riddick's house*. *Patnik's house* was eventually found in Shaughnessy, after retracing our steps and tweaking the architectural requirements.

3x24	TALITHA CUMI	LG

Jeremiah Smith, a renegade alien clone who can transform his appearance, is captured and questioned by Cigarette Smoking Man, but escapes before Alien Bounty Hunter appears.

FAST FOOD RESTAURANT
A&W, 6535 KINGSWAY, BURNABY

Staging a shootout at a fast food restaurant is sensitive. Most fast food restaurants are too busy to entertain business closure, and are very reluctant to endorse any kind of violence. After a rigorous search and impassioned pleas to McDonald's, Burger King, and the like, a generic fast food restaurant and repeat location sated our appetites. As with "Oubliette" (3x08), set dec changed the interior the day before shooting and construction covered all references to A&W. A&W staff were hired to assist props with food and to oversee filming.

Louisa at the Tolko sawmill, used in "Talitha Cumi" (3x24) and "Herrenvolk" (4x01).

SOCIAL SERVICES LOBBY

VANCOUVER CITY HALL,
453 WEST 12TH AVE., VANCOUVER

The final episode of the season afforded the show the least amount of time before air date, and with vacation in sight, it was critical for director Bob Goodwin to complete shooting in the shortest possible time. To expedite the process, Main Unit and Second Unit, along with assiduous crews, would descend upon the City, covering separate locations to complete the task in eight days. In this particular episode, locations assigned to Main Unit included the A&W, *Mulder's family beach house* in Surrey, *a social services office* at the old Woodward's Building, the *parkade* at Woodward's, and the *sawmill* at Tolko Industries in North Vancouver. Six sets were built on stage for both units. Second Unit made the trek to the *beach house,* the *FBI Headquarters lobby* at Granville Square, Crease Clinic at Riverview for the exterior *prison,* and City Hall to film the interior *social services lobby.*

On the day of filming, Main Unit was given an early call time downtown at the Woodward's building and Second Unit was given a 5 p.m. call time at City Hall, in accordance with City filming policy. Upon arrival, Second Unit would pre-light the lobby, set-up cameras, and have all prerigging complete so Bob could leave Main Unit at the end of the scheduled day, arrive at the second location, and resume filming.

Unit manager and Second Unit first assistant director Brett Dowler claimed that there was a pressing urgency to prep the location before the 5 p.m. entry restriction. After some convincing, and in consideration of the rare sunshine that beautiful Friday afternoon, approval to begin some prep was granted. Shortly after 5 p.m., the set was ready for filming. The director showed up after 9 p.m., due to delays at Main Unit. After midnight the crew packed their equipment and left the location, but not quietly. A local resident called to complain about a woman who ironically kept yelling into her walkie, telling everyone to be quiet. The "resident" commented that our activity was the most disruptive over the many years of filming at City Hall. Second Unit quietly returned to City Hall in the following week for reshoots and there were no complaints.

With regard to the use of existing utility poles, several adjustments and precautions were necessary. When Mulder and Scully spot the cable van in the alley behind *Patnik's house,* the cable guy is already descending the pole using a set of handholds. With the advent of cherry pickers and heightened safety concerns, neither hydro nor telco technicians use handholds any longer. In fact, we installed our own under supervision and were required to remove them and fill all holes — to guard against dry rot — when done filming.

The same procedure was followed in the alley behind *Riddock's house,* with David climbing the pole. As a storypoint, Mulder finds a cable box attached to the pole and from it removes a large fuse-like cable trap. Care was taken to stay outside the ten-foot safety radius from all high voltage lines demanded by BC Hydro.

As a final note of interest, poles are jointly used by both hydro and telephone companies. When the issue of jurisdiction arose, as it did when I requested permission to climb these poles and affix objects to them, BC Tel deferred to BC Hydro on the grounds that the latter technically owned the inside of the pole while the telephone company was responsible for only the outside, and our handholds were penetrating the inner portion of the pole. Like some episodes of *The X-Files,* the origin of these ownership rights was never clearly explained.

By the beginning of Season Four, *The X-Files* had reached critical mass in North America. David and Gillian's faces were everywhere and *X-Files*-isms such as "trust no one" and "the truth is out there" were well on their way to assimilation into the mainstream vocabulary.

With the show so popular – and still picking up steam in foreign markets – a concerted effort was made by those "down south" (or so we in Vancouver were led to believe) to rein in the show's budget, which was climbing close to $2 million US per episode. From an accountant's point of view, it may have been logical to assume that it made no sense to spend more on a show which had already reached the status of both a critical and marketing phenomenon.

From a creative point of view, however, reality was very different. Each week, a wildly dedicated audience tuned in to see something at least as good as they had seen the previous week. Better, if possible. The show had to continue to "deliver," and everyone felt the pressure to come up with bigger, better episodes to keep those fans tuned in. If there was a downside, it was that bigger and better usually cost more.

During the first production meeting of the season, as Chris fielded requests to eliminate expensive scenes involving special effects, large numbers of extras, and costly custom-built props, he responded with, "Whatever you want. It's the new me."

"It's the new me" became an in-joke around the production office.

An in-joke since we transported the entire crew nearly 200 miles to film less than half of the season opener. An in-joke because the per-episode budget set for Season Four was consistently surpassed. An in-joke because "The Post-Modern Prometheus" (5x06), written and directed by Chris early in Season Five, came in at $2.8 million US, a figure which director Rob Bowman fell short of by only $10,000 US for his direction on "Killswitch" (5x11).

Crew members speculated on the job security of anyone who might decide to take a serious run at compromising the show's quality through an attempt to reduce costs. In the end, we decided that Chris' "the new me" was really "the old me" in disguise. For us, the more things changed, the more they stayed the same.

– TP

Reincarnation

A sawmill owned by Tolko Industries of North Vancouver was used as a location in both "Talitha Cumi" (3x24) and "Herrenvolk" (4x01). For "Herrenvolk," another mill owned by Flavelle Cedar of Port Moody was also used to film interior night sequences, as the Tolko facility proved inappropriate for interior work. The Flavelle site had recently been closed, and with its turn-of-the-century ambience, offered excellent production value for those spooky chase scenes with the Alien Bounty Hunter.

A deal was made at the end of Season Three allowing us to return to the Tolko site three months later, as Chris had already indicated that this location would again be necessary for the Season Four opener (which was part two).

Tolko Industries burned to the ground in a spectacular blaze one night in late 1997, but this did not signal the end of its use as a location. The site — by then nothing more than a huge parking lot with a single cabin-like office building remaining — was used as an *RV Park* in "Bad Blood" (5x12).

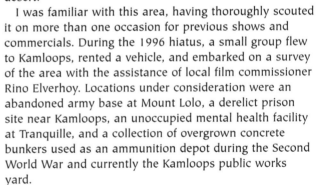

Call sheet notes for "Herrenvolk" (4x01).

| 4x01 | HERRENVOLK | TP |

Jeremiah Smith leads Mulder to a farm where Mulder sees clones of his sister, Samantha. Scully discovers what Smith was doing at the Social Security Administration.

GOLDEN FIELDS
CHAI-NA-TA GINSENG FARM, WALHACHIN

The Season Four opener marked the one and only time that *The X-Files* strayed more than one hundred miles from Vancouver (a very small Second Unit foray to Sedona, Arizona excepted). Chris was intent on placing both story and characters in a region dramatically different than the west coast.

After considering a handful of specific locations and geographies in British Columbia and Alberta - among them the mammoth Mica Dam and Highland Valley open pit copper mine, the moonscapes of Mount Edziza and Spatsizi Plateau Provincial Parks (too inaccessible), the Athabasca Tar Sands project and a deserted airbase near Calgary (too far to travel). Chris' favourite option was the Badlands of southern Alberta, but the distance was prohibitive and we settled on the arid Kamloops/Ashcroft area as an alternative, knowing only that Chris wanted a desert.

I was familiar with this area, having thoroughly scouted it on more than one occasion for previous shows and commercials. During the 1996 hiatus, a small group flew to Kamloops, rented a vehicle, and embarked on a survey of the area with the assistance of local film commissioner Rino Elverhoy. Locations under consideration were an abandoned army base at Mount Lolo, a derelict prison site near Kamloops, an unoccupied mental health facility at Tranquille, and a collection of overgrown concrete bunkers used as an ammunition depot during the Second World War and currently the Kamloops public works yard.

As I recall, the overall response was less than enthusiastic. In fact, a suggestion was made to curtail the survey and catch an earlier flight back to Vancouver. Of the locations we had surveyed so far, nothing really clicked or justified the expenditure of time and effort required to transport crew and equipment to Kamloops.

I was determined, however, that Chris should see a tiny settlement perched high on a plateau above the North Thompson River just east of Cache Creek. I felt that this would make an interesting ghost town while also featuring the desert-like geography of this region. Checking the schedule of flights back to Vancouver, I reasoned that - given the 45-minute drive each way - we could still catch the earlier flight home if nothing panned out.

About halfway to Cache Creek, the terrain begins to flatten and the highway more closely follows the river far below. At this point, huge tracts of farmland emerge, perched dramatically on the plateau between road and river. Chris was intrigued by the enormous, oddly-tented expanses of land under ginseng cultivation, a somewhat serendipitous discovery since I was familiar with the ginseng farms and had not thought them worthy of mention.

Upon our return to Vancouver, location scout Alan Bartolic was dispatched to thoroughly photograph the locations we had picked on the survey. Hence, along with concrete bunkers, an isolated road set amidst golden rolling hills (the road leading to Mount Lolo), and a small town, a geographic focus for the story emerged.

SHANTY TOWN
WALHACHIN

This tiny settlement owes its isolated existence to the horrors of the First World War. As the story goes, this very arid region was originally populated, in the early 1900s, by a group of British remittance men and their families who visualized their own little Garden of Eden. To bring water to their land, they built a network of irrigation flukes high on the hillside, the rotting wooden remains of which can still be spotted in places from the highway. The soil was fertile and fruit trees grew in abundance.

When the First World War began, most of the men enlisted in the British forces and never returned, leaving their widows behind. The orchards fell into neglect and today the site is home to about one hundred people, a strange and eccentric collection of humanity (see *Looking for Normal*).

Several of the houses dotting the dusty main street were built at the turn of the century and have changed little since then. Situated on a narrow strip of land between the river and steeply rising hills, we were impressed by how quickly the "town" ends and scrub brush begins. Fortuitously (for us), a large tract of land under ginseng cultivation existed between the bridge (the only road access to this town) and the first houses approaching town. We were therefore able to "combine" locations for scheduling purposes, as the shanty town of the script is road-accessible only through the *golden fields*, a distance of one kilometre away.

Looking for Normal (TP)

While it may be on the local road maps, the exit sign to Highway 97 between Kamloops and Cache Creek is difficult to spot. Which may be just what the inhabitants of Walhachin, B.C. count on, for this is a town very much at the end of the road.

In retrospect, the decision to use Walhachin as the *shanty town* in "Herrenvolk" (4x01) fit perfectly the mythology which had come to characterize *The X-Files* by Season Four. It was suitably obscure, both in its location and its history, and exuded a charming quirkiness upon first blush.

Upon first blush. I must confess that, like many others in this business, I sometimes ignore initial impressions of a client or situation in an effort to secure a location.

With respect to location scouting and managing, the overwhelming sense of relief which often accompanies the discovery of a *visually* wonderful location after a particularly stressful or demanding search can itself distort one's sense of reality, causing some very important potential problems to be considered insignificant.

This was not what I was thinking as I sped along Highway 97 under a warm July sky on my way to Walhachin for a meeting with key residents about our prospective filming activities. Instead, I hit the brakes hard before pulling a 180 and parking my rental Taurus on the gravel shoulder just east of Savona, a quaint community on Kamloops Lake which, given the derelict sawmill at the edge of town, had probably seen more prosperous days.

Call it professional curiosity or a bad habit, but I have grown accustomed to scouting wherever I go. I keep a loaded point-and-shoot camera in the car at all times for precisely this reason. On this day, the object of my curiosity was a defunct Texaco gas station — now converted into a residence-cum-garage — which sits by itself on a lonely stretch of road, a silent reminder of another era.

Finding a good angle, I brandished my camera and began taking photographs. Lowering the camera, I crossed the highway to take some close-ups of the cluttered front lot, strewn with automotive junk.

Within seconds, a man appeared from what would once have been the office. A few steps behind him, a younger man followed. I put the camera away and prepared to explain myself, as it occurred to me that I may well have been an unwanted trespasser.

We exchanged pleasantries and I explained the camera, saying that I was location scouting for *The X-Files* and on my way to Walhachin. "*The X-Files!* Hell, you're gonna want to hear this story," the younger man exclaimed.

In a vaguely psychotic manner, he explained that the older man was his father, a former shipbuilder in the Kamloops area. "For Chrissakes, my father's father helped run the railroad through this region." The older man just stood there, nodding.

"But something weird happened to dad. He designed and built the first starship in 1960, using his shipbuilding knowledge." He delivered this information with a poker face borne of absolute conviction. This was not the direction in which I had expected the conversation to slide.

"Hell, the creators of *Star Trek* stole his design!" Oh yeah, I thought, looking at my watch for a way out. They were after him, it turned out. As if on cue, dad leaned over to show me a lump protruding from his curly head of hair. "CIA hitmen," the son explained. "They missed that time. He knew too much. He studied levitation with a Tibetan master, who taught him that you didn't need a starship to fly to the stars."

"Well, that makes sense," I said, smiling as I began to look around for a hidden camera or some indication that I was the victim of a practical joke.

No such luck. His next words seemed more desperate. "And then there was KAL Flight 007 in 1984," he sputtered. "He was the real target. CIA hitmen again. At the

"Psychic photographs" become evidence as a psychotic killer – who kidnaps young women and lobotomizes them with an ice pick – is pursued by Mulder and Scully.

DRUGSTORE/ALLEY

MAPLE LEAF PHARMACY,
2406 NANAIMO ST., VANCOUVER

Finding a drugstore would seem an easy task but almost every store we scouted proposed severe time restrictions, and their locations on busy streets would have made filming the driveup/car scenes involving rain towers and major street lockups impossible.

"Unruhe" is a German word for "unrest."

A variety store in New Westminster was our first choice. Although it required major design modifications and decorating, the proprietor was willing to close down for a week. But when the building owner was contacted to discuss the filming proposal, he demanded exorbitant location fees which he felt were comparable to American rates. The search for a location resumed. When informed about the situation, the variety store proprietor threatened to sue the owner for loss of business.

Luckily, and with the grace of alien gods, the owner of Maple Leaf Pharmacy, a quaint drugstore in East Vancouver, was an enormous fan of the show and on that basis alone he granted us use of the location. Many storefronts on the same street as the drugstore were decorated with signage to depict a small American town. Inside the store, set decorator Shirley Inget and her crew stripped store shelves and relocated goods.

The script called for rain. Naturally there was little concern, but as film day approached, the forecast called for continued sunshine and high temperatures. Special effects devised a scheme to outfit two cranes mounted with rain towers, one crane to service the front of the store and the other to shower the rear parking lot.

For the first time in the history of the show, the crew welcomed rain. The cooling effect of the showers made the heat bearable - even the police officers stood directly under the rain towers. It was peculiar to see the block of Nanaimo Street inundated by rain, a contrast to the prevailing sunshine. Director Rob Bowman's challenge was to avoid the sun while filming the exterior scenes. The scheduled day was not completed, so Second Unit had to return to the location to finish interior scenes which again required full re-dressing by the set dec department. After two attempts to film on location in the rear parking lot, the scene was eventually filmed in the parking lot back at the studio.

Dolly grip Peter Wilkie with his gear.

CEMETERY
NORTH VANCOUVER CEMETERY, LILLOOET RD., NORTH VANCOUVER

Our main location at the cemetery was the maintenance/gravel storage area, a perfect place to hide an RV. The reverse angle from the gravel lot showed the cemetery, but the ground-level gravestones made it difficult to tell that the grassy area was a "cemetery." Vertical styrofoam headstones were randomly positioned throughout the cemetery, carefully avoiding existing plaques. During the weekend, however, a visitor to a family plot saw the "tombstones" and was appalled. The visitor called the local newsweekly and condemned use of the cemetery for filming. The front page news headline was our Monday morning wake-up call. Filming proceeded as planned, but within a week a moratorium on filming at North Shore cemeteries was passed in city council. That same week the national newspaper *The Globe and Mail* published an article praising the Toronto film industry for providing funds for cemetery upkeep.

Later in the season, the local newsweekly, having been invited to visit *The X-Files set,* published a special edition called "Inside *The X-Files,*" and featured North Vancouver as a popular film destination.

last minute he cancelled his seat, but *they* didn't know that and blew up the plane anyway. Blamed it on them damn Soviets," he said. By now I was mildly intrigued with both the story and these two characters.

At last, Dad spoke. "Come on in," he said. "I'll show you the documentation and my design for the starship." The son glanced from his dad to me, nodding vigorously. Father and son, standing there in matching grimy t-shirts, arms crossed identically.

As amusing as this was, I had seen a movie called *Cold Comfort* and had no intention of becoming either a hostage or a corpse in an abandoned gas station on Highway 97. "I'd like to take your picture," I ventured. "For my files." The two men beamed as I raised my camera. I then thanked them for the information and turned to leave, promising to relay this information to the show's creator.

"Hell, yes," the son quipped as I crossed the highway and opened the car door. "Maybe you could use it in one of your shows. . . ."

If I'd listened to that inner voice, I would have headed back to Kamloops then, grateful for having just received a divinatory "warning sign." Instead, I wheeled the car around and stepped on the accelerator, concerned that my little detour might actually make me late for my appointment in Walhachin.

The purpose of my visit was to meet with the residents of a handful of homes along the street on which we would be filming. In one case, we would need to access a small house for a camera angle out into the street. We would also be painting this house. The owner lived in Kamloops, and I had made a deal with him and picked up a key the previous evening. The local community hall was to be painted and aged as well. A mobile home further down the road would be *greened out* completely.

In total, six homes would be directly affected by our activities and deals were made, based on the extent of involvement, with each individual or family. Or so I thought. Arrangements for circus parking, use of washroom facilities, and provision for a lunchroom were also made.

I left town feeling confident that most of the details had been dealt with and that Walhachin was pretty much ready for its population to double for a day.

What I hadn't prepared for were the politics and chemistry of a small town. A small town which, I admit, I had come to like very much. First blush. By the time *The X-Files* rolled down the main street on a Monday afternoon, someone had decided that the entire town of Walhachin should be fed from our catering truck. This after residents affected by filming had already been treated to lunch.

One old gentleman whose house was in the line of fire — coaxed by a retired Teamster who happened to live a couple of blocks away — decided to host a drinking party on his front porch, refusing to move indoors until the production had made a substantial contribution to his bar fridge. Once indoors, the party grew to include women and small children. Assistant location manager Ainslie Wiggs, who had gone over at the request of the sound department, was virtually held hostage (she later claimed her glass of juice was spiked with vodka) for the better part of two hours.

Another resident, with whom I had made a cash deal in exchange for allowing our actors to exit her house and walk through her yard, decided that "the money wasn't the thing" and requested that our set electrician rewire her kitchen for 220 amp service, as she'd decided to phase out the woodstove and *go electric*. Our electrician checked her house wiring and suggested that, given the size of the job, I

> Greened out: a number of judiciously placed trees can effectively make an unwanted house or object "disappear."

A small, rural town is home to a clan of deformed inbreeders - a mother and her sons - who do everything they can to keep their family line alive.

POLICE STATION
FORT LANGLEY COMMUNITY HALL, 9167 GLOVER RD., FORT LANGLEY

This episode was set in Home, Pennsylvania and required a small-town feel. To this end we scouted for buildings fronting on a main square or courtyard, as this was where Scully and Mulder's discussion of events in this rather sordid case would occur.

The Fort Langley Community Hall, built in Greek Renaissance style, is a large pale yellow clapboard structure dating back to 1932. With its stately white columns flanking the front entrance, it conveys a sense of history without being pretentious and was a strong contender from the beginning, but because of the distance factor (approximately forty-five minutes from Vancouver), other "lesser" choices were considered and discarded. The hall itself would have been ideal for the construction of at least one set to fill out our shooting schedule, but prior bookings made the three-day art department prep impossible and two sets - the interior of the *police station* and Scully and Mulder's *motel rooms* - were constructed at the nearby Langley Fine Arts School, which was closed for summer holidays.

Fort Langley itself is a mix of new and old, so reverse angles had to be carefully picked to maintain the small-town American illusion. In particular, the fish and chips shop across the street - the one that complained loudly about our presence - would most certainly not have existed in the real *Home*.

We're "Home" (4x03).

As a production note, assistant location manager Ainslie Wiggs was dispatched to buy fish and chips for the entire crew as 12 noon approached on this very sunny August. Perhaps it was the heat - or the burden placed on existing fish stocks by a sudden demand for $250 worth of fish and chips - which caused a harried cook to reluctantly fill our order before closing up shop for the remainder of the day.

4x04	TELIKO	LG

A West African immigrant from a lost tribe who have no pituitary glands preys on African American men, removing their pigmentation in killing them.

DEMOLITION SITE
303-305 RAILWAY ST., VANCOUVER

Japan Town - a Vancouver area once known for its Japanese shops and restaurants - is in one of the more undesirable areas of East Vancouver. The *demolition site* has since been converted into condominiums, in which many film community members live, but its former state of disrepair provided perfect conditions for a building in need of demolition. On a second visit after the location had been confirmed, we discovered old electrical boxes with PCB labels (but, as we found out, no harmful chemicals despite the labels). These would undoubtedly result in site inspections and mounds of red tape which could delay production. Luckily, a simple call to the property manager resulted in the boxes magically disappearing.

DEMOTT AVENUE
500 ALEXANDER ST., AND REAR ALLEY, VANCOUVER

Director Jim Charleton requested that the alley south of Demott Avenue be blocked off to create a dead end. Since all streets have to remain accessible for emergency vehicles, construction developed a rolling wall which could be placed into position across the alley for picture, then easily moved aside.

Vancouver's seedy East Side had a sobering effect on the crew. Preparation for filming necessitates street and sidewalk cleaning and a thorough scan for needles. In this alley, an actor was expected to crawl through a hole in a wall to reach a yard on the other side. As a mound of garbage blocked the other side, we requested permission

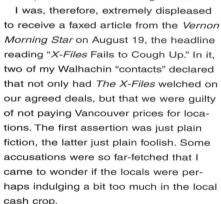

hire a local contractor, which I subseqently did as a gesture of good faith.

Through all this, filming proceeded with a sense of urgency, as Baba Ram's adventure (see *The Lost Squadron*) had caused production to fall behind schedule and we now faced the very real possibility of running out of daylight before completing our day's work.

When filming was finished, I felt confident that everyone was happy and that the show had bent over backwards to accommodate whatever requests were made by residents. A problem with the quality of the repaint on the community hall — a local painting company had been hired — resulted in the hiring of a second subcontractor to fix the job done by the first, at a considerable cost to us. It should be noted that, as we had hired both sets of painters based on local recommendations, any disagreement over job quality should ultimately have rested with the subcontractor and the hall owners. I remained involved only to ensure personally that each side got what they had been promised and were content that we had upheld our end of the agreement.

I was, therefore, extremely displeased to receive a faxed article from the *Vernon Morning Star* on August 19, the headline reading "*X-Files* Fails to Cough Up." In it, two of my Walhachin "contacts" declared that not only had *The X-Files* welched on our agreed deals, but that we were guilty of not paying Vancouver prices for locations. The first assertion was just plain fiction, the latter just plain foolish. Some accusations were so far-fetched that I came to wonder if the locals were perhaps indulging a bit too much in the local cash crop.

For the record, though, Walhachin is a lovely — albeit *strange* — little town and most of the residents extremely good people. Locals were notified of the episode's air date and all those whose homes appeared on film were mailed a VHS copy of the show once it aired. Whether they had a television or not.

"Reports of my death. . . ."

More than one person was upset when word got out that Lone Gunman Frohike was going to "be killed" — a euphemism for written out of the series — at the conclusion of "Musings of a Cigarette Smoking Man" (4x07). Tom Braidwood would still have had his job as first assistant director, but the glamour of being on-screen would be gone.

Not surprisingly, many crew members had strong feelings about this turn of events, since the production draft of the script, written by Glen Morgan and directed by Jim Wong, clearly described Frohike's death at the hands of Cigarette Smoking Man. As one production source later recalled, "Jim Wong instructed the Second Unit crew to shoot it both ways, presumably without Chris' blessing. CSM, therefore, shot Frohike, and didn't shoot Frohike.

The following morning when Chris found out what had transpired, he was angry because he'd already decided not to kill off Frohike. He told production to call the film processing lab and instruct them to not print the dailies showing Frohike's death. Chris wanted to make sure no one viewed that footage.

Assistant location manager Ainslie S. Wiggs on location in Walhachin.

from the owner to remove the garbage at our cost, much to his disbelief. While filming, I was approached by a staff member of a local charity, who asked about the possibility of donations. We placed a permanent donations box in the office and occasional memos resulted in boxes of clothes being donated to the charity.

> After filming "Chinga" (5x10) at the Shop Easy in Port Coquitlam, all the remaining produce, meats, and canned goods were packaged, loaded onto a five-ton, and dropped off at the charity. The butcher cut and wrapped a side of beef which was delivered the following day.

| 4x05 | THE FIELD WHERE I DIED | TP |

Mulder discovers he shares a past life - from the Civil War era - with a woman who is part of a doomsday religious cult.

| 4x06 | SANGUINARIUM | LG |

A cosmetic surgery clinic is the site of a series of deaths. Although they appear to be due to medical misconduct, they are in fact due to the efforts of a man who, through human sacrifice, is eternally youthful.

| HOSPITAL |
| MOUNT SAINT JOSEPH'S HOSPITAL, 3080 PRINCE EDWARD ST., VANCOUVER |

For this episode, our priority was to find a hospital location with an emergency room we could access (most emergencies are active twenty-four hours a day) and ancillary medical rooms. Mount Saint Joseph's had recently made available the entire second floor plus their day surgery room which could easily double as an emergency room and was completely dressed, allowing us the rare opportunity to just point the cameras and shoot. The most difficult aspect of filming at the hospital was refraining from cellular phone use, which could have affected hospital instruments.

| 4x07 | MUSINGS OF A CIGARETTE SMOKING MAN | TP |

The history of the Cigarette Smoking Man is revealed. CSM is a powerful man, controlling everything from elections to political assassinations to award ceremonies, and Super Bowls. He's also a would-be author.

> **TEXAS BOOK DEPOSITORY**
>
> **1190 HOMER ST., VANCOUVER**

If you believe what you see on television, then Oswald and Ray were simply hired guns for a shadowy figure known as Cigarette Smoking Man, the real culprit behind most of the great triumphs and tragedies of the 20th century.

In an attempt to recreate the JFK assassination, much research was done on what Deeley Plaza looked like in 1963. We examined the Zapruder footage and undertook a thorough discussion of existing conspiracy theories. Suffice to say that Deeley Plaza, which is itself a very different place today, never resembled anything in the Vancouver area. Shots were therefore constructed around what could be isolated to pass for the real thing.

We were fortunate in finding an old three-storey building on the edge of Yaletown which actually bore an eerie resemblance to the Texas Book Depository of that era, both inside and out. Currently home to a garment manufacturing business, the top floors of the building served as storage space. The brick walls and massive post and beam construction certainly gave the illusion of a period set. Even the window treatments were a reasonable match.

Unfortunately, this building was far from any location resembling a plaza and views from these windows were completely wrong. So POVs of the Presidential motorcade were filmed in a parking lot at General Motors (GM) Place and from a pedestrian overpass in a nearby park.

Chris and William B. Davis (Cigarette Smoking Man) at the GM Place finale.

Jackie O. never looked so good. Associate casting director Heike Brandstatter was called upon to don the infamous Jackie Kennedy wardrobe for the limo seen in "Musings of a Cigarette Smoking Man" (4x07). The resemblance was astounding, if not unnerving.

The Kennedy motorcade at GM Place ("Musings of a Cigarette Smoking Man" (4x07)).

> Magic hour: also known as "golden hour" or "l'heure bleu"; the short period of time just after sunrise and just before sunset when the sun casts the softest light of the day.

The Lost Squadron (TP)

In the spirit of the lost squadron of historical lore, *The X-Files* also has a story to add to the body of accumulated myth. It is the enigma of *the lost van*. We had ventured out of the Lower Mainland for the first time in more than three years and chosen the Kamloops-Ashcroft corridor as a suitably arid locale to kick off with the Season Four opener, "Herrenvolk."

It was late July 1996 and it was hot. After considerable organization, the shooting crew had assembled on a bluff above the North Thompson River just outside the town of Walhachin, B.C. From there, we had a breathtaking view of the river far below and acre upon acre of ginseng under cultivation to the north and west. With us was a large contingent of "trained" bees and their handlers.

Director Bob Goodwin wanted to take advantage of the warm light of *magic hour* to film the opening shots of the first scene, so the crew had assembled here before sunrise after having been shuttled in buses from their hotels in Kamloops, a forty-five minute drive away.

The cast was assembled and the scene blocked for camera. But there was one problem. One big problem. The shuttle van carrying the hair, make-up, and wardrobe departments — as well as third assistant director Michelle Dutka — had gone missing. Cellular telephone reception in that area was spotty at best, and of no use in our situation. Trunk radios proved similarly useless.

What we did know, standing on that bluff as the sun climbed higher and

| DEELEY PLAZA/THE GRASSY KNOLL |
| ANDY LIVINGSTONE PARK, VANCOUVER |

Recreating a suitable match for a 1963 stretch Lincoln convertible was no easy task for picture vehicle handler Nigel Habgood. Finding a believable location to play as Deeley Plaza was similarly problematic. Thanks go to the Vancouver Parks Board for creating this park in time for its use on *The X-Files*.

After an initial location scout and much discussion, it was decided to film the assasination sequence from overhead, thereby eliminating the background problems associated with time and place. A camera position was identified atop a pedestrian overpass in this newly-constructed urban park. Other angles were "cheated" using a camera crane in a parking lot at adjacent GM Place. In accordance with the "second shooter" theory, low-angle shots from the storm drain were contrived on the ring road around GM Place.

The fourth shooter ("Musings of a Cigarette Smoking Man" (4x07)).

| 4x08 | PAPER HEARTS | LG |

Mulder's belief that his sister was abducted by aliens is called into question when serial killer John Lee Roche suggests that Samantha may actually have been one of his victims.

| BUS GRAVEYARD |
| UNITED AUTO WRECKERS, 10395 SCOTT RD., SURREY |

In preparation for Expo '86 in Vancouver, the British Columbia government replaced existing transit buses with more modern ones. The old buses, still in excellent operating condition, were sold for a song and are stored in Surrey.

Months before we ever needed this location, producer J.P. Finn suggested we scout it with thoughts of taking advantage of this unique location. Photos were taken and shipped to the writers in L.A., but it was not used until this episode, and even then the scene was not long enough to warrant a full day of filming.

The bus graveyard *in Surrey, B.C. used in "Paper Hearts" (4x08).*

| 4x09 | TUNGUSKA | TP |

An extraterrestrial rock is discovered to be carrying the alien black oil. Mulder and Krycek trace the rock's origin to Tunguska, Russia, where they are captured and incarcerated in a gulag. Krycek talks his way out, but Mulder is infected with the black oil. All the while, Scully is stalling a senate subcommittee, who are wondering just where Mulder is.

The senate chamber *built on a sound stage for "Tunguska" (4x09) and "Terma" (4x10).*

higher into the pale blue sky, was that the van *had* left Kamloops on time. From her makeshift production office in a Kamloops hotel, production co-ordinator Anita Truelove had confirmed that much. Beside herself with worry, she had phoned the local hospital as well as the RCMP, fearing the van had met with an accident. What we could not know was that driver Baba Ram had missed the Highway 97 exit to Cache Creek and was now on the Coquihalla Highway bound for Vancouver.

He had evidently realized his error but, rather than turn around and backtrack, had made the decision to take the Logan Lake Road, a gravel road which connects the Coquihalla Highway with Ashcroft just north of Merritt. The logic of his decision remains unclear to this day. When the missing van finally arrived — almost three hours late for set call — Goodwin exhibited amazing restraint, considering his shotlist had been seriously compromised by Baba's tardiness. That considered, it's not much of an exaggeration to say that Bob had homicide on his mind that morning.

Oddly enough, Baba did have the presence of mind to stop in Ashcroft long enough to pick up a sandwich and a soft drink before continuing on. When questioned about the half-eaten sandwich he still clutched in his hand as the van pulled up to set in a cloud of dust, he quipped that it had been a "damn long drive — I got really hungry."

A Teamster collective: (left to right) Mitch, Marty, and Baba.

RURAL RUSSIAN WORKCAMP

GRAVEL PIT, SEYMOUR DEMONSTRATION FOREST, NORTH VANCOUVER

While we can be grateful that the gulags and work-camps of the Cold War-era Soviet Union are a long way away, location managers remain ever grateful that the Seymour Demonstration Forest is a mere twenty-five minutes from downtown Vancouver.

Given the stark landscape demanded by this script, the gravel pit seemed like the natural choice for these scenes. A section of barbed wire fencing was laid in and a navigable path identified for the horsemen. The weather - suitably wet and bleak during filming - added an ominous sense of realism, while making all that rock and gravel appear even more desolate and ominous.

The gravel pit doubled as both a UFO crashsite on "Fallen Angel" (1x09) and as a graveyard for burning Ladas in the Khazikstan Forest during "Patient X" (5x13).

On the day of filming, director Kim Manners arrived on set, took one look at the rubber razor wire fence beneath which David and Nick would later crawl, and demanded it be replaced with the real thing. Art director Gary Allen recalled the moment. "We decided on fake razor wire as a safety precaution, mostly for David. But Kim hated it, and he had a point. It really did look phony." The scramble began to fulfill Kim's request and not hold up production. "The rest of the day," Gary continued, "was spent keeping both actors and crew at least six feet away from that awful stuff. David absolutely hated the whole idea."

SKINNER'S APARTMENT

VIVA TOWER, SUITE 1708, 1311 HOWE ST., VANCOUVER

The issue here was not so much in finding an apartment for Assistant Director Skinner, but in finding a balcony at least ten storeys high from which Alex Krycek - having thrown an assailant to his death - could dangle. The camera was to look straight down to the street, which created a problem in that such a view from almost any other office tower or highrise in town was at least partially obstructed by protruding lower balconies, terraces, or street-level awnings.

Viva Tower was chosen because it fit the above requirements and because of the size of its suites. Very strict filming guidelines meant that specific hours of the day were designated for elevator use. Call times, equipment

The gravel pit doubled as both a *UFO crashsite* on "Fallen Angel" (1x09) and as a *graveyard* for burning Ladas in the Khazikstan Forest during "Patient X" (5x13).

Another dead body.

A split-level penthouse in Viva Tower (Suite 1706) played as a high-end "madam's" condominium in "Avatar" (3x21), an episode which changed Skinner's concept of "safe sex." Three blocks to the northeast, at 1180 Richards Street, is Skinner's old apartment, where he moved after separating from his wife just prior to "Avatar."

load-ins, and exterior filming activities were carefully orchestrated around these restrictions. In such instances, the most stressful parts of the day for the locations department were load-in and wrap-out as, once on the seventeenth floor, the crew remained self-contained, if not subdued.

Care was taken not to reveal either False Creek or English Bay in the background, ironic given the stunning vistas offered from this suite. We were, after all, in the D.C. area. Strictly speaking, this apartment was far more luxurious than would befit a senior FBI agent (unless they were "on the take"), and the art department went to some lengths installing wall plugs to eliminate several rooms, effectively shrinking the true size and opulence of this suite.

As Skinner exits the foyer, the name Viva Tower is featured prominently above the main entrance. From the sidewalk on the north side of the building, gaze up seventeen floors to the northwest corner balcony and imagine yourself as Nick Lea hanging by a handcuff from the railing as he pulls stuntman Tony Morelli over the side.

SEEDY INDUSTRIAL AREA (FLUSHING, QUEENS)
200-BLOCK OF NORTHERN AVE., VANCOUVER

Director Kim Manners envisioned a rundown industrial area where old warehouses and loading docks lined both sides of the street, not unlike the fictional New York setting.

The script called for the placement of a dozen trailer units along one side of the street and a warehouse opposite in which to film a SWAT siege. Another key requirement was the ability to stage gunfire late into the night without disturbing residents. The loading docks along Hamilton and Mainland Streets in Yaletown had a great look, but were too cramped to park our rigs and, in any case, unsuitable for late-night filming due to the growing number of lofts and condos being built in converted warehouses. Ballantyne Pier - before its conversion to a cruiseship facility in the early 1990s - would also have worked well.

The area we chose was light industrial, bordering on a railyard. Businesses in the line of fire included a tile manufacturer, a glass cutter, a steel fabricator, and several artist/woodworkers' studios, all of whom locked up and went home by 7 p.m. The issue became one of access and control for the prep crews, in particular picture vehicle handler Nigel Habgood's container delivery schedule. The ground was carefully marked out in order to spot

Hangin' With the Home Boys (TP)

We returned to an old farmhouse — first seen in "Aubrey" (2x12) — to film what would become the most infamous of all *X-Files* shows, "Home" (4x03). Following a brief review of the "Aubrey" episode and a discussion with the art department, it was decided that because we had never seen this house from its northern or western exposures, featuring it again would not be problematic, considering both the passage of time (almost two years) and our intent to paint and age the entire house to resemble a remnant of the Civil War era.

The paint department went to work, applying fresh coats of cool grey to replace the existing warm yellow hues. The difference was amazing. Next, the tenants were moved out. The house was emptied of furniture and redressed in a style evocative of that era, hydro service to the house was dropped, and telephone poles removed to add authenticity. I then hired the farmer who leased the adjacent fields to create the baseball pitch where the boys would ultimately make a startling discovery at home plate. An exterminator was

Kim Manners directing.

employed to remove a large and pesky nest of wasps which our greens department had the displeasure of stumbling upon while building a pigpen. The set dec department next went to work, skillfully littering the yard with the carcasses of period vehicles, pieces of farm equipment, and bric-a-brac, creating a homestead befitting the horrifying Peacock family.

The property sat next to a major rail line and freight schedules were obtained for the days relevant to filming so that we could plan to work around disruptions. Air traffic from Boundary Bay airport — mostly in the form of flying schools practicing circuits in the airspace above us — was more problematic for our sound department, since air traffic safety precluded them from practicing elsewhere.

Based loosely on a startling feature documentary called *My Brother's Keeper*, this episode aired once and only once on network television. However, it remains one of my personal favourites. So much so that when I received a request from a francophone school in the Kootenays for a donation of *X-Files* memorabilia to be used as awards in their film festival competition, I sent them a fully revised script for "Home," autographed and dedicated by director Kim Manners.

each container as quickly as possible once 5 p.m. rolled around.

Call-time was set for dusk, with the crew working through the night and wrapping at dawn as businesses were about to open for the day. Late into the night, and with steam rising in a back-lit effect which caught a mangy dog wandering through the foreground across wet pavement, an excited Kim looked sideways at director of photography John Joffin and declared that this was "a bitchin', absolutely bitchin' set," a phrase which became a Manners trademark.

Moments before sunrise, Kim - who was suffering from laryngitis and had by now lost his voice - looked over at first assistant director Vladimir Stefoff and whispered, "Let's call it, bud," then flopped into a waiting van for the ride back to his hotel.

| 4×10 | TERMA | LG |

Mulder escapes from the gulag and back to the U.S. as a former KGB assassin comes out of retirement to destroy all evidence of the rock and the black oil.

RUSSIAN PRISON
STANLEY PARK WORKS YARD, OFF PIPELINE RD., STANLEY PARK, VANCOUVER

There were hints of a Russian prison in the previous episode, giving us a head start on finding locations. The abandoned Vocational Institute in Maple Ridge was the first candidate even though it was situated out of the studio zone. Photos of the institute were couriered to the L.A. writers and it was expected that their writing would reflect the location. After reading the script, it was clear that the institute was entirely inappropriate: a more rustic, derelict, makeshift, uninhabitable location would be far more suitable. The essential ingredient was the dirt roads. The combination of run-down buildings and dirt proved to be a difficult find. After an exhaustive search, the idea of the Stanley Parks Works Yard surfaced. Other than the lack of dirt, the location was perfect - a motley group of barrack-type buildings hemmed in by wire mesh fencing.

Initially, greensman Frank Haddad ordered $40,000 worth of potential mud. When Fox vice-president of production Charlie Goldstein got wind of the cost, the number of truckloads was halved. Three production assistants were hired to monitor traffic through the works yard while scores of semi-trucks dumped tons of dirt onto the roads. At the end of filming the dirt was reclaimed by the Park. Frank had shrewdly ordered a quality of dirt that would be useful to the Parks, thereby avoiding the cost of removing it from the site.

> **The 400 cubic feet of much-needed dirt became mud when the rains came.**

Sometimes the simple task of restoring a location to its original state can take several months. In this case, the painters made several trips to the works yard, but the paint wouldn't adhere because of the weather. Finally, on a glorious spring day four months later, paint touch-ups were completed. Well into Season Five, assistant location manager Rick Fearon, armed with a can of "Goof Off," removed some adhesive inadvertently left on several buildings, finally deleting the last remnants of "Terma" (4x10).

Louisa sits outside a cabin in the Seymour Demonstration Forest that doubled as the rural home *of a Russian family in "Terma" (4x10). The X-Files shot in the Seymour Demonstration Forest on more than twenty-four occassions (not including Second Unit).*

Trailer Love

The parking of circus and work trucks is always a prime concern when considering the choice of locations from a logistical perspective.

As the show "grew," so did the crew. And so did the armada of production support vehicles. Bigger, in this case, was not always better. Everything had to be parked somewhere, with virtually every department wanting *their* truck or trailer parked as close to set as possible.

During Season One, both David and Gillian were assigned top-of-the-line twenty-six-foot trailers. For Season Three, David acquired a twenty-eight-foot Airstream trailer (complete with hardwood floors). Transportation co-ordinator Bob Bowe recalls that "by late in Season Four, the Airstream was gone, replaced by a double pop-out thirty-foot King of the Road unit. Which is what Gillian got — factory direct — at the beginning of Season Five." With a price tag of just over $100,000 CDN each, these trailers were both spacious and luxurious, but less than practical.

The units were problematic for two reasons. Not only were they long, but it was technically against the law to use them in their pop-out capacity on city streets, except where one side or the other could be extended over a grass median bordering a sidewalk. They were, after all, recreational vehicles designed for use in RV parks.

The potential danger of another vehicle crashing into David or Gillian's living room — and the associated liability risk for the production company — should have precluded any attempt to use them in their full capacity on residential or downtown locations, but they were a constant concern for locations, particularly where a driver-operator eager to please a "star" showed little or no regard for either common sense or the law.

Caught in the Act (TP)

We were filming Assistant Director Skinner's apartment for "Tunguska" (4x09) in a residential high-rise when trainee assistant location manager Michael Bobroff spotted a naked couple engaging in an erotic act in their apartment across the street. Using only a grand piano for a prop, and with a floor-to-ceiling picture window providing an unrestricted view, most of the shooting crew — myself included — were soon assembled in the kitchen to watch the energetic sexual ballet.

We never knew whether they were performing for the cast and crew of *The X-Files* or the scene was simply a case of wanton lust transcending the boundaries of modesty. In any case, at that moment on that day, their home movie was certainly more interesting than our TV show.

The migrant worker's shantytown, *complete with snow, in "San Joaquin, CA" ("El Mundo Gira" (4x11)).*

FOREST OIL WELL
STOKES GRAVEL PIT, SOUTH SURREY

The tireless search for an Alaskan forest, where an oil well would explode into a column of fire, culminated at a gravel pit in Surrey. Special effects co-ordinator Dave Gauthier and I traversed the landscape in search of an ideal location. We even travelled to a forest area near Mission, B.C., where *Fire Storm* was filming, to get a sense of the magnitude of the fire and the equipment and access required to achieve the effect. After scouting potential locations in Mission, Maple Ridge, and North Vancouver, we ended up in South Surrey. The Stokes Pit offered a gravel field bounded by a border of deciduous trees, which not only provided perfect vistas, but easily accommodated special effects requirements to rig propane lines and hide their equipment behind the trees. Unit parking was also easily disguised by the trees. To achieve the desired effect of oil spewing from the well, special effects proposed the environmentally-friendly ingredients of water, syrup, and a touch of black acrylic, which relieved local environmentalists. The water table at Stokes Pit is very low, and the impact of polluting agents on the drainage system was a major concern.

During filming, thirteen production assistants, six police officers, and six security guards formed a gauntlet around the site to ensure that absolutely no-one crossed the treed boundaries of the site during this day scene.

Second Unit actually set up and filmed the explosion.

4x11	EL MUNDO GIRA	TP

In a migrant workers' shantytown in California, a fungal growth of extraterrestrial origin infects the community, leading the residents to believe they are being terrorized by a legendary monster, El Chupacabra.

TRUCKSTOP
320 SEYMOUR BLVD., NORTH VANCOUVER

Director Tucker Gates was not particularly pleased with the idea of duplicating California's dry and predominantly flat San Joaquin Valley in the Lower Mainland in November. That said, we chose locations as carefully as possible, avoiding anything that looked like a rainforest. The snow, which did fall during this shoot, was another story.

The *truckstop* needed to be vast enough to accommodate the manoeuvering of a dozen or more tractor-trailer units, as a storypoint here involved a cat-and-mouse game between Mulder, an INS agent, and Eladio Buente. We chose a tiny gas bar in the middle of a very large parking lot owned by the Squamish Native band of North Vancouver.

A nondescript gas booth was transformed by the art and construction departments with the aid of a large revolving "gas" sign and a façade. The Squamish band requested that one set of pumps remain open at all times during filming.

The day of filming here was cold but clear, and probably the best weather of this entire episode. While filming other scenes at the Woodlands Hospital site (a *lab*, a *morgue*, an *INS processing facility*) and near the Boundary Bay Airport (our *migrant workers camp*), it snowed. Which meant many crew members running around with shovels, brooms, rakes, and tiger torches, trying to recreate a more believable Fresno winter.

The Goat Sucker strikes ("El Mundo Gira" (4x11)).

Church attic built on set for "Kaddish" (4x12)

4x12	KADDISH	LG

After a number of anti-semites turn up dead in Brooklyn, Mulder posits that a golem – a man-made creature from Jewish folklore – is responsible for the killings.

EXTERIOR WEISS APARTMENT/COPYSHOP/INTERIOR MARKET
WINTER'S HOTEL, 200 ABBOTT ST., VANCOUVER

Gastown is the only area in Vancouver that even remotely resembles residential Queens in New York. The Winter's Hotel was selected to be the exterior of the *Weiss apartment*, with the provision that the neon sign above the door entrance be removed. After being told that the costs for its removal were prohibitive, director Kim Manners said that he would merely move the camera another five feet to avoid the sign.

This Philly Cheese Steak Shack *had customers the next day ("Never Again" (4x13)).*

Built on location. Made to order ("Never Again" (4x13)).

SYNAGOGUE
SHAUGHNESSY HEIGHTS UNITED CHURCH, 1550 WEST 33RD AVE., VANCOUVER

The gothic interior and stained glass windows of this church resembled many New York synagogues. This interior proved to be one of production designer Graeme Murray's most intricate designs and construction co-ordinator Rob Maier's most satisfying accomplishments, while exceeding Kim's expectations. It was the most traditional and ornate edifice created on the show.

Shirley Inget's set dec department dressed the pews, adorned the altar, changed the lighting fixtures, and spread several thousand square feet of specially imported red carpet on the floor. One entire wall of stained glass windows were blocked in by the carpenters and all the walls were painted. Given the extent of prep, crews needed exclusive use of the hall to complete the transformation, and the church was booked for more than two weeks.

Unbeknownst to any of us, other groups had booked events during the same time. Much to our surprise, we learned that a local symphony booked one evening a week for rehearsal, and several other groups required the space on different evenings during our rental. With some clever organizing, and a few donations, alternate venues were found for each group, although providing alternative venues proved as difficult as scouting for specific scripted locations. More than five location crew members were needed.

4x13	NEVER AGAIN	TP

As Mulder takes a vacation, Scully gets entangled with a recently-divorced man, whose new tattoo seems to be spurring him towards acts of violence and murder.

HARD EIGHT LOUNGE
SAMOO PUB, 315 CARRALL ST., VANCOUVER

Production designer Graeme Murray decided that the *lounge* needed something unique – a circular bar, perhaps – and so began the hunt.

It ended in a rather colourful bar in a crime-ridden neighbourhood, and we needed to provide the production crew with a genuine police guard for the duration of filming. Bewildered patrons, many of whom seemed to "set up shop" in the washroom and who might have been quick to turn tail and disappear at the first sign of a uniform, merely grumbled about their loss of (likely illicit) business and went elsewhere. Beyond a very thorough cleaning of the premises before the arrival of the prep crew and the removal of a couple of booths to accommodate an enlarged dance floor, very little was done to enhance the appearance of this watering hole.

The exterior of the *Hard Eight Lounge* was created in a nearby alcove adjoining an Army & Navy department store. Consisting of little more than a construction flat and a set of double doors festooned with a neon sign, its sudden (and rather convincing) presence one morning confused more than one denizen of the streets. A security guard was subsequently posted to ward off thirsty customers.

> This pub is within spitting distance of the Meatmarket Restaurant, which doubled as *Dunaway's Pub* (1x01), a *D.C. coffee shop* (3x15) and the *Hoot Owl Bar* (5x15).

Because of the angles and sightlines necessary to make specific scenes work, the *Philly Cheese Steak Shack* and the exterior of the *Russian Market* were built in parking lots across the street from one another in the 0-block of West Cordova Street. The *Tattoo Parlour* was constructed in an empty retail space at 45 West Cordova Street. Hence, it was possible to cheat camera angles so that the exterior façade of the *Hard Eight Lounge* was visible from inside the *Tattoo Parlour* while the exterior façade of the *Russian Market* was clearly visible from the *Philly Cheese Steak Shack*. The interior of the *Russian Market* was shot around the corner at 209 Abbott Street in a completely redressed convenience store called the Only Stop.

This trick of creative geography allowed production to remain within one block of several locations for three full days, thereby maximizing hours of production versus hours of travel between locations.

4x14	LEONARD BETTS	LG

When a headless corpse walks out of a morgue, Scully and Mulder pursue a man who consumes cancerous tissue from his victims in order to regenerate himself.

THREE RIVERS HOSPITAL/ALLEGHENY HOSPITAL
WOODLANDS HOSPITAL SITE, 9 EAST COLUMBIA ST., NEW WESTMINSTER

This episode proved to be a challenging one to organize. All locations, including scenes of an intersection crash and car explosion, had to be prepared and

A Plane, a Car, & a Whole Lotta Lights (TP)

Very seldom do scripts for episodic television involve trains, planes, or ships. There are two very good reasons for this: time and money. Given the logistics and preparation involved in co-ordinating filming around such big-ticket items, there is seldom enough time to safely and adequately utilize them. Similarly, the relatively small budgets on which most television series must operate preclude the possibility, since the rental of a train or an airplane and the attending personnel is, for the most part, prohibitive.

Having said this, *The X-Files* has done all three. "Tempus Fugit" (episode 4x17) represented part one of a two-parter ("Max" was part two) in which a recurring character — Max — is killed when the passenger aircraft he is flying is mysteriously contacted by a UFO and crashes. In the story, Mulder and Scully speed down an airport runway at night in an attempt to evade their adversaries, and narrowly miss colliding with a large, low-flying aircraft.

A prior relationship with Abbotsford Airport Manager Mike Colmant certainly put us in the comfort zone, but a lot of planning was necessary in terms of shutting down a runway and transporting our Second Unit crew from a staging area to our designated zone, choreographing the action, and prelighting 1,000 feet of tarmac. As best boy Bill Kassis recalled, the latter was completed during a one-day prelight using thirty 4K pars, eight 18Ks, and a dozen generator units. "And that," added director of photography Attila Szalay, "was enough to give my light meter a reading of 'E,' as in, 'not enough light.'" Similarly, three Stinger cranes and two condors were placed at various points along the route. A muscolight — a portable lighting unit carrying nine 12K HMI lights resembling the lights used in athletic stadiums — was imported from Los Angeles.

> Eimo: an unmanned, remote camera, typically used in stunts and special effects set-ups involving a risk to camera operators.

Both muscolight and lighting cranes had to be carefully placed in the threshold of the runway with special attention given to the soft condition of the grass field, since it had been raining heavily for some days prior. Similarly, cranes could be moved into position but not raised until shortly before filming, and their heights in relation to the runway carefully monitored. In all, twenty-one pieces of rolling stock were brought in for this Second Unit event.

Even with the runway closed, Transport Canada regulations were strictly observed in the event of an emergency landing or a late-night straggler, unaware of our presence and attempting to land. To this end, *notams* were issued well in advance of filming to advise anyone flying in the vicinity of our presence. Two meetings, including director Rob Bowman as well as producers and necessary department heads, were held at the airport. The pilot of the DC-6, who represented the owners of the plane, was also in attendance. The Abbotsford Airport was chosen as a location because of the runway length and because the principal tenant had the necessary equipment and expertise on-site to

> Notam: an aircraft advisory.

> Overages: unexpected cost over-runs.

confirmed for filming before the Christmas hiatus and available immediately upon our return in the new year.

To consolidate the exhaustive list of locations, two *hospital* exteriors and two *lab* interiors were filmed at Woodlands, at what was commonly referred to as Studio Four.

> **The big question the crew had about this episode was: how did Betts get around without his head?**

INTERSECTION CRASH
INTERSECTION OF BURRARD AND HASTINGS STS., VANCOUVER

The ambulance crash was one of the show's most ambitious and expensive "vehicle driving" scenes. Filmed downtown in the heart of the financial district among the high-rise canyon, it involved a truck heading northbound on Burrard and colliding with the ambulance heading west on Hastings Street. Six city blocks were reserved to stage the film action and four blocks of curb parking accommodated our work trucks, lighting cranes, and holding areas for picture cars.

Just after 6 p.m. on a cold January evening, the trucks began to arrive. So did representatives of the B.C. Film Commission and the City of Vancouver, ten police officers, an ambulance and fire truck on stand-by, and thirty-two production assistants. A number of lights were positioned on the rooftops of neighbouring high-rise buildings. Each lighting position required a separate generator and a production assistant to guard the power cables dangling off the rooftop, and each building required in-house security to provide roof access. For the main crash scene, four cameras and three *Eimos* recorded the event.

> **As a precautionary measure, bales of hay were propped up against the Marine Building, one of Vancouver's most refined heritage high-rises.**

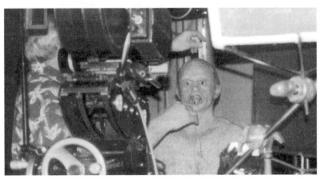

Leonard Betts. With his head ("Leonard Betts" (4x14)).

Water trucks waited for the call for a final street wet down, but due to freezing temperatures it was cancelled. At 3 a.m., Leonard Betts lost his head. So did producer J.P. Finn once he discovered the *overages* associated with the scene.

Leonard Betts (4x14) lost his head over this crash.

Traffic lock-up before the "Leonard Betts" (4x14) crash.

| 4x15 | MEMENTO MORI | TP |

Scully, diagnosed with cancer, comes in contact with a group of women (MUFON), all implanted, all suffering from cancer. With the aid of a clone, and the Lone Gunmen, Mulder infiltrates a fertility clinic, where he finds ova from women, including Scully's.

| LABS AND HOSPITAL ROOMS |
| WOODLANDS HOSPITAL, NEW WESTMINSTER |

By the middle of Season Three, we were looking for a site to replace Crease Clinic at Riverview Hospital, which

POV: point of view.

accommodate our request. Our pilot was a seasoned veteran of water-bombers, which made him a natural choice for extreme low-level flying. Wind conditions would be the deciding factor, with either no wind or a constant headwind being most suitable to maintaining controlled speed and altitude. All said, the pilot practiced his runs for several days prior to filming.

On the night of filming, gusting winds and rain greeted the production crew. After a brief meeting, it was decided to proceed with caution. Several cameras — most of them remote — were placed at various key points according to Bowman's shotlist. The *money shots* involved a POV - from inside Scully and Mulder's sedan - of the DC-6 flying directly at them and missing them by a few feet. For safety reasons, we shot this in cuts and used long lenses where necessary, since any thought of putting a human being in the sedan while the plane made its closest pass was nixed during initial meetings.

This proved an extremely wise deci-

Money shots: in this case, those shots which convey "jeopardy," and sell the scene.

sion, since on the first pass the plane came in low over the parked sedan and the landing gear actually "contacted" the roof of the car, running a two-foot crease down the length of the roof and exploding the front and rear windshields. From my position more than 1,000 feet away, it was obvious that something had happened. Just what was unclear until Second Unit location manager Rob Murdoch and his assistant Sarah Done — who had been at the other end of the runway — arrived with Mike Colmant to inform us of a "small accident." Or perhaps not so small.

An individual sitting in the car would almost certainly have been killed or sustained serious injury. It was also extremely fortunate that the plane's landing gear had not hooked onto the car, as this likely would have flipped the plane end over end and sent it crashing to the runway. The "accident" was blamed on a sudden change in wind velocity. An identical second sedan was brought in to replace the wreck and filming continued throughout the night and without further incident, although the pilot chose to stay well off the deck for the remainder of the shoot.

had become very busy with other film productions and increasingly difficult to book. For years, the Woodlands Hospital site – a large and aging complex comprised of almost a dozen buildings, cottages, workshops, and greenhouses – had provided the film industry with one vacant building, the Centre Building, as a location. Unheated and without water, it was far from ideal. Nonetheless, *The X-Files* had transformed it into a prison and hospital for "F. Emasculata" (2x22).

As luck would have it, Woodlands Hospital began closing down other buildings and cottages early in 1996, and we were first in line to make use of this newfound cache of locations. Under the administrative eye of British Columbia Buildings Corporation's Joy Bissonnette, we would receive exclusive access to this site for a full season and a half, filming scenes for twenty-one separate episodes in virtually every available room, ward, office, hallway, shop, and warehouse. BCBC was more than happy with our organization and performance, and the amount of filming days we provided was about as much as any company *not* in the movie business could manage.

The list of locations and sets for "Memento Mori" was lengthy, and with vacant stage space at a premium, we decided to carry as many sets as possible to the Woodlands site. To this end, four different buildings were used to create a dozen different sets, including an *x-ray lab*, *Scully's hospital room*, a *research facility* and *fertility clinic*, an *incubator room*, a *communications tunnel*, and a *bio-secure room*. Exteriors were also filmed here.

> The sets constructed at Woodlands Hospital – particularly the incubator room – earned production designer Graeme Murray and his crew their first Emmy Award.

Second Unit assistant location manager Rob Murdoch with the crushed car.

An Emmy award-winning set designed for "Memento Mori" (4x15).

4x16 **UNREQUITED** **LG**

A seemingly invisible Vietnam veteran, free from a POW camp after twenty-five years in captivity, is assassinating military generals.

VIETNAM WAR MEMORIAL WALL

**JERICHO PARK,
4000-BLOCK WEST 4TH AVE., VANCOUVER**

We searched every green space in the Lower Mainland for an expansive, groomed, flat field adorned with the deciduous trees that surround Washington Square. Our choice, Jericho Park on Vancouver's West Side, shares similar landscape features. A portion of the wall was built by construction, and CGI technology extended the monument to simulate its real size. A grandstand was erected on location, and with careful direction and a few pass-throughs with mounted police, the scene was completed.

The water drainage system in Jericho Park is not as effective as at other fields. In fact, other than the annual Vancouver Folk Festival, this area is not heavily used. To prevent damage to the grass, trails of plywood were laid to accommodate both construction and shooting crew traffic. Despite our efforts, the field was trashed. But within two days, Frank Haddad and his greens department had completely restored the grass, leaving no evidence of our lengthy visit.

Names of *X-Files* crew members were etched onto the wall.

Blacks: movie jargon for rolls of black duvetyne fabric used to shield a set from unwanted external light.

VIETNAM WAR MEMORIAL WALL

BALLANTYNE PIER, VANCOUVER

To effectively film the night scenes associated with the War Memorial Wall - that is, to avoid the repercussions from the cast and crew of several "all-nighters" on location - part of the set had to be constructed inside an empty building. Unfortunately, finding a free-span building with at least thirty-five-foot-high ceilings was like finding a needle in a haystack.

After viewing more than ten warehouses, the freespan section of the Ballantyne Pier passenger terminal was chosen. Because the north side of the space is exposed to daylight, a wall was needed to simulate night during daylight hours. The solution was to tent the area, but there weren't enough *blacks* available in Vancouver, so a special order was sent to L.A.

A drooping cardboard audience waits for "action" on "Unrequited" (4x16).

After all that, the space was still considered too small to permit action to take place both in front of and behind the bleachers. The rear of the bleachers was eventually constructed next door at the CERES warehouse. Even though the warehouse ceilings were too low, there was no other option, and the view of the wooden trusses in the final cut is barely noticeable.

The grandstand at Jericho Park was dismantled and reassembled inside Ballantyne Pier and another section erected at CERES. Because our sets were in the middle of an operational port facility where large containers were constantly being unloaded, parking for work trucks looked grim. The thought of having five hundred extras a day was even more daunting. Work truck parking was resolved by a neighbouring business which gave us permission to park on its property and the extras were shuttled in each morning by three fifty-five-passenger buses. The parking fee alone totalled $6,000. To reduce the costs of extras, it was initially proposed that cardboard cutouts of people be placed in the rear section of the bleachers. Over 100 life-sized cardboard cut-outs were imported from California and put in place, but after a day in the Vancouver dampness, the "audience" had slumped over.

As a gratuity to North Vancouver, The X-Files donated a bench to Cates Park.

FREEDOM SQUARE
STANLEY PARK PEDESTRIAN UNDERPASS, GEORGIA ST., VANCOUVER

Freedom Square was cleverly cheated using a pedestrian underpass leading to Stanley Park. The pylons blocking the west side of the underpass were removed to allow for picture vehicle access, which included two Hummers. The scene depicts the start of a military parade, and as the procession flows out of the tunnel, the parade is concealed by the concrete cavern. This presented an opportunity to disguise the actual parade length of the parade, which was only about 100 feet.

Filming a parade in "Washington, D.C." for "Unrequited" (4x16).

One of the stipulations of filming in parks is that public access to the area must be permitted. Productions may request that members of the public refrain from walking in front of camera during takes, but that cannot be enforced. When paparazzi discovered that Gillian was filming in Stanley Park, a group of photographers appeared on set but the police would not deny them access. During this time, Gillian was the subject of numerous tabloid articles and became an object of desire for freelance photographers. With an onslaught of security guards, production assistants, and every available crew member, a human blockade was formed, preventing the unwelcomed visitors from capturing the moment.

PENTAGON LOBBY
CANADA PLACE CRUISE SHIP TERMINAL, 999 CANADA PLACE, VANCOUVER

Films and books depicting interiors of the Pentagon were reviewed in order to get the sense of the architecture and scale of the building. Even though the Pentagon suggests power and omniscience, its mundane architecture is utterly disappointing from a filming perpective. The only distinct visual indicator is a maze of concourses which only limited our location options. After viewing two potential locations, the Cruise Ship Terminal - with some design fabrication - doubled for the Pentagon interior.

> Canada Place, with its distinctive white sails, was the Canadian Pavillion during Expo '86. The cruise ship arrival and departure level has been used extensively as an airport terminal for film purposes. This space has only once been used as a *Pentagon lobby*.

4x17	TEMPUS FUGIT	TP

Mulder and Scully find evidence that a commercial airliner may have crashed as a result of a mid-air abduction of Max Fenig by a UFO.

HEADLESS WOMAN PUB
15 NORTH RENFREW RESTAURANT, 15 NORTH RENFREW ST., VANCOUVER

One of the privileges of working on *The X-Files* was the frequent requests - by various individuals and businesses - that their properties be used as locations, and the locations department received regular invitations. On quiet days, our scouts were sent out to investigate and photo-

In one scene at the *Headless Woman Pub*, first assistant director Vladimir Stefoff plays the bartender (uttering the familiar words, "Last call, folks . . . cocktail?"). Assistant location manager Ainslie Wiggs played a tarty barfly, but was edited from the final cut.

Moldy corpses in a migrant workers camp shack ("El Mundo Gira" (4x11)).

Work Hard, Play Hard (TP)

As the show picked up steam and broke new ground, so did the size and scale of the requisite celebrations. From Christmas and end-of-season wrap parties to Golden Globe, Emmy, and 100th episode celebrations, the search for larger and unique locations in which to hold such festivities became increasingly difficult.

Early parties were held in coffee houses and restaurants. The 100th episode party was held in two large ballrooms at the Hyatt Regency Hotel, for which Gillian flew in a funk band from Los Angeles. The final Vancouver party at the end of Season Five was held at the Vancouver Planetarium. An estimated 1,000 people attended, with many fans and well-wishers turned away at the door. The "Trip to Mars" simulator was a popular attraction, and the best-kept secret was the hostess serving bottles of beer from an ice chest in the elevator.

Standing in the bar queue, I glanced around to see two of The Elders leaning against the bar, engaged in a conversation with Deep Throat. Cigarette Smoking Man nudged me from behind as Chris greeted cast and crew on the staircase leading down to the bar and, as usual, Gillian was tearing up the dance floor. The moment struck me as the perfect − surreal − example of life imitating art. It was a perfect *X-Files* moment.

graph these locations, thereby bolstering the massive photo-library we developed over the years.

One of the nine location requirements in this episode was a Washington, D.C. *pub*. Specifically, it had to have a long bar and be large enough to comfortably accommodate both shooting crew and extras. Key to the use of this location was the ability to return here on the following episode, as Chris had indicated that he and writer Frank Spotnitz were working on scenes set here for "Max," the second episode of this two-parter.

At an early concept meeting, we discussed the tremendous cost involved in renting and closing down a functioning bar or restaurant for several days. The "build" option was also discussed and quickly discarded as being not only costly but physically impossible given time constraints and the lack of space on our soundstages. I then produced a fax received a couple of weeks earlier from the owners of a vacant restaurant. Having not yet seen this location myself, I was reluctant to offer the information, lest it prove completely inappropriate for our needs. What the fax did note was that the premises remained intact, a feature which had great appeal to set decorator Shirley Inget. The venue was large and eclectic with good natural light and yes, a full bar. The open floorplan was split between three levels. If there was a downside, it was the large number of windows and skylights, which would need to be "tented" to play day for night. Fortunately, all windows - with the exception of the skylights - were at ground level, which made key grip Al Campbell's job somewhat easier.

This location is where Vancouver actor Brendon Beiser (Agent Pendrell) lost his job – his character was killed.

A deal was made and the restaurant booked for three days with a hold-over clause added. And because the property was for sale, a provision was made allowing us to leave the set "dressed" for the following episode.

Airplane crash site *for "Tempus Fugit" (4x17).*

PARADISE MOTEL

LONDON GUARD MOTEL, 2277 KINGSWAY, VANCOUVER

After four seasons and several hundred locations, it was reassuring to know that we'd not yet exhausted our list of motels, for once again the script called for a character *autocourt-style motel* with individual or semi-detached units, this time fictionally set in Northville, New York.

Three rooms were booked for filming: 326 (Scully), 330 (Sharon Graffia), and 331 (Mulder). Exterior day scenes involving Scully and Mulder's arrival were also featured. Sharon's room was suitably trashed by set dec for the post-abduction scene. As usual, we took over the entire establishment.

We returned to the London Guard Motel for "The End" (5x20).

CRASH SITE

BOUNDARY BAY AIRPORT AND VICINITY, DELTA

Working on *The X-Files* eventually provided every department in production the opportunity to explore an area of their expertise as a once-in-a-lifetime visitation. For the art, construction, and special effects departments, this meant the creation of a full-scale mock-up of a 737 cabin atop a hydraulic gimbal which allowed the set to be rocked and tilted violently in all directions.

For the locations department, the challenge was in providing a lightly-wooded air disaster *crash site* the size of a football field. A clearing was necessary in which to dress the bulk of the wreckage. Similarly, permission was needed to scorch a large meadow and create a small lake around which scores of yellow bodybags were systematically arranged. The set dec department then used air cannons to blast hundreds of rags and pieces of clothing into the trees bordering the site (the real task for the dressers came when it was time to remove them). The entire process, from start to finish, took one month.

This location was also required to be helicopter-friendly, as a chopper would be used for aerial work (establishing the magnitude of the crash) and as picture equipment. Director Rob Bowman originally wanted a *really* big helicopter for picture - the kind which is used for helicopter logging - and we looked at an enormous insect-like Sikorsky S64 SkyCrane, which happened to be sitting idle at nearby Boundary Bay Airport. Unfort-

Marty McInally (right) and Dan Henshaw: camera guys.

Bill Kassis (left) and Attila Szalay: doing much more than putting quarters into telephone booths.

unately, this idea was jettisoned when we discovered that the prop wash – at a height of 100 feet in the air – created 80-kilometre-per-hour winds which would have effectively blown away dressing, equipment, cast, and crew.

Given the other location requirements for this episode – which included a large *aircraft hangar*, a *runway*, and an *airport control tower* - it was pretty much a slam-dunk for our favourite piece of real estate bordering the Boundary Bay Airport. The resulting scenes were both incredibly big, incredibly realistic, and awfully disturbing to anyone who's ever flown in a fixed-wing aircraft.

One of the stipulations demanded by Transport Canada – then the owner of this property – was that it be returned to its natural state upon completion of filming. I admit that, even with head greenskeeper Frank Haddad's repeated assurances that a couple of months of rain would assist in a miracle of restoration (it was early February 1997), I remained skeptical. The degree of devastation was enormous.

Returning here several months later, I noted thankfully that Frank had been correct. Our "site" was, by now, indistinguishable from the surrounding landscape.

HANGAR
BOUNDARY BAY AIRPORT, DELTA

Large pieces of 737 aircraft wreckage were trucked in from North Carolina to simulate a crash site, then moved to the fifty-year-old hangar at nearby Boundary Bay Airport, where they were arranged to resemble the reconstruction of our downed Flight 549.

After a costly round of negotiations with machine shops, flight schools, and individual plane owners, an agreement was reached allowing us several days' access to the hangar to prep this location, film the required scenes, and hold the location for the first day of filming on the following episode, "Max." The owners of small planes hangared in this building were not particularly anxious to leave their valuable aircraft outside in winter weather. Similarly, machine shop operators were reluctant to close up shop for a couple of days, and did so only after receiving generous compensation.

Night exterior scenes were filmed on the tarmac outside, for which several aircraft displaced from the hangar were rented as "picture" aircraft. The chase scene in which Mulder, Scully, and Sergeant Frish realize that they are being followed began outside this hangar and ended

Everyone was happy on The X-Files *sets. Even trainee assistant director Patrick Stark and a dead guy.*

on a runway at the Abbotsford Airport (see *A Plane, a Car, & a Whole Lotta Lights*).

The *Von Drehle Air Force Reserve Installation control tower* scenes were filmed at the Boundary Bay Airport control tower. During the filming of the day establishing sequence, a training helicopter inched its way through the background of the scene, moments before a frantic crew - coaxed by a very excited Rob Bowman - was in position to roll camera. The free production value would have been awesome. Locations was, of course, asked if the chopper could be brought back for take two. After a brief conversation between the aircraft, the tower, and myself, it was decided to move on, as the time required to reposition the chopper was longer than we could afford to wait.

Because this facility remained operational between the hours of 6 a.m. and 11 p.m., night interiors were filmed after 11 p.m. For these scenes - which were split between Main and Second Units - the old hangar across the runway was lit to provide depth. Runway apron lighting was also left on. A 125-foot crane was used to film the overhead reveal of Frith hiding on the tower roof. By the time this scene came up, so had the sun. Well, almost. It was not until this footage came back from the lab that we knew for certain that no reshoot would be required due to loss of night.

While filming "Max" (4x18) at the Vancouver International Airport, director Kim Manners announced that, for the first time, an episode's budget had reached $2 million. The crew cheered.

4x18	MAX	LG

Mulder finds the UFO crash site, and retrieves a piece of alien technology in a knapsack that Max Fenig left for him at an airport luggage claim. While transporting the knapsack, Mulder's flight is itself intercepted by a UFO.

HANGAR
BOUNDARY BAY AIRPORT, DELTA

Several crew members protested the cold conditions in the hangar during the filming of "Tempus Fugit" (4x17), and insisted that the hangar heaters be turned on for the filming of this episode, the second part. Since the heaters had already been established in the previous show as being "off," there was concern about continuity.

Director Kim Manners' intolerance of the cold sparked a creative surge. A wide shot of Mulder and Scully's entrance into the hangar was captured with the heaters "on," thereby establishing the heat that kept everyone warm.

UFO pre-flight ("Tempus Fugit" (4x17), "Max" (4x18)).

I Work for The X-Files (LG)

"Zero Sum" (4x21) required a *playground* to stage the scene where playing children and their teacher are attacked by a swarm of bees. The Connaught Park playground was used. Pheremones — used to attract bees — were brought in by a bee wrangler and applied to the "teacher" and certain areas of the playground. At the end of the day, the bee wrangler summoned the bees back to their nests using the same chemical, and all pieces of playground equipment that had been treated with pheremone were washed with soap and water.

The bee specialists warned that a few stray bees might return the next day, but their ability to survive a winter's night would make this unlikely. In the event that any bees did survive, and returned to the park, they would be unable to find their nest and would likely fly away. Just in case, a production assistant was assigned "bee watch" for the following day.

Vancouver Parks representative John Gray surveyed the park the next day at 11 a.m. and told the production assistant that everything looked fine. Later, Second Unit location manager Rob Murdoch swung by the playground and noticed several bees hovering over the slide. After phoning John with an update, Rob proceeded to kill the bees with his binder. Little did Rob know that his cellular phone was still on and John was listening to everything that was happening at the park.

John overheard one parent ask Rob, who at that time was sitting on the slide, if he was a pedophile. "No," was Rob's reply. "I just work for *The X-Files*."

To make matters worse, a child followed Rob around the playground, asking why he was killing bees. "Mister, bees are our friends," the child insisted. Rob's reply: "I have to kill the bees. I work for *The X-Files*."

4x19	SYNCHRONY	TP

An elderly man from the future tries to change the past by killing the research scientists - including himself - who are responsible for inventing a rapid-freezing chemical.

4x20	SMALL POTATOES	LG

Scully and Mulder pursue a man with the ability to change his physical appearance.

4x21	ZERO SUM	TP

Mulder and Assistant Director Skinner get caught up in a number of attacks by swarms of bees that seem to be carrying the smallpox virus.

TRANSCONTINENTAL EXPRESS ROUTING CENTRE
MAIL-O-MATIC,
2720 SOUTH INGLETON AVE., BURNABY

Automated mail-sorting operations come in all shapes and sizes, but for our purposes we wanted something big and visually interesting. We'd previously scouted all willing candidates for "Blood" (2x03) and shot at this same facility on that episode. The choice was therefore academic.

The bathroom scenes in which the bee attack occurred were filmed in a setpiece on a soundstage to accommodate both special and visual effects requirements. Entrances and exits were filmed on location.

Mail-O-Matic employees were hired as background extras to operate forklifts and sorting equipment, thereby lending authenticity to these scenes.

INCINERATOR ROOM AND SERVICE ELEVATOR
OLD BOILER ROOM, HOTEL VANCOUVER,
900 WEST GEORGIA ST., VANCOUVER

These scenes required a creepy industrial incinerator in which Skinner could surreptitiously dispose of a body. More as a point of reference than as a prospective location, we scouted the City of Burnaby's massive industrial incineration plant, agreeing that it was best "saved" for an episode in which it might be given a starring role.

Ever since touring the Hotel Vancouver from sub-basement to roof as part of a locations promotion for the Hotel, I had been looking for an opportunity to use the decommissioned boiler room in the bowels of the building. Standing two storeys high, it was not only spooky in a gothic sense, but it was big and offered a variety of camera angles.

A preliminary location survey sold it to director Kim Manners, but posted signs warning of the presence of asbestos resulted in the hiring of a company to contain potential hazards resulting from the lining of the old boilers with asbestos fibre. A risk management company was then brought in to evaluate the quality of air. The analysis confirmed that concentrations were within acceptable parameters.

This proved to be a very good thing for all concerned, as Kim had become very attached to the look of this location and time was running out to come up with a suitable alternative. As assistant art director Vivien Nishi noted, "The door opening had to be enlarged to accommodate the body, which required a brick and mortar expert, our metal fabricator, and special effects. This, of course, was done, much to the delight of Kim." Propane flame bars were also added to one of the boiler units to create a flaming inferno for Skinner, but this location was otherwise shot very much as it was.

The exterior establishing shot of the incineration plant was taken from stock footage. The freight elevator scenes in which Skinner entered the facility with Jane's body over his shoulder were shot in the service elevator leading to the sub-basement level of the Hotel.

Main unit assistant location manager Rick Fearon and second unit assistant location manager Fiona Crossley.

| 4x22 | ELEGY | LG |

The ghosts of recent murder victims – killed by a nurse from a psychiatric hospital – appear to people who are about to die.

BOWLING ALLEY
THUNDERBIRD LANES, 120 WEST 16TH AVE., NORTH VANCOUVER

Finding a bowling alley seemed like an easy task and most of the bowling alleys in the Lower Mainland were scouted. It was crucial that the space at the rear of the lanes be large enough to film in and that the system for removing pins could be adjusted to allow a body to drop into the lane. That requirement alone eliminated over two-thirds of the bowling alleys. The additional requirement – for a funky interior – narrowed the options to two. There was also great reluctance by most owners to close down their facility for the three days required for filming. Their commitment to bowling leagues was unfathomable.

"No, really. I'm too warm."
– Kim Manners

An exterior scene scheduled to be shot at the Cassandra House *("Demons" (4x23)) was scrapped at the last minute. This, and an interior made indistinguishable by the set decorating, allowed us to return here to shoot the* Sim House *for "Christmas Carol" (5x05).*

This cottage also played home to the aging victim of government xenotransplantation in "Travellers" (5x15). Key grip Al Campbell requested permission to cut a sizeable hole in the second-storey floor for a lighting effect. His request was denied, but as assistant location manager Ainslie Wiggs left the set she recalled hearing the buzz of a chainsaw tearing through wood. Seven months pregnant at the time, Ainslie couldn't be bothered to investigate the noise. The hole was eventually repaired by the construction department and such acts, thankfully, were not a common occurrence.

Locked: the act of confirming a location for shooting.

Thunderbird Lanes was undoubtedly the most visually interesting interior of all the choices, but the exterior – a generic commercial strip mall – lacked character. The director requested a search for a different exterior, a building more traditional and accentuated by an art deco marquee. Interesting building facades across the street from vacant surface parking lots are rare in Vancouver. All ten alternatives presented were rejected. Finally, it was decided that a sign mounted over the awning of Thunderbird Lanes would resolve the dilemma.

Once the extent of the use of the location was established, creative scheduling, league buyouts, and a location fee meant we were off to the lanes. The crew, of course, bowled during their lunch hour.

4x23	DEMONS	TP

Mulder, undergoing radical treatments to recover suppressed memories, begins to question what he believes about his past, and his family, and his possible role in murder.

WISTERIA COTTAGE
18237-16 AVE., SURREY

"Toddwhich - find a secluded or abandoned two-storey clapboard farmhouse with a dirt or grass driveway and a clean 180 degree reverse." This was the request from executive producer Bob Goodwin, who also penned this episode. Standing beside him, director Kim Manners simply looked at me and arched his eyebrows, as if to say, "Good luck, bud."

A thorough scout of possible candidates took us back to the South Surrey-Langley area. Ironically, it was while on our way to survey another cottage that construction co-ordinator Rob Maier looked out the van window in time to notice this farmhouse. We politely went through the motions of surveying the location for which I had made an appointment, then doubled back.

The property had been for sale for a couple of years and I recall standing in a field dialing the number listed on the "For Sale" sign while the survey group waited anxiously at a distance. Within five minutes the realtor called back to say the owner of the property lived in the eastern United States, having inherited the farm from her mother, and a call was necessary to confirm our intentions. After a scrum with the art and construction departments, I ventured a ballpark figure and a list of requirements. An agreement in principle was quickly reached. Oh, but cellular phones *do* have their place in this world.

One more call was necessary before we *locked* this location. There was much concern over the fact that 16th Avenue was a major truck route and, as such, very noisy during the day. I pitched the City of Surrey on our plan, proposing a detour route for the day of filming, to which they agreed. The entire deal took about twenty minutes, after which we hopped in the van and drove back to North Vancouver.

At this point, the art, greens, and construction departments took over, transforming the farmhouse to conform to both Goodwin's and Manners' specifications.

| CASSANDRA HOUSE |
| 3106 ALBERTA ST., VANCOUVER |

The *Cassandra house* proved a much easier sell than the *Wisteria cottage*. I had watched this house for a couple of years in the hope that we would one day be able to use it as a location.

This craftsman-style heritage home underwent a huge restoration in 1992, effectively saving it from the bulldozer. The main floor was stripped of furniture and filled with computer-enhanced "paintings" of the *Wisteria cottage* - close to 100 reproductions in all shapes and sizes, according to set decorator Shirley Inget. There were, in fact, so many paintings - hung on walls and propped up on easels, tables, window ledges, and mantels - that much of the interior ambience was overwhelmed in the final edited scenes.

Under siege ("Folie à Deux" (5x19)).

| 4x24 | GETHSEMANE | LG |

When a grey alien body is discovered frozen in ice, Mulder and Scully learn that its existence might be part of an elaborate government hoax. Scully also discovers that the same people responsible for the hoax gave her cancer, and identifies a suicide victim's body as Mulder's.

| INDUSTRIAL PARK/DARPA |
| YELLOW PAGES/DOMINION DIRECTORY, 4260 STILL CREEK RD., BURNABY |

The Dominion Directory complex hosted a variety of sets including the exterior *industrial park*, interior *office building*, interior *parking garage*, interior *bio labs*, and interior *stairwell*. Finding this diverse combination of locations was considered a coup except for a major drawback two days prior to filming.

After the technical survey, the gaffer protested the use of the parkade on the basis of its mercury vapour lights. To obtain the desired lighting effect, a new lighting system had to be installed at an astronomical cost. With only two days of prep remaining, alternative parkades were presented to executive producer and director Bob Goodwin but dismissed for various reasons. As the deadline for filming neared, whiling away the last minutes in the survey van, I suggested that we turn out the house lights - as done previously on other episodes - take lights from our truck - the largest lighting package in B.C. - and light the parkade ourselves. The resulting lighting effect looked spectacular.

Filming in parkades is a nightmare as they are built for a specific use; to accommodate vehicles on a daily basis. They are a rare commodity, and are difficult to access for exclusive film purposes. The opportunity to film at the Dominion Directory parkade was unprecedented, especially at 3 p.m. Usually parkades are available only after 7 p.m., which means an entire night of filming.

| SMITHSONIAN INSTITUTE |
| VANCOUVER ART GALLERY, 750 HORNBY ST., VANCOUVER |

Finally, the opportunity to film at the Art Gallery rotunda arose. The spiral stairwell was used to depict the *Smithsonian Institute*. Unfortunately an installation - entitled *Plastic Happiness* and featuring a twelve-foot-long nylon-fabric pig, held aloft with the aid of an air compressor and cables hovered over the stairwell, and would have been clearly discernible in the intended sequence of shots. An exact replica of the stairwell was requested by Bob, even though he knew that no alternative locations existed. There was no doubt, the pig had to go. Robin Naiman, our contact at the gallery, was

Production assistant Robyn Gelka is attacked by the air conditioning.

The main attraction for film productions at the Vancouver Art Gallery are the old courtrooms, one of which was used as the Judacia Archives in "Kaddish" (4x12).

somewhat surprised by our request to remove the "pig," but proposed the question to her staff. Four staff members agreed to remove the installation and then reinstall it after filming.

> INTERIOR SUMMIT CAVE/INTERIOR WAREHOUSE/INTERIOR TENT
>
> SBS FREEZERS, 6228 BERESFORD ST., BURNABY

The "winter" moments of this episode were captured at Seymour Mountain, the Tantalus Range in Squamish, and SBS Freezers. The interior ice caves were initially supposed to be builds, and the quest for warehouse space proceeded. While scouting at the Pacific National Exhibition, Chris called executive producer Bob Goodwin and insisted that the breath of the actors be visible. Word was out: "Chris wants to see breath."

Any special effects alternatives were expensive. A cold storage plant was the most practical and least costly solution. This former meat-packing plant and its freezer room would ultimately produce "breath," but to upgrade the system, a local refrigeration company submitted a quote of $65,000. A competing firm was then asked for a quote, and for a fraction of the original estimate, Chris saw breath.

On the hot, sunny days of mid-May, crew members were outfitting themselves in sub-zero attire.

Special effects coordinator Dave Gauthier. Off to left is art director Greg Loewen.

The ice cave ("Gethsemane" (4x24)) as seen from the inside.

The ice cave ("Gethsemane" (4x24)) as seen from the outside.

A postmortem on *The X-Files'* rumoured relocation to Los Angeles began long before an official announcement of the move was made. Call it wounded pride – many Vancouverites were justly proud that such a smart, world-class television series would call Vancouver home – or an impending sense of loss, but residents (fans and infidels alike) took an active interest in the show's status. Much of the debate surrounded the show's moody "look" and whether or not this "look" could be maintained in the warmer California climate. From the production side, any attempt to replicate a West Coast feel would have proved impossible, especially when the proximity to a more arid landscape allowed for locations – and story opportunities – not possible here.

What is perhaps most poignant is the evolution of *The X-Files'* "look" as it fed on brooding landscapes, seamy downtown neighbour-hoods, and arboreal winter light. This visual aesthetic became, in turn, a touchstone for the distrust, tension, and angst of the nineties. In this sense, the "look" the Lower Mainland gave the show was both tangible and unique.

– *TP*

Show Us the Money (TP)

As is sometimes the case when fulfilling the public relations duties of a location manager, the big productions atone for the sins of their smaller siblings. This is not to say that all big shows are necessarily created equal or that a big show is, by definition, more responsible than a smaller show. The simple truth — as distasteful as it may be — is that money has a palliative effect on wounds and acts of indiscretion (real or perceived), which enable certain productions to achieve what others cannot. And while there is no substitute for creativity, deep pockets open reluctant doors.

On more than one occasion, *The X-Files* was cited (ironically enough, by other productions) as being guilty of inflating location costs around Vancouver, an accusation accompanied by fiction as much as fact. There is no doubt that when we, as a film unit, moved into a neighbourhood, we *moved in*. With a prep crew whose numbers sometimes rivalled those of an entire shooting crew on other productions, there was no such thing as a subtle presence or minimal disruption. Scripts were large and ambitious, demanding elements usually associated with feature films. We made this clear to all concerned from the beginning. Better to map out a worst-case scenario than to understate the terms of our presence. The last thing we needed was to be accosted by a group of angry merchants or residents during filming, hurling accusations that they were misled or lied to.

Night filming was almost always accompanied by at least two lighting cranes and access to adjacent yards and rooftops — sometimes a block or two away — for additional lighting requirements. The use of wind and lightning machines, as well as raintowers, was common. And while we always attempted to schedule such

The story of how the Lone Gunmen came to be: a woman who was involved in producing a paranoia-inducing gas solicits help from three men at a computer convention.

NEWSPAPER OFFICES

THE DOMINION BUILDING,
207 WEST HASTINGS ST., VANCOUVER

The first episode of Season Five was unusual in more than one way. With the exception of a very brief appearance by Mulder, David and Gillian - who were still filming the first *X-Files* feature *Fight the Future* in California - were absent from this show. The episode was hence written around Vancouver's own Lone Gunmen.

The location requirement for our Baltimore, Maryland *newspaper office* exterior led us to the kind of traditional big-city building evocative of the Hearst publishing era. For this reason, we chose the old TD Bank building which, ironically, sat kitty-corner to what was once a real newspaper office building.

It is perhaps unfortunate that scenes were not written to showcase the interior of this building, which is particularly notable for its ornate hallways and stairwells. It is also unfortunate that this neighbourhood, on the edge of skid row, is so tender (see *Show Us the Money*).

This building faces Victory Square and the oft-used Victory Alley, which played as a Washington, D.C. *street* and *drug hang-out* in "Wetwired" (3x23).

A Lone Gunman: Tom Braidwood outside the Ovaltine Café.

CONVENTION CENTRE

ROBSON SQUARE CONFERENCE CENTRE,
600 ROBSON ST., VANCOUVER

As early as July 1997, producer J.P. Finn had warned me that a large convention centre would be required as the key location for this episode. With Season Five prep still several weeks away, I made a shortlist of possibilities, although there was really only one choice.

Director Kim Manners was concerned that a bland, sterile environment would only detract from the story. With so much screen time devoted to this location, he insisted that it offer something visually unique. The defining features here were a tiered ceiling and a large mezzanine area from which the main hall could be seen (and filmed). All other available choices of location (with the exception of the Pacific Ballroom at the Hotel Vancouver) were simply large, windowless conference halls.

Availability was a key issue. David had booked a holiday upon completion of his work on the feature. That meant he was unavailable to production for over a week after we were to begin filming. The shooting schedule was therefore split between "Unusual Suspects" and the season's second episode, "Redux." We completed six of our eight-day schedule on "Unusual Suspects" and shot the first three days of "Redux." We then returned to the Convention Centre to complete David's work upon his return, before moving to a warehouse to complete Day Eight on the schedule. The following day, "Redux" recommenced filming with Day Four work.

It was an awkward and costly arrangement which required locations to "hold" the conference facility for an additional four days. In all, *The X-Files* occupied the Robson Square Conference Centre for seventeen consecutive days in order to shoot five days of film and facilitate a massive "dress" and "strike." Also dressed and shot were the lobby and foyer, which meant that events in the adjoining theatres - those not being rented to house our large contingent of extras - were either moved elsewhere or rescheduled around filming days.

We were very fortunate to be filming this show in late August, which was the "low season" for convention and conference hall bookings. At any other time of year, a booking such as this would not have been possible.

> Props master Ken Hawryliw was cast as the computer nerd whom the police wrongfully hauled off to jail, all the while mumbling the lines: "I didn't hack into anyone's computer . . . Seriously, guys, I've got a circulatory problem . . . I have a tendency to fall down a lot. . . ."

effects early in the evening, this was not always possible due to late calls or lengthy and complicated set-ups. The polling of neighbourhoods thus became standard procedure prior to any night filming, whether we needed the extra time (after the usual 11 p.m. noise restriction kicked in) or not.

The easiest — and perhaps fairest — way to deal with resistance was to relocate the protesters (usually to a hotel room) for the duration of the shoot, something many television shows could not afford. Cash payments, which we likened to extortion, were avoided except in extreme situations. If someone wanted money in exchange for their co-operation, we usually tried to find an alternate location.

I found out one hot August afternoon in 1997 that finding an alternative was not always possible. We were prepping the first episode of Season Five, "Unusual Suspects," the first show to be written around the Lone Gunmen. The script called for a *convention centre*, for which we used the lower level of the Robson Square Conference Centre. It also called for the exterior of a big-city *newspaper office*, for which the Dominion Building at 207 West Hastings Street seemed ideally suited. The neighbourhood was rundown enough to convey the sense of a big American city, in this case Washington, D.C. My biggest potential problem — or so I thought — was keeping well away from a retail sewing supply outlet at the west end of the block infamous for the owner's opposition to filming anywhere near its doors. Hypocritical, since many costumers and seamstresses employed in the film industry regularly shop there for fabric and supplies.

I warned director Kim Manners that this location could be problematic for this reason and he assured me that he would have no problem staying well away from that end of the block. A deal was signed with the owners of the Dominion Building and an agreement in principle reached with the woman who ran the confectionary kiosk directly outside the front doors of the building, as her business was directly in the line of fire. Resident letters were circulated.

We also intended to stage an abduction around the corner of the Dominion Building in the 400-block of Cambie Street, for which police were to be used for intermittent one-way traffic lock-ups (for no longer than three-minutes). I knew that, in the past, there had been problems involving film crews and a handful of small businesses in the half-block north of the alley, specifically in and around a particular residential hotel. To this end, I intended to restrict our activities south of the alley. What I was not prepared for was the near-violent reception from a half-dozen irate merchants who surrounded me and proceeded to verbally accost me about crimes committed by film crews in their block.

This despite the fact that we were still several days away from filming at this location and our activities here were to be brief (about two hours, as it turned out). When I finally managed to calm everyone down enough to have a rational discussion, the situation became clear. An earlier production had promised compensation as part of a "deal" to film in front of these businesses, but the production had disappeared upon completion of filming, reneging on their promise.

A funny thing happens to disgruntled human beings once they've been given the opportunity to vent in the face of their adversary (which I clearly was): they become reasonable and almost sympathetic to your cause. No one likes to be ignored, especially when they have a valid complaint. All the more so when the perceived villain is a large

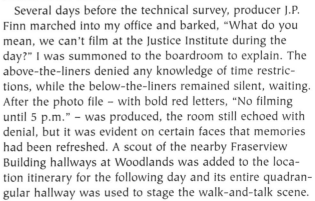

5x02	REDUX	LG

Scully discovers the origin of her cancer, as Mulder discovers - in a secret research facility - the truth behind the existence of the aliens he has believed in for so long.

INTERIOR DARPA

JUSTICE INSTITUTE, 715 MCBRIDE BLVD., NEW WESTMINSTER

The interior of the *DARPA facility* was intended to reflect a modern high-tech facility with an imposing, impenetrable security entrance leading to a large open lobby and connected to an endless maze of corridors. Long corridors were of paramount importance in order to stage a five-minute walk-and-talk. As previously mentioned, large lobbies and long hallways are scarce resources in Vancouver. The limited number of potential locations available allowed filming on weekends only and were dismissed on that basis alone. The main contender, the Justice Institute, permitted filming after 5 p.m. While scouting the institute with the director, producer, and department heads, I mentioned the time restrictions. I suggested the use of the Fraserview Building at Woodlands for some of the hallway scenes as an alternative to filming at the Institute for two full nights, but prep continued with the intent to film all of the interior *DARPA* scenes at the institute.

Several days before the technical survey, producer J.P. Finn marched into my office and barked, "What do you mean, we can't film at the Justice Institute during the day?" I was summoned to the boardroom to explain. The above-the-liners denied any knowledge of time restrictions, while the below-the-liners remained silent, waiting. After the photo file – with bold red letters, "No filming until 5 p.m." – was produced, the room still echoed with denial, but it was evident on certain faces that memories had been refreshed. A scout of the nearby Fraserview Building hallways at Woodlands was added to the location itinerary for the following day and its entire quadrangular hallway was used to stage the walk-and-talk scene.

Although hours of filming at the Justice Institute were restricted, we were given permission to build the security booth between the lobby and the busiest corridor – the hallway leading to the cafeteria. A wall, with a three-foot doorway, was constructed in the corridor.

Permission was also requested to test a special helium balloon to be used for lighting purposes. With a diameter of five metres (seventeen feet), this contraption had a frame at the bottom to accommodate four 4K HMI lights that shone up into the balloon, essentially creating a giant lightbulb. This lighting effect would maintain the illusion of daylight as night fell upon the glass-domed atrium lobby. The test was approved but what no one knew was that in order to inflate the balloon, a loud electrical air blower, much like a large, powerful hair dryer, was to be used.

On the day of filming, cabling proceeded well in advance of the time restriction, and lights were hauled in, one at a time, in an attempt to conceal our clandestine activity. By 5:30 p.m., the crew had arrived to an almost completely lit location.

INTERIOR/EXTERIOR DARPA
YELLOW PAGES/DOMIONION DIRECTORY, 4260 STILL CREEK DR., BURNABY

The interior of *DARPA* came back to haunt the locations department. While the entire lobby and the constructed security booth at the Justice Institute was filmed, an alternative lobby was required to show the approach to the security booth.

Just when they thought they saw the last of us (at the end of Season Four), we returned to the Dominion Directory with a special request: to film in the lobby during a work day. Generally, filming during the day at an active facility is not permitted. But this was a special request and the building management had become comfortable with our presence. The scene had to be shot in daylight and it was impossible to complete the scene between the end of the day at 4:30 p.m. and sunset at 8:30 p.m. In consideration of our past association with them, Dominion Directory officials gave us permission to film during the day. With careful and considerate prep and the excitement generated by David's presence, a smooth day of filming was chalked up. Again, the proceeds for filming were donated to a charitable fund.

company or a representative of a large industry. I listened intently to their complaints, pointing out that, while *The X-Files* had never filmed in this block before, we had, many times, worked out of the parking lot around the corner and next to the vacant Woodward's building. "Had we ever caused them grief before?" I asked, knowing that the answer would be, "No."

I cut to the chase and asked what they wanted for compensation for loss of business, given the fact that we would be filming over the lunch hour on a Friday afternoon in the summer. *$200 for each business* was the quick response. It seemed reasonable enough, but given that there were nine separate businesses here, $1,800 stuck in my throat. What was really happening was that our production was being asked to apologize for the entire industry. I pondered this for a few moments before agreeing to their demand. We shook hands and, as I was leaving, the owner of the residential hotel taunted me: "We'll never see you again, will we?" I took him into his office, where I expressed my own displeasure at being called a liar, and told him that I would take a great deal of pleasure in not only proving him wrong, but also in personally delivering each and every cheque to each and every merchant. Which is exactly what I did upon completion of filming.

Given the phenomenal growth rate of the movie industry in British Columbia (some twenty percent per annum) and the difficulties associated with managing that kind of rapid growth, such scenarios are, perhaps, impossible to avoid. And while there exists a degree of dishonesty amongst some merchants or small businesses in any city, the overwhelming majority are content simply to be heard and treated reasonably.

Don't they know who we are?

Filming for "Redux" (5x02) involved some amount of studio work. A Lions Gate Studios' office building and its vacant second floor was a promising solution. The Studio approved our use of the space, but the following day, they called to tell us that there were prospective tenants. They wanted to back out of our agreement. Given that we rented three stages on a long-term basis, producer J.P. Finn was asked to help resolve the situation. After all, he was the person who, when denied a curfew extension by City of Vancouver officials during the filming of a Season Three episode, responded by saying, "Don't they know who we are?" The answer was, "Yes, but no matter what some Teamster said about *The X-Files* having the keys to the City, it's not true." North Shore Studios knew who we were, and a phone call from J.P. secured the second floor for our use.

William B. Davis (Cigarette Smoking Man) trades his Morleys for a microphone.

5x03	REDUX II	TP

A microchip Mulder took from the research facility is implanted into Scully's neck, and sends her cancer into remission. Cigarette Smoking Man is shot after trying to recruit Mulder by arranging a meeting with Mulder and his sister, Samantha.

THE RACETRACK
HASTINGS PARK RACECOURSE, EXHIBITION PARK, VANCOUVER

The Elders may have shown scant regard for human life, but they certainly loved their horses. Evidently, so did the sniper. And when it comes to thoroughbred racing, there's only one place in town to go. We'd established a connection between the Well-Manicured Man and horse-breeding on "Tunguska" (4x09), locating his ranch at Lone Rock Farms. It seemed logical that we should eventually find him at a *racetrack*.

Filming at the track can be tricky, especially during the racing season, when film companies must contend not only with morning practices but with late afternoon racing four days a week. Here we were lucky enough to slip in with a Second Unit crew after morning practice on a day when "the ponies" were not running.

GEORGETOWN STREET
400-BLOCK OF WEST CORDOVA ST., VANCOUVER

A scribbled note on the script page describing this location read "think Gastown," for not only was Vancouver's Gastown area the only believable match for Georgetown, but it was an area very familiar to both Chris and his writing team.

Key to identifying a precise section of street was the proximity of a parking garage from which a sniper would follow Mulder and the Cigarette Smoking Man's sidewalk conversation in the crosshairs of his rifle. A six-level parkade was chosen and level four identified as the point from which the sniper would shoot. Levels four through six were subsequently booked and closed to the public during filming.

A window in a building opposite the parking garage was then chosen to double as the Cigarette Smoking Man's apartment, for his implied death would also be filmed on this day. During a preliminary scout, we'd looked at another parkade across the street from one of Vancouver's more famous hotels and strip clubs. Eight of us made a late-morning visit to an "empty" room in the hotel, startling an old gentleman sleeping off a night of drinking. He stood quietly dazed in his underwear as I explained our presence and apologized for the disturbance.

A false wall or "return" was erected in the office into which our window faced. It was built to match the Cigarette Smoking Man's apartment interior, a setpiece constructed on one of our soundstages. The existing window - which was sealed - was then carefully removed by a glazier and our own custom-built window installed, as a requirement in this scene was that the sheer curtains blow gently in the breeze. The breeze was created by suspending a large electric fan from the exterior of the building just out of camera frame.

Both City Hall and the police department were very helpful with traffic control on this busy route. Unfortunately, and to David's displeasure, an unscheduled cruise ship arrived at the nearby terminal during filming, unloading 300 very curious tourists into the middle of our location. With handicams rolling and autograph pads in hand, many could not believe their good fortune at having walked off a cruise vessel and onto an *X-Files* set. With every available production assistant already controlling pedestrian traffic at key points of access, we were overwhelmed by eager fans oblivious to our requests to maintain distance, and David was surrounded. A local security company was hastily called in to provide both a bodyguard and additional guards for crowd control.

> The stairwell in which the sniper ascends the parkade was unsuitable at this location, as it was very narrow and completely enclosed. Director Kim Manners wished to shoot this sequence with a combination of high-angle shots and a substitute stairwell was found at the Atrium Inn (2889 East Hastings St.). The scene was shot by the Second Unit crew the day of their shoot at the Hastings Park Racecourse.

(l-r) Director Rob Bowman, David, and first assistant director Tom Braidwood discuss a scene in downtown Vancouver.

2-Jay Way (TP)

The 2-Jay's Café appeared as a repeat location in "Redux II" (5x03), where a *diner* was required in which to stage a meeting between Mulder and sister Samantha. The original intention had been to pick a diner in Steveston, as the scripted scenes required a visual relationship between the interior of the *diner* and Cigarette Smoking Man's car, which would be angle-parked outside with headlights illuminating Mulder sitting at his table.

A suitable diner — which permitted angle parking and addressed our primary concerns — was found in Steveston, south of Vancouver. The fact that most of the scenes being filmed here were night scenes made for easier negotiations with merchants, most of whom would be gone for the day by the time we arrived. At the last minute, however, David — who was in virtually every scene being shot at the diner — got wind of an impending all-nighter at a location far from home, and this choice was abandoned in favour of the 2-Jay's Café in downtown Vancouver. It was, for the crew, a popular decision, as no one wanted to see another Saturday morning sunrise from behind the wheel of a vehicle.

There were some real problems associated with filming these particular scenes at the 2-Jay's Café. It had been decided to move as much night work as possible to day in order to wrap by 2 or 3 a.m. For the grips, this meant tenting the entire front of the building out to the edge of the sidewalk. Similarly, the delicate nature of the dialogue scenes required not only traffic control on the street, but control of the tenants of a rooming house directly above the café. Police officers working around rush hour restrictions would deal with vehicular traffic but the residents of the Arco were another story.

After lengthy discussions with a representative of the Downtown Eastside Residents' Association (DERA), it was suggested that any attempt to control the activities of residents of the rooming house — heavily populated by drug addicts and alcoholics — would only create a larger problem on the day of filming. As the DERA representative was quick to point out, "You may not like the way these people live, but they are also citizens with rights."

In representing the interests of residents of Vancouver's Downtown Eastside, DERA attempts to fulfill many roles. With regard to the film industry, at least one DERA rep must be employed by each film company filming in this difficult neighbourhood, ostensibly to act as a liaison between the film company and the disenfranchised or less-stable element within the community. So, if a problem arises with a local resident at any stage in the filming process, the DERA rep is immediately called to help resolve the situation.

In this case, a plan evolved whereby residents were offered a free room for the night in another hotel in Vancouver's Downtown Eastside. Only those who refused the offer outright and who seemed very likely to create trouble for the production crew — there were two — were offered twenty dollars in exchange for being quiet and co-operating with our crew. In order to extend this offer, location scout Alan Bartolic made several harrowing trips through the halls of the Arco, collecting names in an attempt to gain a sense of the degree of co-operation we might expect.

5x04	DETOUR	LG

Ancient creatures with glowing red eyes who live in the forests of Florida are attacking people in the area, providing a distraction for Mulder and Scully, who are headed to an FBI seminar.

CLEARING IN WOODS/HIGHWAY
SEYMOUR DEMONSTRATION FOREST, NORTH VANCOUVER

Filming this episode - which was written to include mostly day scenes - involved a constant battle with daylight and the weather. It was the first and last time that Main Unit shooting was extended to ten days, which meant that the remainder of the year's schedule had to be adjusted. With over twenty shooting days in total, a record was broken. Luckily, most of the show was filmed in the Seymour Demonstration Forest and, given its close proximity to the studio, return trips could be arranged on clear days.

> This episode marked our twenty-fourth Main Unit visit to the Seymour Demonstration Forest.

While Main Unit was shooting in the early days of the schedule, the helium lighting balloon - first used by the electrics department at the Justice Institute - was set up for an exterior scene of Mulder and Scully stranded in the forest at night. Gale-force winds swept away the balloon and in consideration of safety all lighting cranes were dismantled, and the night ended early. During the following week, the rains descended, adding texture to the imagery but limiting daylight hours.

> The greens department had a crew of twenty-two working on this episode, the largest Frank Haddad ever needed.

Canadian director Brett Dowler and forest dweller in "Detour" (5x04).

| 5x05 | CHRISTMAS CAROL | TP |

Scully receives a number of phone calls from an unknown source, which lead her to a young girl, Emily, who turns out to be her daughter.

| 5x06 | THE POST-MODERN PROMETHEUS | LG |

A small town in Indiana is terrorized by a peanut-butter-sand-wich-eating, Frankenstein-like monster who has a fondness for Cher.

POLLIDORI'S HOUSE
BURRVILLA, DEAS ISLAND PARK, RIVER RD., DELTA

Chris' black-and-white episode presented one of the biggest challenges of the season. With ten huge locations on the plate, the survey bus transported the team to Richmond, Delta, Ladner, Downtown Vancouver, East Vancouver, and finally North Vancouver, all within ten hours.

> "That's one thing I really wish I'd done." – Cher, on her refusal of Chris Carter's request that she guest star as herself at the end of "The Post-Modern Prometheus" (5x06). A Cher look-alike was used instead.

Scully and Mutato ("The Post-Modern Prometheus" (5x06)).

Pollidori's house was an exceptional find, with its grand Victorian architecture, its remote setting, and the aspect of a road in front of the house allowing for an unob-structed view of the tarped premises. There was one major drawback to the house: it was a crafts retail outlet for part of the year and when scouted, the business was

Fortunately, the majority of tenants opted for alternate lodging for the night. What I later learned was that several residents checked into the other hotel and immediately sublet their free room *by the hour* to "friends." They then showed up at the 2-Jay's and demand-ed their twenty bucks (word was out). A glance at Alan's list revealed that they had already opted for the free room.

One major problem arose that night with a resident on the second floor. Unfortunately, his room was immedi-ately above our set. Refusing to relocate, he disappeared at around 3 p.m. (call-time) and returned to col-lect his twenty dollars at approximately 6 p.m. Returning again at 9 p.m. (this time in an intoxicated state), he proceeded to hike the volume on his stereo to warp nine, making the recording of dialogue scenes all but impossible.

During the ensuing forty-five minute delay to production, the DERA rep and a police officer paid the man a visit, but were unable to resolve the issue. Assistant location manager Ainslie Wiggs finally lured him downstairs, promising to give him another twenty bucks to co-operate. When he became violent and abusive, it was suggested that a bed for the night – courtesy of the Vancouver Police Department – might be found "a few blocks away." Neither myself nor the attendant offi-cers saw his incarceration in a city lock-up as just resolution to this prob-lem, but when the man kicked in the back window of the paddywagon, he was taken away.

Location scout Alan Bartolic with Mutato ("The Post-Modern Prometheus" (5x06)).

Some scenes for "The Post-Modern Prometheus" (5x06) were filmed in a Vancouver residential neighbour-hood. A few days after we had wrapped out, a woman called with a concern. It seemed that, since our appearance, her sewing machine would only function in "reverse." She was wondering if our generators might have done something. Our only recourse was to send flowers and apologize for our trickery.

gearing up for Christmas. The interior decor, largely resembling Martha Stewart on a bad day, inspired Chris' vision and he requested a similar theme without the Christmas references. Within two days, four staff members, a moving company, six set decorators, and three production assistants pooled their efforts to remove any semblance of Christmas. Then set dec constructed their own Martha Stewart set.

The X-Files was the first film company to use this location. A number of series and movies have shot here since.

The wrap was awful. No one could remember what went where. Of course no one had taken photographs to document the space "before," but with the crew's creativity unleashed, the store was restored to its original state. Almost. A missing door mat cost the production $25.

Down the road past this house was the clearing used for the peanut butter vigil. A few days after we confirmed our filming days, we were informed that the field had been previously booked by a boy scout camp group. In November. We reimbursed the troop for their booking costs, made a donation, and, to the delight of the group, invited them to set.

Two lighting cranes and the helium lighting balloon illuminated the deciduous forest surrounding the clearing. While Main Unit filmed in the field on a clear Friday night, the balloon hovered over the field in complete view of an adjacent highway. Second Unit was assigned to shoot the exterior lightning storm outside of Burrvilla. Around 5 p.m., Main Unit moved from the Ladner Post Office – where the town riot took place – to Deas Island Park, on the heals of the Second Unit move in.

This episode won production designer Graeme Murray and his art department a second Emmy award for Outstanding Art Direction for a Series in 1998.

Set decorating for "The Post-Modern Prometheus" (5x05).

EXTERIOR SWALE/DEEPER WOODS

MAPLEWOOD FLATS WILDLIFE SANCTUARY,
2600-BLOCK DOLLARTON HWY., NORTH VANCOUVER

A *swale* was required to stage the scene for the appearance of the grandfather and a pig. We consulted the *Oxford Dictionary* for a definition, but it wasn't listed. Nor was it listed in other dictionaries. The true meaning was finally revealed in *The Meridian* and the hunt for "a gully or low-lying depressed landscape" was on. The quest for a filmable site - easily accessible for equipment and safe for walking - along the edge of a land depression was depressing. After visits to properties in Surrey, Vancouver, and the Seymour Demonstration Forest in North Vancouver, a mound off a parking lot at Maplewood Flats was selected. It wasn't a swale, it was a mound. In the end it didn't matter as the scene was cut.

FARM/BARN

2981 - 41B ST., DELTA

The configuration of a farmhouse that looked onto a barn (that could be burned) was one of the most immediate and urgent requirements of this episode. The initial plan to construct a false barn façade to burn was estimated to cost about $40,000. For half the price, the same effect could be achieved by constructing a false front with fire retardant materials covering an existing barn.

Scenes for "Killswitch" (5x01) were also filmed at this location.

Just days before construction on the barn façade was to proceed, the carpenters voiced their concerns about the health ramifications of working inside a barn that housed mice. The locations department was asked to have the barn interior disinfected. Location scout Alan Bartolic consulted five infectious disease specialists and concluded that bleach and power washing would remove the dust particles associated with mice feces. The cleaners - dressed in moon suits and respirators - washed the problem away.

Chris Carter was nominated for Best Director by the Directors Guild of America for directing "The Post-Modern Prometheus." He invited ten crew members – including Louisa – all expenses paid, to the awards ceremony at Century Plaza in L.A. It was a Hollywood spectacle with greats including James Cameron, Francis Ford Coppola, and Steven Spielberg in attendance. Most importantly, it wasn't raining.

In "The Post-Modern Prometheus" (5x06), the barn catches fire, which prompted special effects co-ordinator Dave Gauthier's utterance, "If you build it, I will burn it."

In L.A. after the Directors Guild of America awards.

Squatters' Rights (TP)

I believed we had found the perfect location for the *retirement home* scripted in "Emily" (5x07). First discovered while filming scenes for "Memento Mori" (4x15) in an adjacent apartment building, the Glen Hospital was now vacant and being considered by the city for re-zoning for condominium redevelopment. No one had filmed here previously and, given the redevelopment schedule, it was unlikely that anyone would film here after *The X-Files*.

I contacted the new owner of the property and pitched him our filming proposal. He liked the novelty of the idea, realizing that it would be a one-off deal. Arrangements were made to take a location survey of essential department heads through the building as a precursor to negotiations. Departmental requirements were subsequently discussed and a prep schedule hammered out. An insurance certificate and a location agreement were faxed to the owner's office, and a cheque requisition drawn up for the negotiated amount. We then agreed to meet on Monday morning (it was now Friday afternoon) to exchange a set of keys for a cheque, since the paint department required access no later than Monday afternoon to begin a repaint.

I tried several times to reach the owner by telephone on Monday morning, only to be told he was "unavailable." Explaining our prior arrangement and my plight — which was growing more desperate by the hour — I convinced the receptionist to give me the owner's cellular phone number. It was 12 noon when I finally reached him and, judging by the clamour in the background, I knew there was a problem.

He frantically informed me that he was at the Glen Hospital with a number of police officers, desperately trying to dislodge a group of squatters who had moved in over the weekend. To paraphrase his words, "there are twenty or thirty people here . . . women with small children and babies . . . they're even

5x07   EMILY   TP

Scully and Mulder, while searching for a cure to Emily's illness, determine that she is linked to the alien-hybrid clones.

RETIREMENT HOME
GLEN HOSPITAL, 1036 SALSBURY DR., VANCOUVER

Every now and then the unique opportunity arises to make use of a location which is about to disappear or be forever transformed. Such was the case with the Glen Hospital, a defunct retirement home we discovered nine months earlier while filming scenes for "Memento Mori" (4x15) next door at a three-storey brick apartment building (*Kurt's apartment* in that script).

When Chris described this location, the Glen Hospital came to mind immediately as the choice. It was vacant and slated for redevelopment, although its designated Heritage-A status saved the main structure from the wrecker's ball. A location photofile was couriered to Chris in Los Angeles, who gave it the thumbs up, and a survey was arranged.

This structure was originally built in 1908 by an Australian realtor and auctioneer. The hospital was the perfect location for *The X-Files*. It was creepy and odd, with a long main hallway off which a number of private and group dayrooms were located. Much of the hospital equipment - wheelchairs, walkers, beds, and dishes - remained, as if the new owners had simply locked the doors and walked away. The untended grounds outside lent to these scenes a visual sense of angst and foreboding for which *The X-Files* had become famous. Looking at this building from the street, you just knew some terrible secret was about to be revealed from within.

After near-disaster was averted during the negotiation process - life once again imitating art (see *Squatter's Rights*) - a cleaning crew attacked the interior of the building to prepare it for the onslaught of the paint, construction, and set dec departments. The old furnace in the basement - while still operational - needed a speedy overhaul in order to generate enough heat to dry paint and keep the prep crews warm.

This was the one and only time this location was ever used by a film crew, as redevelopment began soon after we wrapped.

5x08   KITSUNEGARI   LG

After Robert Modell, the Pusher, escapes from prison, Scully and Mulder discover that there is another Pusher, a woman Modell is trying to reach.

PRISON CAFETERIA

OLD BOILER ROOM, GEORGE PEARSON HOSPITAL, WEST 57TH AVE., VANCOUVER

Daniel Sackheim returned to direct his last episode of *The X-Files* in Vancouver. The technical survey lasted a record-breaking twelve hours.

After dismissing at least ten possible prison cafeteria locations, a local hospital's vacant boiler facility that was being used to store derelict equipment was finally chosen. Its main attractions were the lattice-framed windows, cinderblock walls, and balcony which looked like a guard-patrol station. To create the prison cafeteria set, all of the equipment had to be removed, the walls painted, wire mesh fencing installed, and the kitchen and lunch tables dressed.

> This location became Father Gregory's church in "All Souls" (5x17).

The facility was just being cleared out when the technical survey bus arrived. Underneath all the junk was a series of concrete protrusions. Filming was only five days away and the intrusions needed to be removed. At a cost of nearly $1,500, jackhammers solved the problem. After the concrete dust settled, power washers removed all evidence and the walls and ceiling were painted. When the location was prepped and ready for shooting, its appeal was easy to see. And the site didn't have to be returned to its pre-shooting state. Only set dressing had to be removed.

> On shoot day, David and Gillian accepted an invitation to visit patients at Pearson Hospital.

SPORTING GOODS STORE

GREAT OUTDOORS, 201 LONSDALE AVE., NORTH VANCOUVER

We couldn't locate a sporting goods store that might look like it was in a small town. As prep time closed in, executive producer Bob Goodwin insisted that a decision be made immediately. The exterior chase and police drive-up scenes required street lock-up during business hours, restricting our options. We settled on a store in North Vancouver situated on a controllable street. Its exterior scale was right, but the interior required major dressing to reflect more of a runners and t-shirts type of outlet.

> Second Unit had to return to this location the following week, as Main Unit had forgotten to capture an establishing shot.

cooking food in the kitchen. . . ." While expressing genuine shock, I had to ask the obvious question: "How does this affect our arrangement? My paint crew needs to get started this afternoon." His reply was chilling. "Maybe we don't have an arrangement. Call me back in two hours. I have to go now."

I called him back at 2 p.m. to find him in his office and in a more philosophical mood. The squatters had been coaxed to leave and calm had been restored. "How badly do you need this location?" he asked. "Is there somewhere else you can go? You know, I really don't need this kind of publicity." He then explained that the squatters were really protesters attempting to draw attention to the issue of a lack of affordable housing in the area. The last thing he needed was a high-profile television show drawing attention to the situation. I replied that there was, by now, nowhere else we could go, given the prep schedule and our first day of filming, which was five working days away. "I'll talk with my partner. Call me back in one hour," he said.

At 3 p.m. we spoke again. To the owner's credit — and our benefit — he decided to let us proceed, on the condition that *The X-Files* provide round-the-clock security on the property — commencing immediately — for the duration of our presence, which was to be fifteen days. Within half an hour, we had our keys and the art department and paint crew were on-site by 4 p.m.

Security reported that, over the next few days, protesters made late-night visits to the hospital, essentially to taunt the guards. On one occasion, the police were called in when a break-in was attempted. By the weekend before filming, all was quiet. Word had evidently reached the street that further attempts at occupancy would be futile. The first of two days of Main Unit filming passed, *almost* without incident.

You better get over here right away.

This ominous message from my assistant appeared on my voicemail at approximately 7:45 p.m. Within five minutes, I was on location. So were twenty or thirty placard-toting protesters, a television news crew, and sixteen police officers. Production had ground to a halt, as we were filming night exteriors and the protesters were standing in the background of our shot. While the police figured out how best to resolve the situation, first assistant director Vladimir Stefoff — who was fuming over the delay — approached the group and offered them a choice.

So far, filming had been disrupted for almost an hour and, with an 11 p.m. neighbourhood curfew looming, he was nervous that this incident might cost us our day. As Stefoff would later relate, "I told them that if they refused to move, we [the crew] would be here all night . . . and the next night and the next night after that . . . until we completed our work. If, however, they moved to the opposite corner now, we would complete our work and be gone, giving them a chance to do what they had to do."

Stefoff cuts an imposing swath at the best of times, all the more so when angry. One by one, the protesters moved across the street, followed closely by the arrival of a paddywagon, at which point they vanished into the night.

Stefoff made the ten o'clock news and filming continued without further incident for the remainder of this day and the next. Additional Second Unit work the following week went unhindered.

Greensman Frank Haddad and construction co-ordinator Rob Maier recreated the hazelnut orchard on a sound stage with 200 hazelnut trees, which were recycled for use on later episodes. By the end of the season, only twigs remained.

| 5x09 | SCHIZOGENY | TP |

The past haunts a woman counselling teenage children who appear to be victims of abuse, and who are linked to the strange deaths of their parents.

ORCHARD
HAZELGROVE FARMS, FORT LANGLEY STAGE, LION'S GATE STUDIOS

"Schizogeny" was known amongst the crew as the *killer tree* episode. Not only was *Lisa's house* chosen partly because a large willow tree stood in close proximity to the upstairs window of this two-storey clapboard farmhouse - a window from which Lisa's father is pulled to his death - but an additional hero limb measuring more than twenty-feet was affixed to the tree to create a more sinister and believable culprit.

The night scenes in the orchard - those in which a character is dragged to his death beneath the mud by a killer root - were both time-consuming and tricky to stage. It was therefore decided to recreate a portion of the orchard on a soundstage to give production maximum control over all elements of filming, including the weather.

The construction department built a large, elevated platform to accommodate the actor's demise beneath the mud. The greens department trucked in 200 hazelnut trees - greensman Frank Haddad bought an orchard for $1,000 - and "planted" them in pre-cut holes in the platform, which was then covered with dirt and leaves. Blacks were hung around the perimeter of this remarkable set to simulate night and hide the soundstage walls. The pit into which the actor disappeared was then filled with sterile peat moss and topsoil.

Once this episode was completed, the trees were selectively stripped of dead wood and recycled for subsequent episodes, until they dried out to the point of being unusable.

A hazelnut orchard recreated on a soundstage at North Shore Studios for "Schizogeny" (5x09).

| 5×10 | CHINGA | LG |

Scully investigates a series of bizarre deaths in a small Maine town, in which a little girl's doll is the culprit.

SUPERMARKET
SHOP EASY, 2535 SHAUGHNESSY ST., PORT COQUITLAM

We needed a *supermarket* for an unusual self-mutilation scene and selected Shop Easy in Port Coquitlam. Filming not only required store closure prior to Christmas, but involved stripping an entire aisle and lining it with stand-up freezers to reflect images. Two days prior to prep, set dec discovered that their freezer units were too wide to fit through the store doors. We had to make arrangements to remove the front windows of the store so a crane could be used to move the freezers through the openings. This became an overnight job for set dec, locations, and the store staff.

> During the filming of the self-mutilation scene, a customer, who had somehow found her way onto set, meandered through the aisles. She stopped, looked around in confusion, then darted from the store.

The shot of Scully driving an open convertible had been established on a relatively sunny day the week prior to shooting this pull-up scene, which in the script takes place minutes later. On film day the skies were overcast and rain was imminent, but it was imperative not only to complete this scene on this particular day, but to ensure that the two shots would match. To make the transition from sun to cloud, filming in a covered environment was needed, and at the last minute, a covered gas station was proposed. A Save On Gas in North Vancouver was our only saving grace. The end result is that when Scully goes to get gas, the weather changes.

> This episode was written by horror guru Stephen King, although Chris revised the entire episode as it originally read like a feature film script, and would have been impossible to shoot within the eight-day schedule.

Car Pool (TP)

While filming scenes for "Schizogeny" (5x09) at a farmhouse in one of our rural municipalities, the local police force provided us with a few moments of off-set humour. Two officers had been booked for traffic control on the country road in front of the house. Both officers subsequently arrived in one cruiser. It was early December and very cold. Even the muddy fields and shoulders of the road had frozen solid by sundown, which at least made the parking of work trucks more efficient.

I suggested to the officers that they attempt to procure a second vehicle, as we would be filming late into the night and the temperatures were expected to drop well below zero. After some discussion, they were released from set to make the run back to the police vehicle compound to get another car.

A half-hour later, the first officer showed up in the original cruiser and informed me that, due to a vehicle shortage, there had been some difficulty in finding a second vehicle. Not to worry, though, his partner would be along presently.

When the second officer finally arrived, it was at the wheel of a van used for impaired driving roadchecks, which was evidently all he could get his hands on. I thought it a brilliant move in terms of traffic control. Cars speeding along this road were apt to show scant regard for a garden-variety police cruiser, but when faced with the possibility of a roadside breathalyzer check, the level of co-operation went way up.

Shopping The X-Files *way ("Chinga" (5x10)).*

Blow-Up à Deux (TP)

There's an unwritten rule in location managing: *Never show a director a location he/she cannot use.* The script for "Killswitch" (5x11), written by William Gibson, called for three explosions and a shoot-out in a *diner*. The protocol to detonate explosive devices within Vancouver city limits has become necessarily stringent over the years, meaning that a great deal of preparation and lead time is required.

I had applied to blow up a cargo container at one of the container facilities on the Vancouver waterfront. For maximum visual effect, the explosion was scheduled for night. We anticipated that special effects co-ordinator Dave Gauthier's "recipe" would propel a fireball 150 feet into the night sky. After choosing the location, we scheduled a meeting with the City of Vancouver, the Vancouver Police, the Vancouver Fire Department, the Vancouver Port Corporation, the B.C. Film Commission, representatives from the container terminal, the explosives division of Natural Resources Canada, and the production company. Discussion included technical aspects of the explosion (how much detonator cord, how much black powder, time delays, size of fireball), logistical issues such as containment of debris, shockwaves, advance public notification, crowd control, additional 911 staffing (to handle the increased volume of calls), and traffic control on both North Shore bridges.

An agreement in principle was reached and all concerned seemed satisfied. The outright refusal that came from the Vancouver Port Corporation several days later was completely unanticipated. I had assumed — perhaps overenthusiastically — that we had already cleared any obstacles.

A senior official with the Harbour-

| 5x11 | KILLSWITCH | TP |

Scully and Mulder combat an artificial intelligence which has taken over orbiting weapons platforms in order to survive.

SWINGBRIDGE
WESTHAM ISLAND BRIDGE, CANOE PASS

While on a location technical survey for "Schizogeny" (5x09), our bus passed over an old swingspan bridge. Chris leaned over and whispered his intention to feature the old bridge in an upcoming episode. Moments later, I was on my cell phone with Lorna Leslie at the B.C. Department of Highways, establishing the parameters within which we could be use the structure.

As this bridge was the sole access to an island farming community in the Fraser River, any disruption of traffic would have to be late at night and kept to a minimum. Notification to local residents began two weeks prior to filming. The real problem for us occured with the mechanics of the bridge itself, originally built in 1908. The swingspan was added in 1912 when it was discovered that the bridge was too low to permit the passage of fishing vessels. The tiny five-horsepower engine which rotates the platter cannot be operated with vehicles parked on the swingspan.

We were also warned that no more than five people could stand on the swingspan while it swung, and that they should stand as close to the centre as possible. These technical points were questioned by certain members of the production, who were determined that the scene be shot as written since, in the original draft, Scully's car is trapped on the swingspan as it rotates. On an early scout, director Rob Bowman leaned over the bridge railing to watch his rather expensive sunglasses slip from his head and disappear into the murky river. If you believe in omens, what happened next will come as no surprise.

On the day of the technical survey, the bridge operator was asked to swing the span to demonstrate the physics of the structure to our various department heads, who had all crowded to the edge of the span. As if by divine example, the bridge swung open, then jammed. Several minutes passed as the operator manually reset the system.

Evidently, the weight of fifteen people combined with the momentum of the swing had caused a misalignment which, while not uncommon, created an inconvenient and time-consuming delay. Oddly enough, this little misadventure inspired a major change in the way the scene was finally written and blocked, as the possibility of Gillian becoming stranded on a swingspan in the middle of a river late at night was a risk no one wished to take.

A storypoint in this scene occurs when Scully and Esther realize that an armed military satellite has locked its sites onto the laptop computer in their possession, and is about to vapourize them with a particle beam. Esther throws the laptop off the bridge, causing the weapon to shift its aim. The beam narrowly misses them and a plume of steam and water erupts from the river.

Permission to stage this effect in the river took the better part of thirty days to obtain, and involved agencies as diverse as the Coast Guard, the Fraser River Harbour Commission, the Fraser River Estuary Management Program, Environment Canada, the Department of Highways, and the Department of Fisheries. The overriding concerns were with navigational hazards and possible damage to the foreshore of this fish-bearing estuary. Modifications to Dave Gauthier's special effects proposal were made as requested before filming was allowed to proceed.

I explained the difficulties I was experiencing in securing permission from the various agencies to one of the residents of a cluster of houseboats moored 100 feet downstream from the bridge. With a chuckle, he pointed to the houseboats bobbing in the gentle current. "Just where do you think the toilets on those things empty, anyway?" He wished me luck and walked away.

> This episode was written by Vancouver writer William Gibson.
>
> The only other swingspans in the Lower Mainland straddle the Pitt River, the Fraser River at Annacis Island, and the middle arm of the Fraser River in Richmond. None of these were ever considered due to their high traffic volumes.

RUINED FARMHOUSE
2981 - 41B ST., DELTA

This location required three specific components. In the episode, Mulder approaches a ramshackle farmhouse, stopping his car on the country road out front. He notices a utility pole on the far side of the road, from which an unusually hefty service cable is strung. He follows the cable to the farmhouse and into an adjacent stand of trees, where he disappears. Emerging on the other side several minutes later, he spots a lone trailer sitting in a clearing. The service cable leads directly to the trailer.

The farmhouse we chose was indeed abandoned and visually perfect, but the stand of trees beside it was

master's Office informed me that the Port had decided that such an activity was not in their "best interests."

As it was, the cast and crew of The X-Files was about to take a well-deserved two-week Christmas holiday, which gave me some wiggle room to come up with an alternative plan. Other container facilities — not on VPC property — were considered, and it was finally decided to truck in as many containers as needed to an alternate site, the massive back lot at BFI Recycling in Burnaby. As a location, BFI was remote and easily controllable, since it fronted the Fraser River and was bordered by either industrial or undeveloped land.

A new meeting was held, this time with City of Burnaby officials replacing their City of Vancouver counterparts. The filming of all scenes leading up to the explosion were then shot as scheduled at the original container terminal, while Second Unit was dispatched to BFI to film the explosion sequence. The entire process was hence doubly expensive and very time-consuming, but went off without incident.

As a footnote, I happened upon an article in a local community newspaper some months later concerning safety issues and the handling of dangerous goods on the Vancouver waterfront. With the growing number of residents buying lofts and condos immediately adjacent to the docks and rail lines, special interest groups were busy lobbying the Canadian government in an effort to curtail certain practices on the waterfront which they perceived as dangerous to the immediate neighbourhood.

This would seem to suggest the presence of political motives which our presence could not help but highlight, for better and for worse. Either that or, as the Vancouver Port Corporation explained to us, they were concerned with the effect such an explosion might have on the largely non-English-speaking crews of foreign vessels in port and the inability to convey to these crews the nature of our activities.

A more comical situation developed after filming our favourite explosion for "Killswitch" (5x11). I had arranged that our hero trailer be blown up on a large tract of uninhabited land adjacent to the Boundary Bay Airport. Once again, the necessary meetings were held and subsequent precautions taken. Given our proximity to both the airport and the freeway, we decided that the optimal time for this explosion was between 9 p.m. and 10 p.m., when both air and freeway traffic would be light or non-existent. Similarly, it was still early enough in the evening that whatever sound might be heard would not wake those living on nearby farms.

The explosion went off flawlessly at 9:59 p.m. with a fireball erupting 100 feet into the sky and dissipating within ten seconds. The attending police and fire deparment crews inspected the site to their satisfaction and went home, leaving the production company to clean up as much as possible in the darkness. My biggest concern with this

choked with blackberry bushes and the adjacent fields were mudpits. Employing creative geography, a stand of trees and a clearing in which to blow up the trailer were found at our favourite recurring location near the Boundary Bay Airport (see *Blow-Up a Deux*). Director Rob Bowman simply walked Mulder around the corner of the house and let him disappear. The camera then picked him up emerging from the trees at Boundary Bay.

Two utility poles existed more or less where we wanted them - on the roadside and in the front yard of the farmhouse. With the help of BC Hydro, hundreds of feet of cable were strung by the set dec department. Other than using the interior for a camera position, no filming was done in the house, although it was cleaned thoroughly upon completion of filming. Moments before the camera rolled, art director Gary Allen used his creative touch to carefully break the kitchen window, a storypoint in the script.

Known locally as Read House and built around 1898 by immigrants from England, the Delta Heritage Advisory Commission has strongly recommended it - built in an architectural style known as "four-square" - be preserved as a heritage landmark. As of the late 1990s, the farmhouse remained unoccupied, a target of repeated vandalism.

> This location was also used in "The Post-Modern Prometheus" (5x06), although it was the huge barn at the back of the property which received the camera's attention.

5x12	BAD BLOOD	LG

Scully and Mulder remember, very differently, the events that led to the death of a teenager suspected of being a vampire in rural Texas.

The phony graveyard for "Bad Blood" (5x12).

5x13	PATIENT X	TP

Mulder, now believing that alien abductions are a conspiratorial government cover-up, has difficulty understanding why UFO abductees are gathering and being burned to death.

RUSKIN DAM
DEWDNEY TRUNK RD., RUSKIN

"Patient X" marked the beginning of the final two-parter *The X-Files* would shoot in the Lower Mainland. Chris requested a spectacular location to stage a UFO abduction scene. He was presented with a variety of options, including Squamish Chief Mountain, Cleveland Dam, and Stave Lake Dam. The script ultimately reflected the industrial gothic architecture of the Ruskin Dam, and its unique setting, which incorporated a bridge approach and powerhouse with a roadway running across the top of the dam.

In preparation for the filming of night scenes, a five-day pre-rig was initiated. *Par cans* were placed along the bridge superstructure itself and along the base of the powerstation. Eight 1200K *par lights* were mounted on the dam buttresses to illuminate the dam, spillway, and reservoir below. Twelve *redheads* were then mounted under the bridge to crosslight the reservoir and dam. Four 4K par lights provided further illumination for the reservoir and spillway. Finally, three lighting cranes – each carrying two 18K HMI lights – were strategically placed around the perimeter of the site to fill in and supplement the lighting already established.

BC Hydro, owner and operator of the site, allowed us to control the flow of water through the dam gates, which made for a spectacular visual effect when standing on the adjacent bridge. On both episodes, helicopters were used for night lighting effects and filming, a disruption which annoyed some local residents.

location had been the enormous new glass hothouses being built in a field about one kilometre east of our location as the land was flat and offered no buffer. Fortunately, no shock waves capable of damaging these hothouses were produced, or so I thought at the time. The following afternoon, I received a call from the film liaison with the Corporation of Delta demanding to know "what the hell had happened" the previous evening. She explained that several people, living as far as ten miles away, had called to complain about a large boom that had "shaken homes" at about the same time as our explosion had occurred. One resident called me, explaining that an antique plate had fallen off his wall and broken as a result of the shockwave from the explosion.

As curious as I found this, having observed nothing overwhelming from where I stood at "ground zero," I felt obliged to replace the plate, which was gratefully accepted. To this day, I do not believe that the boom reported by numerous residents of the Delta area had anything to do with our activities that night. Perhaps it was a result of an uncharacteristic thunderstorm that had rocked the same neighbourhoods the previous night with similar results.

The flow of water from the lake above was controlled by six gates in the dam. Opening each gate five centimeters (about two inches) – which produced a spectacular waterfall – cost $200 and our final bill – for water alone – was $1,500.

Well before filming commenced, a town meeting was held at the Hydro offices in Ruskin, involving the B.C. Film Commission's community affairs officer Tom Crowe, BC Hydro staff, local residents, Louisa, and me. Aside from explaining in detail our filming requirements, we listened intently as individuals in the packed conference room expressed their concerns and, in some cases, opposition to our presence. In a meeting which at times grew heated, allegations of misrepresentation and past broken promises by film crews and Hydro staff alike were raised and addressed.

As a gesture of good faith, *The X-Files* agreed to a sizeable donation in support of a local playground restoration fund. A hundred or so autographed photos of David and Gillian were also dispensed within a two-minute period.

Ruskin Dam bridge used in "Patient X" (5x13) and "The Red and the Black" (5x14).

| 5x14 | THE RED AND THE BLACK | LG |

Scully and Mulder learn that alien rebels are burning UFO abductees in an attempt to thwart alien colonists.

RUSKIN DAM
DEWDNEY TRUNK RD., RUSKIN

As this show was a continuation of "Patient X" (5x13), the Ruskin Dam was again a key location. Creating the lighting affect above the Ruskin Dam bridge for the night-time UFO abduction scene was restricted by the location and by the time it would take to film the complicated abduction sequences. It was impossible to position cranes close enough to the bridge to give the range, height, and flexibility to create the complicated effect, so we decided to build a replica of the Ruskin Dam bridge on a set, in a space that could accommodate its sixty-foot height. The only available complex in the Lower Mainland was a seven-storey "A" Frame stage in Delta, so it was booked for a month.

Par cans/lights: use parabolic reflectors to focus the light.

Redheads: a 1K tungsten light; create light similar to household lighting.

Prepping the crashed UFO for "The Red and the Black" (5x14).

Ruskin Dam bridge setpiece: an exercise in creative geography ("Patient X" (5x13) and "The Red and the Black" (5x14)).

| UFO CRASH SITE |
| STOKES PIT, SOUTH SURREY |

The crash scene was to include a blazing trail of fire leading to the flaming UFO. The ideal setting would have been a large rural field accentuated by low-lying brush. The brush would have to be trimmed and slightly charred in order to create the illusion of a skid line, and the ground would have to be excavated to bury propane lines. Additional space was required for a construction camp.

On February 11, construction set up camp in Stokes Pit and began to build the UFO. To capture the real essence of the UFO, metal sheets – not metallic-painted plywood – were used for the exterior. With the exorbitant costs associated with metal construction, the position of the UFO in the earth was modified to reveal only two-thirds of the craft, saving construction the ordeal and the cost of building an entire ship. With very little prep time, one of the largest tents in the Lower Mainland was set-up on-site to accommodate the construction of the ship. Just shortly after the tent was erected, it collapsed as a result of gale-force winds. Although a valuable day of prep was lost, new tents were erected and work proceeded. A trail burn was created by the greens department and a depression in the gravel was excavated for the final placement of the stationary craft. Special effects rigged the trail burn and UFO with a maze of propane lines.

Although Stokes Pit is situated in a remote area of Surrey, city noise bylaws are still applicable: nothing too loud after 11 p.m. Most of the evening was spent filming the Alien Bounty Hunter climbing a fence and by 10:30

UFO crash site ("The Red and the Black (5x14)).

Map Game (TP)

Coming up with new and unusual locations with which to satisfy the story needs a visually-oriented series such as *The X-Files* was one thing, but getting a shooting crew of sixty-plus people to these locations — week in, week out — was a task of a different sort. David sometimes joked that he suspected some kind of kickback arrangement between us (as location managers) and the most farflung municipalities surrounding Vancouver to entice shows like *The X-Files* to film there. This because many of the storylines dictated remote settings not to be found ten minutes from Vancouver. In David's case, at least he didn't have to drive those distances himself, although at times (the drive to Ruskin Dam for "Patient X" (5x13) and "The Red and the Black" (5x14) was a good hour each way) he must have felt like he might just as well have.

Well-crafted maps were a fixture of each crew member's day, as was breakfast off the catering truck upon arrival on location for a day's work. This is not to say that problems never arose. Signs could blow down in heavy winds or become obscured by fog. Over-zealous municipal road crews sometimes removed signs from the highway as fast as they were installed, claiming that they were a dangerous distraction to other motorists. On at least one memorable occasion ("Conduit" (1x03)), the location van carrying both production assistants and the requisite location signage to be placed at intervals on the highway leading to *Lake Okobogee* (aka Buntzen Lake) became lost itself and that, combined with a small error on the map, left several crew members driving around the countryside wondering why they'd missed the turn-off. Having said that, one must admit that some individuals are simply *directionally impaired,* and no amount of cartography or signage will change that.

It was a crisp, sunny morning in late February 1998 as the crew assembled

p.m. it was apparent that the explosion would have to be delayed. Because city officials were on site, the curfew was relaxed for an additional half an hour. At approximately 11:30 p.m., the explosion went off with a muffled thump, not the big bang that was anticipated, and the giant fireball and the metallic glow of the ship were lost in a cloud of smoke. The site was finally wrapped three weeks later.

> This location doubled as an Alaskan oil well in "Terma" (4x10).

Carpenters building the UFO on location ("Patient X" (5x13), "The Red and the Black" (5x14)).

FORT WIEKAMP
B.C. PARKS WORKS YARD, BASE OF SEYMOUR MOUNTAIN, NORTH VANCOUVER

An entrance to a military-type base was required in North Vancouver. A quick perusal of photofiles under the category of "Works Yards" yielded a suitable option. Seymour Resorts occupied half of the site and B.C. Parks used the other half. The open sheds were filled with equipment which had to be relocated so we could park military vehicles in their place. After the laborious tasks of removing row upon row of ski lifts, installing a wire mesh gate, cleaning up the site, and then placing a trailer, an austere, militaristic compound was created. Another small set for *The X-Files.*

5x15	TRAVELLERS	TP

Mulder, a year before he begins work on the X-Files, investigates the death of a man who was a victim of xenotransplantation experiments by the government in the 1950s and who, when he was killed, whispered, "Mulder."

5x16   **MIND'S EYE**   LG

A blind woman who can see, in her mind's eye, everything her killer father sees, is investigated by Mulder and Scully.

BUS DEPOT
HASTINGS PARK RACECOURSE, EXHIBITION PARK, VANCOUVER

Bus depot options in the Vancouver area are limited, particularly when looking for a depot that resembles an Atlantic City terminal. Vancouver's downtown terminal was too upscale and alternative buildings were considered and dismissed. At this point creative location planning was warranted. The race track terminal was suggested, dismissed, suggested again, and reconsidered. When suggested for the third time, an appointment to view the site was already in the works. Buses could be parked outside the front doors, a simple flat across one wall would partition the area from the remainder of the building, and with rows of seats and lockers, all one had to do was relax and wait for the next bus.

Dolly grip Peter Wilkie ("Mind's Eye" (5x16)).

5x17   **ALL SOULS**   TP

Scully experiences visions of Emily as she investigates the deaths of young women who are found in positions of supplication, their eyes burned out of their sockets.

ST. JOHN'S CHURCH
ST. AUGUSTINE'S PARISH, 2028 WEST 7TH AVE., VANCOUVER

When this script was released to production and I began to think of possible locations to play as *Scully's church* in

> Guest star Lili Taylor was nominated for an Emmy for "Mind's Eye" (5x16).

on a quiet country road near the Canada-U.S. border to film a scene for "Travellers" (5x15). Given the fact that, at the end of Season Four, we had filmed "Demons" (4x23) at a deserted farmhouse less than a mile from where we now stood, finding this location should have been unproblematic.

But there was indeed a problem. David's stand-in, Jaap Broeker, was nowhere to be found, and we were about to block the scene. Other crew members had passed Jaap enroute, driving his Renault Le Car, so we knew he was in the vicinity. Just about the time I received a call from the production office announcing that a somewhat irate Jaap was on the other line on his cell phone asking for directions, a production assistant at the highway exit radioed set saying that he had just seen Jaap drive by, heading for the U.S. border crossing. I then got on the line with Jaap and turned him in the right direction. Upon his arrival on set, the scene became comical as Jaap realized that he alone had missed a well-marked exit on a clear day, no small feat considering the number of times crew members had found their way to really obscure locations under truly adverse circumstances.

Maps to locations are customarily drawn from the production office to the location. The following day's map was changed to reflect Jaap's own home relative to the location. It became The *Jaap Broeker Memorial Map*. This incident spawned a set joke, as Jaap had been cast as a television psychic in "Clyde Bruckman's Final Repose" (3x04). Ask *The Stupendous Yappi* to locate a murderer or predict the future — *no problem* — but never rely on this man to find his way to set in the morning.

The confessing Father was played by producer J.P. Finn, who reprised a role he first played as Chaplain on "The List" (3x05).

The "White" Side of Town (TP)

Location surveys turn up all manner of things. One memorable morning we were scouting locations for *Father Gregory's church* in "All Souls" (5x17). The survey group had just said good-bye to Crusty, the somewhat bizarre "manager" of the old Station Street Theatre (and yes, he did look a little like a live-action version of *The Simpsons*' Crusty the Clown) and had crossed the street. As we filed past a parked car, I looked down to see the lone occupant frantically shovelling a small pile of white powder up his nose, completely oblivious to the immediate presence of eleven strangers.

Much later, I would recall this moment to an irate hotel owner, who was complaining bitterly (before the event, of course) of loss of parking for his patrons, as we had elected to film our *bad neighbourhood* scenes here. When I suggested that the person in the car might not be the type of clientele condusive to repeat business (they have this nasty habit of dying suddenly), he immediately became a more reasonable human being and agreed to a *wait and see* approach.

fictional New England, this parish topped the list. Photos were presented to director Allen Coulter and a copy of the script delivered to the Catholic Archdiocese, whose permission would be required to film here.

As a safety measure, several other churches were surveyed while we awaited word from the Monseigneur. None had the ornate physical presence of this lovely brick structure and we were fortunate that the script was finally approved for filming.

Initially, only exterior scenes involving Scully and Starkey were shot here. Second Unit was subsequently sent back to film additional interior scenes, written after a rough edit of the episode had been viewed. The church housed several confessional booths, which were too small and awkward to permit the filming of the scenes as written. The art and construction departments subsequently designed and built our own confessional in the church hall next door, but moved it elsewhere to accommodate scheduling demands. Those scenes were shot at a later date in the Pacific National Exhibition forum, where the set was rebuilt.

FATHER GREGORY'S CHURCH
OLD BOILER ROOM, GEORGE PEARSON HOSPITAL, WEST 57TH AVE., VANCOUVER

The basic concept for Father Gregory's Church involved anything but a conventional church, as Father Gregory was anything but a conventional cleric. The word "makeshift" came up more than once in attempting to describe director Allan Coulter's sense of what this location should be.

Various halls and vacant warehouses were scouted, as was the old Station Street Theatre, before the subtle suggestion was made that perhaps we should re-visit a location used by Louisa as the Prison Cafeteria in "Kitsunegari" (5x08). This location had left a less-than-pleasant taste in the mouth of producer J.P. Finn, who could not forget the substantial sum of money spent in transforming an old boiler room into a cafeteria. I reasoned that the money had already been spent on this location and that the real task lay in limiting the "damage" this time around.

Allan immediately fell in love with this old building, although the exterior offered only very limited angles due to its residential surroundings, which looked nothing like a down-and-dirty inner city neighbourhood. And while very little was done to the interior - set dressing was minimal - the front exterior of the building was aged to indicate the desperate plight of

Father Gregory's ministry.

Ironically, the lovely high windows that were so much a part of this location's attraction presented a problem for production. With so much interior day work scheduled here, there were concerns that the light would shift so dramatically during the day that the grips and electrics would end up fighting a losing battle to maintain continuity. That, or they would simply lose the light entirely, as it was only late March.

The solution to this dilemma involved *plugging* a couple of the windows entirely, while building special light-diffusers to mount over the others. And while the results were mixed, the overall effect was achieved with the help of two days of overcast skies. Father Gregory's Church may not have been ornate, but it certainly had soul.

5x18	THE PINE BLUFF VARIANT	LG

Mulder goes undercover to infiltrate a militia group that wants to infect the public with a deadly biotoxin.

VOGUE THEATRE
DUNBAR THEATRE, 4555 DUNBAR ST., VANCOUVER

This neighbourhood movie theatre had recently closed and *The X-Files* seized the opportunity to use it. Because so many days were required to prep, shoot, and wrap, there were no other options. Luckily, the Dunbar Theatre featured the architectural and design characteristics of a small-town cinema situated within an appropriate neighbourhood context. Special effects make-up artist Toby Lindala created the deceased theatre audience in his shop. When he brought them to set, there was nowhere in the theatre to store the "fake" cadavers, so he placed them in the craft services room. Many of the crew lost their appetites that day.

MULDER'S APARTMENT EXTERIOR
1010 SALSBURY ST., VANCOUVER

Mulder's original apartment exterior on York Street had a change in property management and even though the apartment had been established through the years, the new fee structure of $5,000 for filming a short exterior scene was undeniably extortionist and a greedy attempt to hold the film industry at ransom. I informed the new management representative that by requesting such fees,

Plugging: the practice of "removing" an unwanted door or window by installing a painted wall.

Tom Braidwood on location at the London Guard Motel ("The Pine Bluff Variant" (5x18)).

they could kiss the local film industry goodbye. The producers and director - equally outraged - agreed, and an alternative apartment was selected.

BANK
BANK OF CANADA BUILDING, 900 WEST HASTINGS ST., VANCOUVER

The majority of banking institutions welcome filming (after business hours, of course), but depicting the institution in a robbery situation is generally frowned upon. The bank used in this episode was once the Bank of Canada Federal Reserve. The vault in the basement is probably the only structure in Vancouver that could withstand a major earthquake.

The bank, vacant at the time, provided the perfect venue for the robbery and as well allowed for daytime filming. The interior layout was adapted for the action sequence and the script revised to reflect the location. When discussing Mulder's exterior drive-up scene, director Rob Bowman was informed of the parameters of street closure restrictions and time constraints for traffic lockups; traffic had to "flow." In his usual optimistic manner, Rob acknowledged the guidelines and told us not to worry, that everything would be "hunky dory."

The exterior scene included an entourage of FEMA experts and police and SWAT team members. Mulder screeches to a halt on the Hornby Street side of the bank. For picture purposes, barricades were placed on the street and sidewalks to cordon off the the area and rescue vehicles were randomly parked along the street. The four police officers on duty assisted this complex scene by detouring traffic and giving us exclusive access to the street. By afternoon rush hour, however, the street was cleared of our presence, and regular traffic flow resumed.

On the following day at this location, there was only one police officer on site since there was very little exterior filming involved. As the exterior establishing shot of the bank evolved into a larger scene at the last minute, we requested a second police officer. In the interim, the officer on duty discovered that $40,000 in American dollars lined the top layer of the pallet of "fake" cash in the vault and reported this news to the police department. The dreaded call to shut down production was received and with Constable Bob Young absent from the department, I quickly resolved the problem by informing officials that a second officer was on route to provide additional traffic assistance and that the officers would remain on site for the rest of the shooting day. Rightly so. As the police explained, one officer could not possibly

When David and Gillian arrived at the *bank* location ("The Pine Bluff Variant" (5x18)), curious crowds started gathering.

The mother and child at the bank during the holdup scene ("The Pine Bluff Variant" (5x18)) are the wife and daughter of Todd Pittson.

SWAT team ready for action.

deal with an armed robbery should there be any attempt to abscond with the $40,000. Although the props department decided to conceal the "real" money on set, within minutes of call-time, news of the money had spread like wildfire.

When I asked the producers why I wasn't informed of the presence of money, I was told there was a need for secrecy.

There's real money in there. $40,000 worth.

| 5x19 | FOLIE A DEUX | TP |

Office employees are preyed upon by their boss, who appears to one employee – and Mulder – as a giant bug-like monster.

| STARN HOUSE |
| 500-BLOCK EAST 11TH ST., NORTH VANCOUVER |

During the concept meeting for this episode, the words "tract home" were used to describe this location. Over the course of the series, "tract home" came to mean "a neighbourhood of cookie-cutter houses," where each home closely resembles the next in architectural style, size, layout, and landscaping. This phrase evoked an ideal image with screen references to the pastel community featured in the movie *Edward Scissorhands* and the fictional community of *The Truman Show*. It was an ideal image which bore little in common with the architectural realities of the Lower Mainland, with the exception of a small post-Second World War community on the North Shore called Norgate (these homes were too small) and a suburban development in Richmond (too upscale).

After examining sixty or seventy photofiles with director Kim Manners, we zeroed in on a suburb in North Vancouver developed in 1989 and began a block-by-block search for a bland, modern home in which to situate our murderous creature. Given the specific requirements for

The Kernoff House, featured in "All Souls" (5x17), is one block north of the Starn House, in the 500-block of East 12th St.

"Folie a Deux" (5x19).

Lights Out (TP)

The end of "The End" (5x20) came just minutes after 1 a.m. on April 30, 1998. It came with a bang — a round of gunfire from a prison guard's sidearm — rather than a whimper. After months of rumour in the local media and Chris Carter's dramatic announcement at the 2400 Court Motel on March 27, the end seemed almost anticlimactic.

Anticipating an 11 p.m. or midnight wrap, crew members not part of the shooting crew began arriving at Crease Clinic (Riverview Hospital) in the early evening. Pulling into the parking lot at 9 p.m., I was amazed by the array of crew vehicles seldom — if ever — associated with the shooting crew.

Crew members had gathered in clusters around the main entrance to Crease Clinic in anticipation of the final "wrap." Notable among them were producer J.P. Finn, production designer Graeme Murray, art director Greg Loewen, construction co-ordinator Rob Maier, props master Ken Hawryliw, special effects co-ordinator Dave Gauthier, assistant location manager Rick Fearon, set decorator Shirley Inget, costume designer Jenni Gullett, Chris' assistant Joanne Service, and, of course, Chris himself. Gillian had departed half an hour earlier after delivering an emotional farewell speech to this, her extended Canadian family. She also presented each crew member with a midnight blue bathrobe containing the inscription: *1993-1998 Goodnight Everybody I Love You — Forever G.A.* The previous evening — also at Crease Clinic — David had said his farewells, presenting each crew member with a Chuck Taylor basketball, autographed with *Thanks for five years of great work. I had a ball.*

While waiting for wrap, we joked and reminisced about great feats and near disasters, and about how *The X-Files* had transformed our lives during its five-

interior floorplan and position of exterior windows relative to a clean view of the side of the house upwards to the roofline (all in the name of monster action), the search only grew more frustrating for location scout Alan Bartolic, whose obsession with the perfect house fueled an unsolicited weekend scout.

With day one of principal photography approaching and no obvious choice in the bag, executive producer Bob Goodwin suggested that perhaps an older home might help create a spookier atmosphere and provide more workable choices. This was, after all, an episode about a monster bug. The original concept was abandoned and, within hours, the location survey van had pulled up in front of this turn-of-the-century home in North Vancouver. And while it bore no resemblance to a "tract home," the specifics of geography were adequate to meet Kim's blocking requirements.

A platform was built to straddle the peaked roof, allowing the special effects crew to assist our creature in its ascent up the back of the house and onto the roof. A hole was also drilled through the overhang to permit cabling. Windows were replaced with "safety glass," care being taken not to break the fragile original stained glass inserts. Hydro, telephone, and cable services to the house were then relocated to allow for crane shots and the monster's safe ascent up the back wall.

After lengthy discussions about the look of the monster, it was decided that "less was indeed better," as there was an overriding concern that the monster not appear hokey. The onscreen monster – more shadow than substance – was the product of a combination of an actor in Toby Lindala's bug-suit and CGI. It was nonetheless important to provide a location in which the monster's path could be incorporated into existing walls and ceilings while maintaining a seamless match with technology.

VINYLRIGHT
12340 HORSESHOE WAY, RICHMOND

An *armoured car ploughs through the wall of a building and into the cafeteria to end a hostage-taking.* This was the preliminary description received from the Los Angeles office when asked for any available information regarding this upcoming episode. *There's also a house and an apartment complex. Should be pretty straight-forward.* The words *straight-forward* – heard so often during the past five years – had become code for "we hope you're well-rested" and cause for alarm. History had proved there was nothing straight-forward about *The X-Files.*

The scenes involving the armoured car necessitated that the interior of the *Vinylright office* and *cafeteria* be constructed on a soundstage. Kim envisioned a low-slung, modern building located in an industrial park as a suitable exterior and production designer Graeme Murray had proceeded accordingly. With a large build already in progress, it was imperative that the locations team find a location to match the set. There would be no modification of the set to accommodate location problems. Kim also demanded roof access for stuntmen and complete control of the adjacent parking lot and street for the placement of picture vehicles.

After discussing three possibilities, we decided on location scout David Caughlan's find, a new and unoccupied building large enough to permit the construction of an interior set *(Mrs. Loach's kitchen)*. The physical location of the property in a large industrial park with numerous vehicular access points allowed for detours on the adjacent street with only minimal disruption to neighbouring businesses. As luck would have it, the shooting day fell on Easter Monday, making this normally busy area very quiet.

Near-disaster came when the property owner disappeared on urgent business just as the location agreement was to be signed. With construction co-ordinator Rob Maier camped outside my office – his well-worn quip, "You're killin' me, bud," very appropriate here – and no appealing back-up location in place, I spent two very anxious days by the telephone. The owner was finally located and a copy of the agreement faxed to him for signature. His family members were, it turned out, fans of the show.

> While Main Unit was filming scenes at this location, the Second Unit crew - in radio range and less than a mile away - were busy filming scenes on a rural road which would later appear in *The X-Files* feature film, *Fight the Future*.

The big rescue in "Folie a Deux" (5x19).

year sojourn in Vancouver. And while the mood was relaxed and anticipatory, the look on the faces of so many was that of overwhelming fatigue. Nobody talked about their "next show," a major preoccupation with so many of us in the film industry.

When the final shot rang out and first assistant director Tom Braidwood called wrap from the end of a long, very familiar hallway on the main floor of Crease Clinic, a line formed as crew members shook hands and hugged one another. Equipment was quickly loaded into trucks and the crew assembled in what had once been a morgue set for an impromptu celebration which included speeches, a champagne toast, and the requisite photo opportunities with Chris and director Bob Goodwin.

A casual exodus of very tired human beings followed, and in less than an hour, it was all over.

Todd and Chris at wrap ("The End" (5x20)).

Chris couldn't believe the crowd size at the GM Place Finale.

GM Place: a cast of thousands.

They lined up for miles to be extras for "The End" (5x20).

| 5x20 | THE END | LG |

A boy with the ability to read minds is proof of a genetic link between humans and an alien race.

SPORTS ARENA
LOCATION: GENERAL MOTORS PLACE, 800 GRIFFITHS WAY, VANCOUVER

Now that the show's tenure in Vancouver was officially over, "The End" was an appropriate title for this episode. The tribute to Vancouver was masterminded by Chris, who initially suggested GM Place as the ideal location, but given the cost considerations for one day of filming a chess match scene, alternative venues were scouted, but ultimately rejected. The script – without naming it – clearly called for GM Place, and the stadium proved to be a perfect and most spectacular location.

The stadium booking was a gamble. We had committed to the largest venue in Vancouver knowing that a few thousand seats needed to be filled, and knowing that 500 extras would not suffice. Organizing the event was a major undertaking. A media specialist was hired to promote the event and hopefully draw a few thousand fans to be spectators, to witness the filming of the final scenes, and to see Chris, Gillian, David, and other cast and crew members.

It was a good thing that we prepared for large numbers of people, because more than 10,000 people turned out for the event, some having lined up as early as 7 a.m. for the 5 p.m. opening. Over 100 event security staff and five police officers were hired for crowd control, and they were forced to turn away hoards of people at the door, as by then the stadium was at capacity. The crowd even sat quiet during takes. Executive producer Bob Goodwin was heard to say, "You couldn't pay people to be so great."

Even though this one scene cost over $85,000 in location-related costs, the production value was priceless.

At one point Chris and I stepped outside the stadium to check on the crowds. The lineups stretched on forever, doubling back on themselves. He reacted with surprise and I remembered seeing him during Season Two, as the show was beginning to capture the attention of fans around the world, sitting quietly on the veranda of *Mulder's mother's house*, oblivious to the activity around him. I heard him say, softly, "I can't believe this."

E P I L O G U E (LG)

It was at the 2400 Motel on Kingsway in Vancouver that Chris announced to the crew that *The X-Files* would be leaving Vancouver. He arrived on set after lunch, gathered the crew together and read the official memo from vice president of production Charlie Goldstein confirming the move to L.A. The tears in Chris' eyes sparked waves of emotion in the crew; *The X-Files* family was to be disbanded. Some crew members, anticipating the news, wore sunglasses on the cloudy day. Some immediately flipped open their cellular phones – no time for grief – and started inquiring about other jobs.

We all knew the show would end, but when it finally happened, we felt a sense of loss. All those years working together had developed intimacies. It was unavoidable given the amount of time spent at work. As art director Greg Loewen said: "We spent more time with each other than with our spouses." We had been thrown into a pool with strangers and the subsequent stream of arguments, grudges, laughter, caring, and crying solidified us as a family. The show might be over, but we all had fond memories.

I was sitting in the lunchroom at the Eldorado Hotel on Kingsway and Nanaimo when Chris called. Obviously this was not his first call divulging the news. His voice said it all. Chris said that I was integral to the show. He said, "You were the show."

I'm sure he said the same to everyone.

David bids Vancouver adieu at the GM Place finale.

Gillian says goodbye the Canadian way.

Mulder and a peanut butter sandwich ("The Post-Modern Prometheus" (5x06)).

"Shooting in Vancouver has just been a dream, which is why I am back here again." – Chris Carter on the set of his new series, *Harsh Realm*, March 1999

POSTSCRIPT (TP)

A private screening of *The X-Files* feature film, *Fight the Future*, was held in Vancouver on Sunday, June 14, 1998 in a downtown theatre. Six weeks had passed since the last official day of filming the series in Vancouver. Some crew members had moved on to other productions, some had taken time off, but most of us – and several local cast members – showed up for the screening. Given our intimate history with *The X-Files* we were an extremely curious audience.

The feature was filmed in California and Texas during the Season Four hiatus, although a small Second Unit crew was dispatched to a glacier north of Whistler – everyone sworn to secrecy. The script and production information were closely-guarded secrets. Most of us in Vancouver knew only that the working title of the film was *Blackwood*, and if anyone knew more, they weren't talking.

In the lobby before the screening – during a reunion of sorts – Chris chatted enthusiastically about the filming of the feature film and the challenges of creating innovative visual effects. The viewing itself was characterized by an eerie silence, with occasional laughter and applause. Afterwards, Chris stood in a receiving line, soliciting responses to what we had seen.

As people headed for the exits, Chris confessed how nervous he had been before the screening. It was more intense than the butterflies he felt at the press screening in Los Angeles the week before. With the press, he said he was relieved when the audience responded at what he felt were the appropriate moments. Here in Vancouver, on the other hand, he was less certain of the reactions. The silence was difficult to interpret since the audience – people who were familiar with David and Gillian's every facial twitch and voice modulation – seemed to sift through each frame for meaning and subtext, wanting to assess whether the feature was true to the spirit of the series.

The reception was largely enthusiastic; a well-earned grade from the toughest collection of critics imagineable.

As the last of us left the cinema, I quietly presented Chris with a gift on behalf of the B.C. Film Commission. It was their way of showing their appreciation for his tireless support of the Vancouver industry. It was their way of saying, "Thanks," and "Let's do it again soon."

Chris made the sentiment a reality when, in March and April of 1999 Vancouver became home to the filming of the pilot for his new Fox series *Harsh Realm*. The crew list read like an invitation to a family reunion.

Photo: Rob Murdoch

Louisa Gradnitzer and Todd Pittson are
employed in the thriving Vancouver film industry.
They were the location managers for *The X-Files*
during the five years the television series
was produced in Vancouver.

X-TOURS

A Vancouver tour guide is offering tours
to locations where *The X-Files* was filmed.

Tour options include:

Quick X-Tour

Cruise X-Tour

Agent X-Tour

For more information contact:

604-609-2770

1-888-250-7211

www.x-tour.com